NOSTRAI

C000311219

Engraving of Nostradamus (Mary Evans Picture Library)

NOSTRADAMUS

Prophecies of Present Times?

by

DAVID PITT FRANCIS

The Aquarian Press
An Imprint of HarperCollins*Publishers*

The Aquarian Press
An Imprint of HarperCollins*Publishers*
77–85 Fulham Palace Road,
Hammersmith, London W6 8JB

Published by The Aquarian Press 1984
First paperback edition 1985
9 11 13 15 14 12 10

© David Pitt Francis 1985

David Pitt Francis asserts the moral right to
be identified as the author of this work

A CIP catalogue record for this book
is available from the British Library

ISBN 0-85030-517-9

Printed and bound in Great Britain by
Mackays of Chatham PLC, Chatham, Kent

All rights reserved. No part of this publication may be
reproduced, stored in a retrieval system, or transmitted,
in any form or by any means, electronic, mechanical,
photocopying, recording or otherwise, without the prior
permission of the publishers.

Acknowledgements

I am indebted to a number of people with whom some of the ideas in this book have been discussed, including, in particular: Mr Dennis Gillett of Oxford and the late Mr G. G. McHaffie of Edinburgh, both of whom read and commented on the manuscript. I should like to express gratitude to a number of others who took the trouble to correspond with me after the appearance of the first edition.

I am particularly indebted to Mr Edgar Leoni, whose correspondence resulted in some of the minor corrections made to the present edition. Though his work does not investigate the biblical sources of Nostradamus's material and is not easily accessible to United Kingdom readers, it is listed in the revised bibliography and would certainly repay careful study. His critical viewpoint is similar to mine, though we have arrived at these positions independently of each other.

I am also indebted to Mr Ellic Howe, who drew my attention to an original collection of work of K. E. Krafft, including a surviving Portuguese translation of his exposition, listed in the revised bibliography.

My thanks are also due to my editors at the Aquarian Press, Michael Cox and Simon Franklin.

Although I have frequently produced my own translation of Nostradamus's work, acknowledgement is due to a number of early translators, whose work was consulted in the process, and some modern ones, including those of James Laver and Edgar Leoni for occasional use of their varying translations.

Quotations from the Bible are sometimes given in my own translation (e.g. p. 275), but acknowledgement is due to the divsion of Christian Education of the National Council of the Churches of Christ in the USA for occasional use of the Revised Standard Version of the Bible.

D. Pitt Francis
Hertford

Dedicated to the Greatest of all Teachers
—and to the unknown student.

Contents

		Page
Prologue		9

Chapter

1. Seer, Scientist, or Biblical Scholar?   13

    *The Man and the Enigma – The Centuries – The
Statistics of the Stanzas – Nostradamus and Modern
Inventions – Nostradamus and the Revelation of
John – Some Possible Explanations*

2. Nostradamus and the French Monarchy   33

    *Babylon – The Seven-branched Candlestick – Three
Kings – The Huguenots – The Bourbons*

3. Nostradamus and Revolution   72

    *Cromwell and the Long Parliament – The Glorious
Revolution 1688–9 – The First French Revolution,
1789 – Nostradamus and Napoleon I – The
Revolutions of 1830 and 1848*

4. Nostradamus and the Second World War   108

    *The Great Divide – Calling the Tune – The Failure
of Peace and the Rise of Hitler – Two Preludes to War
– The Outbreak of War – Domination and Decline*

5. Prophecies of Present Times   143

    *The State of Israel and The Coming of Antichrist –
Plagues and Popes – Nostradamus, Science and
Present Times – Interpretational 'Fudge'*

6. Towards an Explanation   176

   *Nostradamus and Astrology – Six Contributing
   Factors*

7. Precognition, Coincidence and the Doomsday
   Message   219

   *Patterns in Obscurity – Obscurity and Biblical
   Quotations – The Bible and the Doomsday Message –
   The Doomsday Framework*

8. The Last Mystery   254

   *A Scientist Before his Time? – The Unexplained
   Hardcore – A Theory of Prophecy – A Final
   Reflection*

   Bibliography   279
   Statistical Appendices   283
   Index   301

Prologue

The name of Nostradamus conjures up a variety of images. Some dismiss him as a 'quack'; others have visions of a sixteenth-century astrologer peering into a bowl of water on a brass tripod, trying to foresee the exact details of the French Revolution, of Hitler's war, and of modern inventions . . . My own interest in Nostradamus is related, firstly, to the statistical study of short-term prediction and, secondly, to my interest in long-term biblical prophecy; in respect of the latter, the works of Nostradamus seemed to challenge my belief in the superiority of biblical prophecy over other predictive writings.

Let me explain both these interests more fully. First of all, I wanted to know why some predictions succeed and others fail. I had for some time been intermittently interested in the writings of Nostradamus because they seemed, unlike most non-biblical predictive writings, to have long-term prophetic value, spanning many centuries. The matter came to a head when I was on holiday in Brittany in August 1982 and read a French poster crediting Nostradamus with success in foreseeing some recent political event. At the time I had been preparing a paper for a conference of university teachers[1] to explain Z-tests. These tests are thought to be useful in predicting business failure, and use formulae based on characteristics such as (a) ready cash resources, (b) rate of profit and (c) the extent to which a business uses borrowed funds.[2] They use measurements that are quite easy to

---

[1] D. Pitt Francis, 'Predictors of Corporate Failure – Old Models and New Directions', Association of University Teachers in Accounting, S.E.A.G. Conference Papers, Hatfield Polytechnic, September 1982.

[2] See, for example, R. J. Taffler and H. J. Tisshaw, 'Going, going, gone – Four Factors which Predict', *Accountancy*, March 1977.

explain, and are sometimes very accurate predictors, so accountants naturally prefer them to crystal balls!

When I presented my paper in September 1982, the discussant suggested that some tests work simply because of the effect that they have on people. The unassailable logic of his argument went as follows. If a banker seriously believes a given bankruptcy test (or Z-test) to predict the failure of a business, he will withdraw his loans from those clients for whom it forecasts disaster. Other bankers will follow suit, leaving the client without funds. So the client fails anyway, and the prediction of business failure becomes self-fulfilling. The situation thus resembles a surgery discussion in which a doctor tells his patient that diagnostic 'tests' prove conclusively that the patient will die within minutes. So, to save the patient from death, the doctor calmly takes a revolver out of his drawer and subjects the patient to euthanasia instead!

Both examples – serious and frivolous – perhaps illustrate one of the dangers of believing that even a supposedly scientifically-based prediction is necessarily of value. Other examples will be given later. Let me now explain my second interest, for it is a more long-standing one. In 1969 I wrote a small privately circulated commentary on the biblical prophecy of Daniel.[3] I followed this in 1973 with a commentary on the Revelation of John[4] and revised and extended this commentary for a larger readership in 1983.[5]

My background in Theology might seem to some to make me biased *in favour* of biblical prophecy, and *against* the predictive value of non-biblical 'prophecies'. But this explains the very nature of my concern in writing this book. No one who believes in the Bible should dismiss the prophecies of Nostradamus lightly if they appear to challenge one of the main reasons for believing in its superiority as a spiritual guide. Shortly I shall show that the Bible contains prophecies with fulfilments that span thousands of years. There is no doubt that some people are gifted with a natural short-term insight, but few have the long-term insight that the Bible claims for itself:

---

[3] D. Pitt Francis, *The Message of Daniel* (privately circulated, 1969).
[4] D. Pitt Francis, *Meditations on the Last Message of Jesus* (1973).
[5] D. Pitt Francis, *The Most Amazing Message Ever Written* (Castle Books, 1983).

declaring the end from the beginning
– and from ancient times things not yet done,
saying 'My counsel shall stand, . . .
. . . and I will accomplish all my purpose'[6]

This biblical claim to give knowledge of future events is one of the true tests of prophecy.[7] So any challenge to that superiority must be seriously considered and answered, whether it comes from Nostradamus, Malachy, Old Moore, Jeanne Dixon, Buddha, Mohammed – or whomsoever.

The two 'qualifications' (if they are to be regarded as such) have driven me with a sense of mission and urgency to write an unbiased work on Nostradamus. For my interest in biblical prophecy makes me aware of the biases from which many biblical commentators may suffer; on the other hand, my knowledge of Z-tests has helped me to generate formulae by which most of Nostradamus's successful predictions can be explained. I have tried similar techniques[8] to discriminate between successful and unsuccessful prophecies by 'weighting' a number of causal factors so that the formula for successful prophecy can be found. Some of these 'factors' or explanatory variables are listed later in this chapter,[9,10] but there are measurement problems, as I shall show.

This approach, I believe, makes this work unique. The most detailed writings on Nostradamus are 'commentaries' that differ from each other, and there is even one concordance. These are listed in the bibliography at the end of the book and are the works of people who viewed

---

[6] Isaiah 46:10 (RSV).

[7] Deuteronomy 18:18-22.

[8] This technique, known as multivariate discriminant analysis, is explained in most statistical texts.

[9] These 'weighted' variables can be considered by mathematically-minded readers as components of an equation:

$$Z = V_1X_1 + V_2X_2 + V_3X_3 + V_4X_4 \ldots \text{etc.}$$

where Z is discriminating factor (success, as against failure), X_1, X_2 etc. are each of the explanatory variables listed later in this chapter, and V_1, V_2 the proportions by which each is important.

[10] 'Weighting', of course, serves to emphasize the more important of these explanatory factors.

Nostradamus with great reverence, comparing him with ancient biblical prophets, such as Isaiah and Daniel. They never considered debunking him, and their main objectives seemed to have been either to agree or disagree with previous commentators in interpreting him. In microcosm, they are just like those medieval biblical commentators who never dared look too critically at the received text of the Bible, but contented themselves with looking intently at the history of their own times for some new 'application' or interpretation of prophecy. At the other end of the spectrum there are a few who, because of pseudo-scientific disbelief in all prophecy, or because of vested interest in believing the Bible to be superior, against all odds, have prejudicially debunked Nostradamus.[11] Somewhere in the middle, poised halfway between these two extremes, pretending complete lack of bias, is the 'Micropaedia' comment of the 1974 edition of the *Encyclopaedia Britannica*:

> Because of their cryptic style and content, the prophecies have continued to create much controversy. Some of them are thought to have prefigured historical events that have occurred since Nostradamus's time. Others, having no apparent meaning, are said to foretell events that have not yet occurred.[12]

Such are the extremes of absolute credulity and of utter disbelief, and the apparently disinterested 'middle-way' between them. My position is not simply that of being somewhere in the middle, but of being able to look critically at all shades of opinion on the subject. In summary, I have attempted to look at the biases from which biblical commentators suffer when interpreting obscure predictions and to examine all the factors that contribute to the success of a given set of predictions. If this can be done successfully, then Nostradamus's predictions will no longer be considered solely on their own merits as a set of sixteenth-century forecasts that 'happened' to be correct, and in addition some contribution will have been made to the science of prediction.

---

[11] See, for instance, *Déclaration des abus, ignorances et séditions de Michel Nostradamus* (Avignon, 1558).

[12] *Encyclopaedia Britannica, Micropaedia* (1974 edition), vii, 416, 'Nostradamus'.

1
Seer, Scientist, or Biblical Scholar?

The Man, and the Enigma

For over four hundred years, with the sole exception of Bible prophecy, no set of predictions has stimulated such an infectious interest as those credited to Nostradamus. They were consulted with religious fervour by some members of the French monarchy, and held in high regard by them until 1781, when they were officially condemned by the Church, by being placed on the *Index Librorum Prohibitorum*, only eight years before the French Revolution. In the nineteenth century, Nostradamus's ten Centuries (sets of a hundred verses each) were denounced as Satanic by Protestant religious fundamentalists, and Nostradamus himself was regarded as something of a witch. The present century has witnessed spasms of revival of interest in his writings, partly because they seemed to provide detailed descriptions of some modern events, such as the atomic bombing of Hiroshima, and partly because of their effect on the course of the Second World War after Hitler had been introduced to them by Frau Goebbels. Hitler's interest is indeed curious. He frowned on the Bible and on Christianity, because of their Jewish origins, yet failed to appreciate that Nostradamus, whose works he seemed to worship, was also a Jew.

Hardly a month passes without the probability that some new event has been pronounced by Nostradamus. For example, quatrain I:63 foresees a period of relatively safe air travel, followed by 'battles'. Could this be a reference to the advent of air-travel competition, of the kind that forced Sir Freddie Laker into insolvency? If Nostradamus *is* so accurate, then he deserves an answer. But before trying to answer the enigma, let us look at the man himself.

Born at Saint-Remy in Provence on 14 December 1503, Michel de Notredame (Nostradamus) was the grandson of a Jewish corn merchant who married a Gentile girl called Blanche. In 1512, when he was nearly nine years old, the family converted from Judaism to Catholicism. His grandfather taught him Latin, mathematics, Hebrew, Greek, and some astronomy. His interest in astronomy is important, because it appears to have been a scientific rather than an occult one. He lived before the great divorce of astronomy from astrology, yet held the Copernican theory that the earth was round and encircled the sun, before Galileo was condemned for similar beliefs.

In 1525 he obtained a bachelor's degree in medicine and spent the next four years as an itinerant healer moving between Toulouse, Bordeaux and Avignon trying to cure victims of plague. Though he may have studied occult literature at Avignon, whose library was known to have held such books, there is no direct evidence that he did so. In most respects he seems to have been more of a scientist than an occultist. He refused to bleed plague victims; his book of medical remedies[1] is modern in approach; his astronomy (as we have seen) was in advance of its age; his attitude to image-making (though he was nominally Catholic) was that it was idolatrous; and he developed a love-hate relationship with the religious philosopher Julius Caesar Scaliger, after completing his doctorate in medicine a few years later.

This friendship took him from Toulouse, where he first practised, to Agen, where he married and had two children between 1534 and 1538. In 1538 both his wife and children were killed by the plague, which he had earlier been[2] so successful in treating. His wife's family made attempts to sue him for the return of his dowry, and this began a series of reverses for him, during which he was later accused of heresy, and he commenced a period of wandering. In 1554 he was again preoccupied with the treatment of plague and

---

[1] Nostradamus, *An excellent treatise on Contagious Infirmities* (London, 1559).
[2] J. Laver, *Nostradamus, The Future Foretold* (Mann), p. 29-30. See also 'Nostradamus', *Encyclopaedia Britannica, Micropaedia* (1974 edition), vii, 416.

made his base in Marseilles. By this time he had married again and was engaged firmly in the study of astrology. He produced an almanac from 1550, partly helped by a former mayor of Beaunne, and later by his own son, César. The so-called Centuries of Nostradamus are reputed to date from 1555, but the only edition to survive from that year to recent times contained only three of the ten Centuries and part of a fourth.[3] During the last eleven years of his life he became famous as an astrologer, partly because of the Centuries, but also because of his 'scientific' knowledge of astronomy. I shall show in Chapter Six that his use of, and belief in, astrology may have been overrated by many in their attempts to explain the Centuries on astrological lines. Let us now turn to the Centuries and see what we can make of them.

The Centuries

The writings of Nostradamus are virtually unique, because several of his quatrains indisputably relate to events many decades ahead of his own time. In this respect, he differs from the great majority of 'fortune-tellers', who may be able to predict events that are a few years ahead of their predictions but would never pretend to know of events centuries into the future. Most make their predictions about individuals or governments. They must be fulfilled in a single lifetime, and the great majority of personal predictions, from simple premonitions to horoscope readings (using successful data), are fulfilled within an average period of less than thirty years from the time when they are delivered.

There are, of course, some rare exceptions. I have already mentioned the Bible. Some biblical prophecies have very long fulfilment spans. One of the prophecies of Moses[4] in the second millennium BC presented the Jewish nation with a 'thumb-nail' sketch of its history from that period to modern times, including a series of identifiable invasions, its dispersion by the Romans in the first century of our era, and the return to its homeland in the present century. Even if the book of Deuteronomy had been written later than the time of

---

[3] Nostradamus, *Les Propheties de M. Michel Nostradamus* (Bonhomme, Lyons 1555).

[4] Deuteronomy 28 and 30.

Moses, as some scholars maintain, such a prophecy would still be long-term in its validity. Later Old Testament prophecies[5] in the sixth century BC foretold the destruction of Tyre by Alexander the Great in the fourth century BC in vivid and astonishing detail. A large number of other cases of valid long-term biblical prophecy could be given. Further, the Bible often helped to ignite prophetic foresight in its interpreters, who, though wrong in their interpretations, became valid prophets in their own right when commenting on its prophecies. For example, expositors of the Book of Revelation of John[6] were led by their interpretations to assume, from the early seventeenth century, that the Turkish empire would decline in the nineteenth and twentieth centuries of our era. Well-known writers, such as Joseph Mede[7] and Isaac Newton[8] held these beliefs, and their truth has been confirmed within the past century.

But, other than Nostradamus (and to a *much greater extent* than his writings), the Bible is the only main exception to the theory that most valid prophecies do not have long fulfilment-spans. There are only a handful of other well-researched cases. Buddha, in the sixth century BC, was reputed to have accurately predicted the entry of Buddhism into China in the first century of our era, but there are no manuscripts that survive to prove that the prophecy did not postdate the event, and it was a single prophecy without much detail. In the twelfth century, a Cistercian friend of Bernard of Clairvaux, Malachy of Armagh (1094-1148), predicted the papal succession to the end of the twentieth century, using a series of mottoes, and some of his intuitive flashes were remarkably accurate. But they have little real value in the scientific study of prediction, for it can be reasoned that:

(i) some of the cardinals who are responsible for choosing each successive Pope are aware of Malachy's prophecies;

---

[5] Ezekiel 26:14.
[6] Commentaries on Revelation 9 and 16.
[7] Mede, *Apocalypse* 3.
[8] Newton, *Observations on the Prophecies of Daniel and the Apocalypse of John* (London, 1732).

(ii) it is quite easy for each successor of the papal chair to 'participate' in fulfilling Malachy's prophecies, if he wishes to do so; and

(iii) within a given 'lifetime' it is quite easy to find events that fit each successive 'motto'.

Nostradamus is the great exception to the principle that fulfilment-spans are usually short. No other famous non-biblical prophet produced nearly four thousand lines of closely-packed detail about events centuries beyond his own lifetime. What explanations can be rendered for this remarkable achievement?

His short-term prophecies can be explained, like all other short-term predictions, by simple reference to his own psychic gifts. These are evidenced by the incident that was reputed to have occurred during Nostradamus's visit to Italy in the late 1540s when he addressed a young monk as 'Your Holiness'. The monk, Felice Peretti, within twenty years of Nostradamus's death, became Pope Sextus V. If the story is correct, it is evidence of a 'gift' of personal intuition; but we must be cautious about jumping to a conclusion that these gifts necessarily spring from a knowledge of astrology, the practice of crystal-gazing, or of some other branch of the occult sciences. I have already shown that Nostradamus was as much a scientific astronomer as an astrologer – for his age tended to mix the two sciences – and it would have been difficult for him to have studied the one without also studying the other. Yet he was to some extent, anti-astrological. Not that he tried to debunk astrology – nor would have it been entirely correct for him to have done so, for recent researches suggest a strong correlation between birth-patterns and personal characteristics. But, like the prophets of Israel before him[9] he perceived that astrology

---

[9] The warnings are found in passages such as:

'You are wearied with your many counsels, those who . . . gaze at the stars' (Isaiah 47:13 [RSV]).

'Learn not the ways of the nations, nor be dismayed at the signs of the heavens' (Jeremiah 10:2 [RSV]).

Conversely, there are a few pro-astrological references.

'The stars in their courses fought against Sisera' (Judges 5:20).

was not without its dangers and could lead people into wrong directions, and as most of the astrologers of Nostradamus's times were unreliable, his warnings were even more appropriate.

For example, there are direct warnings, as in VI:100:

> *Let those who read this verse think about it maturely*
> *and let the profane, unknowing crowd stay away.*
> *Let astrologers, fools and barbarians keep off*
> *Whoever does otherwise, let him be priest to the rite!*

To couple the astrologers of his day with barbarians and idiots may sound like an insult to those who look today for helpful correlation between birth charts and personal characteristics. But Nostradamus lived at a time when astrology in Christian circles was at its peak and when the distinction between astronomy and astrology had not been clarified. He was not simply trying to be 'biblical' in his apparent condemnation of astrologers; as the last line indicates, he is trying to tell us that there is a truer science of prediction, and that such science is a sacred one.

The distinction between astrologers and 'sacred ones' is clarified in a later stanza (VIII:71):

> *The number of astrologers will become so large*
> *that they will be driven out, and banned, and their books censored*
>
> . . .
>
> *None will be assured from the sacred ones*

Some of his predictions, assumed to have astrological references, are in fact curious 'puns' on language. The mention of a 'sickle' early in his prophecies may seem like an astrological reference to Saturn, but perhaps may instead refer to 'd'Estang', while it has been shown that 'Taurer' much later is not 'Taurus', but a variant for 'Tory' or a reference to a local church. I shall discuss such cases as they occur. There is no doubt of his 'reputation' as an astrologer because he was asked to cast horoscopes for the dowager Catherine, whom he could scarcely refuse. But his knowledge of astrology was incidental to his greater gifts. Were these gifts acquired by using other occult practices?

He condemned many of these with greater zeal than that

which he vented on astrology. For example I:42:

> *The fire is extinguished, and the devilish gatherings*
> *Seek the bones of the demon of Psellus*

could be a reference to Psellus, a writer on demonology who lived some centuries earlier, or it would be a corruption of 'Phallus' and indicate the sexual nature of some witchcraft practices of Nostradamus's time. In either case, he is not at all complimentary about the practices, and we cannot imagine his indulging in them.

Alternatively, was he a 'diviner' or a 'scryer'? There is only one apparent reference to divination in the quatrains, where he is also explicitly a participant. It refers to a wand, a flame, a tripod and the sprinkling of hem and feet with water.[10] This is usually taken to mean that there was a bowl of water on the tripod, into which Nostradamus was assumed to gaze in order to obtain his inspiration. The mention of a wand passing between the legs of the tripod is obscure, but at least, the whole thing seems, at first reading, to indicate some practice of magic. The lines (I:1-2) actually read in translation:

> *Sitting solitary at night in secret study*
> *It is at rest on a tripod of brass*
> *A scanty flame comes out of the solitude*
> *and prospers that which should not be believed emptily*
> *The wand in hand is placed between the branches* [tripod's legs]
> *He sprinkles fringe and foot with water* [literally 'with a wave']
> *A voice, be afraid, he trembles, robed!*
> *Splendour divine – God is near!*

Note, firstly, that the lines do not refer to a bowl of water on the brass tripod, but that a flame rests on them. Secondly, as the first line indicates, the lines are not about magical practice, but about *study*. Thirdly, the reference to the scant flame in the third line has a double meaning, for in French the word is *exigue* (= slight or scanty), which is similar to the

---

[10] *Centuries* I:1-2.

word *exegete* and its Latin equivalent. The study is to *interpret*
something or other. It is not *empty* ('solitude') inspiration
(line 3) to assist *empty* (*croire vain*) beliefs, but the study of
something that is positively symbolic.

So, the connection with magical practices may be entirely
superficial, and even Laver,[11] who suggests that Nostradamus copied the ritual practices of the fourth-century
Neo-platonist philosopher Iamblichus, may also have been
entirely wrong. If the other quatrains of Nostradamus are to
be interpreted symbolically, why should not these two also
be symbolic in meaning? 'It', resting on the brass tripod, is
clearly the flame. Thus, we can infer that the brass tripod
held the only lamp with which Nostradamus 'burned the
midnight oil' in study. It caused him to reflect on the Deity –
on God. This would have been quite easy, for the figure of a
tripod holding a lamp is a close depiction of the Neo-
platonist doctrine of the three primal hypostases,[12] the three
'substances' or 'faces' of God – a teaching that later affected
the Church as the doctrine of the Trinity. Note that there is
no reference in the stanzas to a bowl of water. Indeed, the
only reference to water is *l'onde*, which also means a 'wave'.
Bodily distractions have to be swept aside (splashed clean)
while the 'waves' of inspiration do their work. There is a
series of collapsed biblical references, including those to the
practice of feetwashing,[13] and the fringes of garments.[14] The
whole impact of the two introductory stanzas is that external
distractions must be held in check, while inspiration (in
interpretation) does its work. In this sense they are innocent
of any suggestion of 'black magic' and compare favourably
with medieval mystical writings such as *The Cloud of
Unknowing*[15] and the writings of the pseudo-Dionysius.[16]

Nostradamus may thus be cleared of being *simply* an
astrologer, or *simply* a clairvoyant. He was much more than
that; but what *was* he?

---

[11] J. Laver, *Nostradamus: The Future Foretold*, p. 43.
[12] See E. O'Brien, *The Essential Plotinus*, pp. 90–105, or any other translation or
paraphrase of Plotinus's *Enneads*.
[13] John 13:1–11.
[14] Exodus 28:33–34; Matthew 9:20.
[15] C. Wolters (tr.), *The Cloud of Unknowing* (Penguin, 1961).
[16] C. E. Rolt (tr.), *Dionysius the Areopagite: The Divine Names and the Mystical
Theology* (SPCK, new edition, 1940).

The Statistics of the Stanzas

The predictions, published in 1555, are grouped into Centuries (sets of one hundred, four-line stanzas, or 'quatrains'). The first impression that these stanzas give is that they are not arranged in any apparent order. There is no 'time-series' or chronological order of prediction from Nostradamus's time to our own, but each of the ten Centuries contains prophecies relating to each of the periods between the sixteenth century and our own time, and thus each set of a hundred stanzas (Centuries) also contains a small residuum of unfulfilled, or at least unidentifiable, predictions.

Thus, if we take *one* interpretation of the first Century as an example,[17] the proportion of assumed fulfilments is shown below, using several accepted modern interpretations of Nostradamus.

Time Period	Number of Stanzas
1555–1600	18
1601–1700	5
1701–1800	16
1801–1900	20
1901–1983	25
Future twentieth century	4
Unidentifiable	12
Total	100

This table illustrates the apparent jumble, and it is sometimes claimed on behalf of Nostradamus that he deliberately jumbled the historical order of the stanzas so that they would escape easy interpretation. The proportions of fulfilments (with the above date-intervals) in the other Centuries are different, but the order is equally 'random'. There are a few cases where groups of stanzas in a given Century relate to a single event or set of events. For example, there is a high concentration of stanzas relating to the French monarchy of

---

[17] For this analysis I used Cheetham's interpretation, with some modifications.

Henri III's time in the first half of Century III. Also, in the middle of Century VIII, there is a group of apparent predictions of the English monarchy during the Civil War, while Century IX has a seemingly high 'cluster' of predictions relating to the House of Bourbon. Predictions of the French Revolution are also apparently clustered in Centuries I and IX. But these exceptions are only illusory. If a well-known statistical test, known as the *chi*-squared test[18] is applied to the above frequencies to test the relationship to later Centuries they can be proved 'random', not significantly different from later ones, though there are more unidentified stanzas in later Centuries, perhaps because people have thought less about them.

This randomness seems like ammunition for cynics, who sometimes suggest that the prophecies contain so many movements backwards and forwards in history that it is quite easy within four hundred years to identify any number of random events with each of the stanzas. Yet the apparent disorder is probably the greatest clue for the real investigator, for it would have been much too easy for Nostradamus simply to have placed them in historical order. Any number of other arrangements are possible. For example, the 114 suras of the Muslim Qur'an seem to be 'disarrayed' to a casual reader, for the 'creation' narrative appears late, and later events are arranged early on. But this is because the suras are placed in order of size.[19] Nostradamus's predictions appear to be arranged *topically*, some of them showing his scientific insight, and some based on the Bible; and there are whole sequences of stanzas indicating that he 'drew' (whether subconsciously or by interpretation[20]) on his knowledge of the biblical Apocalypse of John.

---

[18] For a fuller description of this test, see the appropriate entry in D. Pitt Francis and C. A. O'Muircheartaigh, *Statistics: A Dictionary of Terms and Ideas* (Hutchinson-Arrow, 1981).

[19] See G. Margoliouth and M. Rodwell, *The Koran* (Dent, 1909) for a rearrangement from the order of the Arabic text to a near-historical order.

[20] Using the interpretation of I:1-2 suggested earlier, Nostradamus's stanzas could contain either a 'studied' interpretation of biblical prophecy or a comment on subconsciously absorbed sections of it.

Nostradamus and Modern Inventions

Let us now explore the 'scientific' and 'biblical' bases of Nostradamus's insight, before trying to provide a number of possible explanations of the apparent accurate fulfilment of many of his prophecies. First, the scientific insight, which will be explored in detail in Chapter Seven.

One of the earliest of these predictions describes the invention of the submarine, and the firing of a missile from it:

> *When the fish that journeys over land and sea*
> *Is cast on the shore by a great wave –*
> *its shape, strange, smooth and horrific*
> *– the enemies soon reach the walls from the sea* [I:29]

This prediction is not only an example of Nostradamus's knowledge of inventions to come, but also of the principle of 'topical arrangement' suggested in the previous section. It comes only four quatrains later than his prophecy of Pasteur, and though that quatrain may mean something different in context, the 'Pasteur' prophecy *could* mean medicine before its time. He was certainly not the first to conceive of the submarine as a possibility. In fact, over fifty years earlier, the painter Leonardo da Vinci had sketched a drawing of a submarine in one of his notebooks, together with plans of missiles that could be ejected from them. He wrote: 'The evil nature of men is such that they will practice assassination by breaking the hulls of boats and wrecking them . . .' Nostradamus would have needed no foresight to be able to copy the works or words of Leonardo. His genius lay in arranging this information alongside other prophecies of scientific invention that have also been accurately fulfilled.

For example, the very next stanza predicts death and pillage despite 'palm-branches'.

> *Despite the signs of palm-branches,*
> *– afterward, death and pillage,*
> *– good counsel arrives too late* [I:30]

On first reading this seems like a prophecy of a reversal of peaceful intentions, but it is, in fact, an extraordinary prophecy of nuclear war, in which he not only 'drew' on his knowledge of the direction of modern inventions, but also on his knowledge of biblical prophecy. At some time between the eighth and fourth centuries BC, the Hebrew prophet, Joel, had written:[21] 'I will show wonders in heaven and on earth – blood and fire and pillars [lit. *palm trees*] of smoke'. This was an early biblical prophecy of nuclear war, and used a Hebrew word for 'pillar' (*timorah*) that derives from the word for 'palm-tree' (*tomer*) because the pillars of ancient buildings were often structured to look like palm trees. The word is frequently used in the Old Testament for an artificial palm tree,[22] and aptly describes the spreading shape of a 'cloud' of nuclear 'smoke'. As a Jewish Catholic, Nostradamus acquired a thorough knowledge of Hebrew from his grandfather, Jean.

The prediction, held in isolation, is remarkable enough but its position in the Centuries is even more remarkable. Not only is it a curious piece of *double-entendre,* but it occurs immediately after the submarine prophecy,[23] thus indicating that nuclear power will have originally been discovered with 'peaceful intent'. Yet it associates the submarine with nuclear power (e.g. nuclear warheads) and describes the great havoc that such weapons (as Polaris and its successors) can cause.

Nostradamus and the Revelation of John

Many of Nostradamus's quatrains look like cryptic apocalyptic writings of the style that imitates biblical prophecy, yet recasts its symbols. In Jewish history, such 'apocalypses' were common from the third century BC onwards, and I have shown elsewhere[24] that the Revelation of John was intended to be a Christian 'answer' to such cryptic, apocalyptic writing. Medieval interpreters did not know this, however, and often imagined that the Book of Revelation was simply a sequential political prophecy. Nostradamus would have been aware of their interpretations, some of which were fulfilled, because history sometimes tends to be self-repeating. It may have required an effort on his part to have arranged the

---

[21] Joel 2:28-30.
[22] Ezekiel 41:19-20.
[23] See 1:29 above.
[24] D. Pitt Francis, *The Most Amazing Message Ever Written* (Castle Books, 1983).

'scientific' stanzas I:25-30 in a sensible topical order, but it would have required very little effort to have consciously or unconsciously reproduced some of the themes from the Apocalypse of John in the very order in which they occurred there. Take, for example, the following sequence, again from Century I.

Revelation of John	*Nostradamus*
1. A warrior with a bow (6:1-2)	1. A reference to 'Mars' (I:15)
2. Bloodshed (6:3-4) associated with the 'seventy-sevenfold' reference to Cain (see Genesis 4:24)	2. Blood to be shed, and a reference to 'seventy times' (I:15).
3. 'Archer' symbols (6:1-8)	3. Reference to Sagittarius, the 'archer' (I:16)
4. Plague, famine and death in that order (6:5-9)	4. 'Plague, famine and death' (I:16)
5. Plagued earth (6:7-8)	5. 'parched earth' (I:17)
6. Earth soaked with blood to be avenged (6:9-10)	6. Land and sea soaked with blood (I:18)
7. 'Souls under an altar' (6:9)	7. Snakes around an altar (I:19)
8. A 'great earthquake' (6:12)	8. 'Shaking of land and sea' (I:20)

Does this sequence seem to be unconvincing? It is one of a number of such sequences. Some of the items contain several specific elements of detail that are also in order, as the 'plague, famine and death' of 4; but even if each of the eight elements only contained one item the chances of their being arranged in the same given order would be 1:8! (a mathematical factorial notation) which means 1/40320. But the chance that, in the mass of possible items, the same elements themselves occur in both the Apocalypse and Nostradamus is much greater and it is not the only case of such a sequence. Others occur in later Centuries.

This is not to say that Nostradamus provided the 'best'

possible interpretation of John's Revelation. His viewpoint was conditioned by the limitations of the time in which he lived, and history tends to be self-repeating, as far as interpretations of John's Apocalypse are concerned. For example, he used the cipher 'Babylon' of Revelation 17 to mean Paris because, just like ancient Babylon (situated between Tigris and Euphrates), Paris is also situated on two rivers (the Seine and Marne). Such a meaning would never be accepted by modern biblical scholars, but was useful to Nostradamus, because Revelation's predictions are capable of multiple fulfilment in the vast time-continuum of history, and Nostradamus 'cracked' only one set of meanings of its ciphers – something akin to what is known as the 'historical' school of interpretation, whereby interpreters such as Newton, Mede and Eliott were able to predict some events in the future of France, including the French Revolution.[25]

Some Possible Explanations

The challenge of Nostradamus is an outstanding one on two counts. To a materialist, who believes that the future cannot be predicted successfully, the success of Nostradamus in doing so has to be explained. To the Christian fundamentalist, who may believe that only biblical prophecy accurately anticipates future events, the astonishingly reliable detail of some of the Centuries can present a curious problem. The second part of this chapter attempted to show that Nostradamus was no charlatan but an educated healer, who was, in many respects, ahead of his time. We have seen that Nostradamus was not simply an astrologer, a crystal-gazer, or a black magician. On his own admission he was deeply engrossed in interpreting something. If so, what was he interpreting? Lastly, we have seen that though the Centuries appear to be jumbled, they seem to be arranged in a topical order, reflecting his knowledge of science and of biblical prophecy. If this is so, then scientific foresight and biblical interpretation may be added to the list of part-explanations of

---

[25] See Mede, *Apocalypse 3*; Newton, *Observations on the Prophecies of Daniel and the Apocalypse of John* (ed. 1732); Elliott's *Horae Apocalyptae* was later (nineteenth century) but followed the same 'traditions' in interpretation as the two previous authors.

his foresight. This being done, we are now in a position to offer some preliminary explanations of his success in forecasting future events.

The *first* of these explanatory factors is *random fulfilment*. Toss a coin, and there is a 0.5 chance of obtaining a desired head or tail. The chance of a 'six' is less (0.16̄) if a die is cast. If no time limit is specified there is always a greater chance that at some remote time any given combination of events (or cluster of numbers) can occur (or be cast), and this chance increases with the passage of time. If all of Nostradamus's predictions provided only one fulfilment-date and no other, and each fulfilment date had been matched exactly by a fulfilment, the Centuries would be easily vindicated. In some cases, however, the prediction actually failed in its intended fulfilment.

To quote two examples:

1. In Presages CXLI he predicted the details of the events surrounding his death. He would return from an embassy, put away the King's gift and fall on a bench near his bed, where he would be found dead. However, the date of his death was wrongly predicted.

2. In I:51 he implicitly quoted Roussat's work, and thus predicted a revolution in 1702. The revolution did not come until nearly ninety years afterwards.

So there is a statistical case against Nostradamus, a case that, in a sufficiently long time-span, all its details will be fulfilled, and that when there were references to specific dates these did not see the events that were sometimes intended to fit them.

Secondly, some early fulfilments can be attributed to a *personal gift* of foresight. This gift may be intuitive or logical and varies from one person to another. Some small fulfilment-spans can be anticipated, because of existing conditions. The death of Brezhnev in 1982 could have been foreseen, so could the Falklands crisis. At the time of writing there is a likelihood of a conflict between Venezuela and Guyana over territory around the Esequibo river. Not everyone has the intuitive foresight of a Jeanne Dixon. Some may project trends, as in Alvin Toffler's *Future Shock*; others may construct a model of the future, while yet others may engage in collective 'polls' of opinion about the future. Douglas McGregor, of the Massachussetts Institute of Technology, and Hadley Cantril, of Princeton University, both independently encouraged people in 1936 to make forecasts about near events, including Hitler's war and other matters, and the extent of 'collective' accuracy was astonishing. Later in 1953, Richard Auerbach, a New York primary school headmaster repeated the experiment, this time using children, by trying to get them to project the world of 1978. Their projections were locked away, and examined in 1978. Again the projections were astonishing.[26]

Astrological studies of correlation between horoscopes and character profiles suggest that astrology has some predictive value. However, in all these cases, the timespan between prediction and fulfilment is a short one (less than a century), and there is no evidence that it could be used successfully to explain much of Nostradamus's apparently long-range perception of the future, though the statistical explanation (see above) enhances accuracy, given that the timespan is not specific.

A *third* set of explanations, as we have seen, involves *prescriptive prophecy*. If a doctor tells a patient that he (the patient) is ill, it may have the effect of making him feel worse than otherwise would be the case. In the same way, an accountant (misusing accounting information) may judge a firm to be nearing bankruptcy. A bank takes the accountant's opinion and refuses credit. Other banks follow suit, and thus an otherwise healthy firm can easily be bankrupted.

A *fourth* explanation is similar, except that the 'subject' of the prophecy voluntarily fulfils it. It is *participative fulfilment*. The popes probably know of the prophecies of Malachy of Armagh mentioned earlier in the chapter, and some may have set about trying to fulfil them. Similarly, Hitler, who believed Nostradamus, attempted in some respects to fulfil Nostradamus's prophecies, as I show in Chapter Four.

A *fifth* reasonable explanation is *interpretational 'fudge'* – the variety of conflicting and diverse interpretations that hang on a single line. When the Pythoness at Delphi was consulted

---

[26] Full details are provided in the research studies concerned, but a popular summary is provided by D. Colligan, 'Your Gift of Prophecy' (*Readers Digest*, December 1982, pages 116–119).

about the battle between Lydia and Persia she wisely but ambiguously replied that if it occurred a great empire would be overthrown. It was a 'heads I win – tails you lose' prophecy. Both contenders were great empires, and one had to be overthrown. In this context is the obscurity that surrounds much of Nostradamus's crabbed French. For example, an anagram of only six letters may have up to 720 meanings, dependent on the arrangement of the letters,[27] though most arrangements may not have necessary meanings. But there are sufficiently obscure arrangements of anagrams to suggest the most diverse meanings. For example, Lonole is variously interpreted as Oliver Cromwell by James Laver and as London by Erika Cheetham in two equally convincing interpretations of one of Nostradamus's stanzas.

These five explanations exhaust many of the non-specific prophecies – those that seem to have 'worked out' because of chance, perceptiveness, involuntary and voluntary participation on the part of the subject, and the very fact that obscurity of language often enhances the chance of prophetic fulfilment because of the variety of interpretations that such obscurity can produce.

We can also add two more sets of explanations. The first of these is *scientific perceptiveness*. Nostradamus's foresight regarding modern inventions was not unique. This is because we all possess the desire to imagine the impossible, and then set about accomplishing it. I showed earlier that Nostradamus was not alone in anticipating the invention of submarines; Leonardo da Vinci, for example, had done so fifty years before him. Several factors combine to produce scientific predictiveness in people.

The first of these is that design often anticipates discovery by several hundred years. The ancient Greeks were known to have made some progress towards aeronautics; the Egyptians had used Pythagoras's theorem long before Pythagoras propounded it; and other pieces of important data, such as the value of *pi* (to calculate the circumference of a circle) are known to have been discovered independently by different people at different times.

Secondly, inventions are not necessarily accredited to their

---

[27] The number of combinations is 6!, a mathematical shorthand for $6 \times 5 \times 4 \times 3 \times 2 \times 1 = 720$.

'first' inventors, who often live and die in obscurity – thus there is another time-gap between first discovery and popularity.

Thirdly, scientific vision entails 'hit-and-miss' speculation about seemingly impossible inventions – as is clear from much science fiction writing. This very 'scientific vision' itself thus produces expectations, goals and objectives in the minds of people who would like to see them invented.

A fourth factor is that the very expectation of such discoveries carries considerable popularity, and that this, itself, drives people to work, trying to discover how a particular feat (such as radio communication or underwater travel) can be accomplished.

Finally, as with the first factor above, there is no necessary time scale. If people sufficiently believe that a given invention is 'possible', some will carry on working until it is realized. Thus, although I have listed *'scientific perceptiveness'* as a *special explanation* of the accuracy of Nostradamus's predictions, it does combine some of the earlier explanations. Apart from the discovery-popularity 'lag', it combines random speculation with a large element of prescriptive and participative fulfilment. If some 'prophet' can 'dream up' a seemingly impossible feat, and the desire to perform it becomes sufficiently popular, some people will carry on trying to discover how it can be accomplished, until it becomes a reality.

A seventh explanation, or set of explanations, derives from a knowledge of biblical prophecy. This was discussed briefly earlier in this chapter. If the Bible's prophetic claim is correct, and it reflects Divine foresight of human events – as some of the cases quoted earlier, such as the history of Israel and the destruction of Tyre, suggest – then any human 'prophet' can be reliable to the extent that he consciously or unconsciously interprets or recasts biblical prophecy. Some of Nostradamus's predictions, such as his prophecy of the re-creation of the State of Israel, clearly fall into this category, for such an event was foreseen much earlier by Biblical prophets. Even false prophets of a much lower moral calibre, and of much more spurious intentions than Nostradamus, are known to have made 'capital' for themselves, by reinterpreting biblical prophecy. To use a simple illustration, Moses 'warned' Pharaoh that the waters of Egypt would 'become blood' (whatever that meant). The Bible tells us that subsequently: 'the magicians of Egypt did the same by their secret arts'.[28]

It is difficult to imagine that the waters of Egypt 'became blood' twice. It is much more probable that the 'magicians' realized the reliability of Moses' prediction, and simply copied it, claiming it to be their own, and telling a credulous Pharoah that Moses had obtained it from them. Anyone who reads Nostradamus's work will realize that his prophecy of the restoration of Israel is accurate; but it needs a working knowledge of the Bible to give it the credit for having predicted the event nearly 3,000 years earlier.

Finally, there is the *ex eventu* explanation – that some prophecies of Nostradamus may have been written (or 'tampered with') after the events to which they relate occurred. Some biblical scholars are often quick to point out that later books of the Old Testament, such as Daniel, which contains a summary of the histories of Greek dynasties of Egypt and Syria from 330 to 165 BC, may have been written after the event. This is not the place to discuss such a claim, but it is fairly certain that some alterations occurred to the Centuries after Nostradamus's death. The first edition (1555) of the Centuries is incomplete, and only contains the first few centuries. It is also known that there were forgeries later attributed to Nostradamus, such as that relating to Mazarin, Richelieu's successor[29] and that relating to the final supremacy of Louis XIV.[30]

There, then are the eight factors that have helped to make the prophecies of Nostradamus successful predictions of future events. None of these alone is sufficient: all are necessary. Even so, not all of them will necessarily explain the 'genius' that has survived as 'Nostradamus', and the purpose of this book is to find out how far they can do so.

Thus, this book is not a simple 'translation' of Nostradamus's quatrains with some of the 'likely' fulfilments. Such a task has already been undertaken by many, including Erika

---

[28] Exodus 7:22.
[29] See Laver, *The Future Foretold* (Mann), pp. 103-104. Two stanzas were inserted in editions of the Centuries at the time of the civil war between the Frondeurs and the Cardinal in the seventeenth century.
[30] This occurs in some editions at the end of Century X.

Cheetham – though some of her assumed 'fulfilments' are now out of date. Instead, the book is an elaborate investigation, in which an impartial 'scepticism' (if such exists) has to be assumed. Chapters Two and Three discuss Nostradamus's prophecies of the French monarchy and of various revolutions, with the object of assessing, among other things, how many of the assumed predictions could have been consciously fulfilled by the French monarchy and how much prophetic material written by Nostradamus had to be reinterpreted when the French Revolution occurred.

Many of the fulfilments of Nostradamus's prophecies are clustered: they occur at times of greatest interest in his predictions, when people were puzzling over his writings, wondering how obscure passages could have been worked out, or how important events could have been foreseen by him. Thus, Chapter Four moves forward to the Second World War, and Chapter Five examines modern (i.e. late twentieth century) fulfilments of the Centuries. Chapter Six will show the weakness of the astrological explanation and assess the importance of other factors, such as Nostradamus's scientific foresight, his use of biblical prophecy, and the ingenuity of interpreters. These are examined in Chapter Seven.

An unexplained 'hardcore' will remain, to form the basis of a theory. Thus, this book will try to demonstrate that someone with an outdated knowledge of scientific invention and Biblical interpretation *could* (and therefore can!) demonstrate overwhelming powers of foresight. If this was possible in the leisurely unsophisticated times of Nostradamus, how much more possible is it to do so in our own days!

2
Nostradamus and the French Monarchy

Babylon

Throughout the first chapter, I have argued that Nostradamus was much more than a 'mere' astrologer, and that his apparently extraordinary gifts of foresight were attributable to other factors, including his anticipation of scientific invention and his knowledge of biblical interpretation. This theory seems to cut across all previous impressions of him, which have resulted mainly from the fact that he was consulted on astrology by most of the French 'notables' of his day. These included the dowager Queen Catherine (1519-1589) widow of Henri II and a member of the corrupt Medici family, who had bought their way into power in Italy two hundred years earlier and occupied the papal chair on at least three occasions, as Giovanni (Leo X: 1475-1521), Guilio (Clement VII: 1478-1534) and Alessandro (Leo XI: 1535-1605). Though she was nominally Catholic in deference to her papal relatives, and was primarily responsible for engineering the infamous massacre of the Huguenots in 1572, she was rather a Jezebel, who was reported to have dabbled in every kind of magic, black and white.

Faced with such a woman, who intermittently occupied the French throne after the death of Henri II in 1559, while three of her sons reigned and died, Nostradamus could scarcely refuse to cast horoscopes and give advice on what, in his days, despite his own denunciations,[1] was regarded as a respectable science. As a Jew, he was more vulnerable than most, so he adopted a slightly compromised role. He saw

---

[1] Centuries VI:100.

himself as a kind of 'successor' to the biblical Daniel, with a reputation for knowledge of occult sciences, but having the perceptiveness to realize that they are often useless in themselves. He would have appreciated that history often repeats itself, that John in Revelation[2] had recast the model of Babylon to mean the Roman world of his day, and that he could, with equal liberty, apply the same model to a corrupt sixteenth-century Paris, with its ties to a decadent papacy. To do so was not necessarily even a Protestant reaction, and Marzieh Gail[3] has shown that the Popes themselves used the term 'Babylon' in denunciation of each other in the days of the Triple Papacy, centuries earlier.

I am not suggesting that there is necessarily a parallel between Daniel and Nostradamus, but that he may have used some of the biblical data about Daniel — who was 'taught in the arts and language of the Chaldeans',[4] and 'chief of the magicians'[5] — in order to excuse his compromised position.

However, the historical parallel between the Babylon of the sixth century BC and sixteenth-century Paris speaks for itself, as the following summary shows:

BABYLON AND PARIS — THE REPETITION OF HISTORY

Sixth-century Babylon	*Sixteenth-century Paris*
1. Situated on two rivers: Tigris and Euphrates.	1. Situated on two rivers: Seine and Marne.
2. Corrupt, dowager widow of Nebuchadnezzar tries to retain control of kingdom at the end of neo-Babylonian dynasty (to 538 BC).	2. Corrupt, dowager widow of Henri II (d. 1559) tries to retain control of kingdom[6] at the end of Valois dynasty (1559-1589).
3. Dowager queen respects and consults Daniel.[6]	3. Dowager queen respects and consults Nostradamus.[7]

---

[2] Revelation 17 and 18.
[3] Marzieh Gail, *The Three Popes* (Hale, 1972).
[4] Daniel 1:4.
[5] Daniel 4:9.
[6] Daniel 5:10.
[7] J. Laver, *Nostradamus, The Future Foretold* (Mann), pp. 52-54.

Sixth-century Babylon	Sixteenth-century Paris
4. Babylonian throne occupied by weak successors to Nebuchadnezzar II (i.e. Amil-Marduk, Neriglassar and Nabonidus [with Belshazzar]) for nearly thirty years.	4. French throne occupied by weak successors to Henri II — by Francis II, Charles IX and Henri III, respectively — for a period of thirty years (to 1589).
5. Persecution of religious opponents.[8]	5. Persecution of Huguenots, including the massacre on St Bartholomew's day 1572.
6. A powerful tributary (Cyrus II) waits to take control when Babylon is in anarchy. His religion is Zoroastrian.	6. A powerful tributary (Henri of Navarre) waits to assume power when Paris reaches its nadir of anarchy. His religion is Huguenot.
7. Cyrus overcomes Babylon and renounces Zoroastrian for Babylonian religion.[9]	7. Henri of Navarre becomes Henri IV and renounces his Huguenot faith for Catholic teaching.
8. Cyrus proclaims civil and religious liberty, resulting in the restoration of[10] Judaism and return from exile.	8. Henri IV enacts the edit of Nantes (1598), by which all religious minorities were tolerated, and the Huguenots allowed to worship publicly.
9. The Persian dynasty lasted 200 years and ended with another period of decadence and the conquest by Alexander the Great (c.333 BC).	9. The Bourbon dynasty lasted exactly 200 years and ended with another period of decadence, the French Revolution (1789), and the rise of Napoleon.

Some of these parallels are obvious to us, and though some of them would not have been obvious to Nostradamus, he could easily have speculated about them. He would realize that when a strong-willed widow acts as a debased regent for her weak children and outlives them, this often presages the end of a dynasty. There are Old Testament parallels

---

[8] Daniel 3 and 6 and apocryphal appendices; also Jeremiah 29:22
[9] Cyrus Cylinder (A.N.E.T., ed. Pritchard, OUP, 1950).
[10] Compare Ezra 1:1-4 with 9 *supra*.

elsewhere: Jezebel was imported into Northern Israel from Zidon, and her reign terminated the decadent dynasty of Omri; Athaliah performed the same disservice for the Kingdom of Judah a generation later; and there are non-Biblical parallels in both Egypt and China. The symbol of Babylon, however, provided the best parallel for Nostradamus, for he interpreted the 'Babylon' city of the Apocalypse of John[11] to mean Paris. This is evidenced in the writings of most of his commentators. It is difficult to imagine that when he wrote of 'Babel' in 'newspapers', or of 'a city watered by two rivers', or 'he will lead a great army of red and white, and they will go forth against the king of Babylon',[12] that he was not referring to Paris. Thus, if he interpreted the 'Babylon' of John's Revelation to mean sixteenth-century European Paris, it is plausible that he would consider himself as a kind of 'Daniel' in it.

The Seven-branched Candlestick

Given that Nostradamus used John's Apocalypse as a model for predictions, he would have commenced with its earliest vision, a Jewish *menorah* or seven-branched candlestick. John had used it of seven Christian churches in Roman Asia that were near and dear to him. Nostradamus would similarly have appropriated the symbol to mean the House of Valois — a dynasty near and dear to himself. It was appropriate for Henri II died in 1559 leaving seven 'branches' or descendants. The *menorah* predates Moses. It is a reminder of the Creation story of Genesis,[13] of the seven planets, of Jewish weeks of years, and perhaps the symbol is associated with Joseph and with a well-known story of seven years of plenty, followed by seven years of famine.[14] The association is by no means 'forced'. In Hebrew, the word for stalk in the dream of Pharaoh is *qanah*, a word that is translated 'branch' in the account of the seven-branched candlestick and also means 'descendant'. The ready association between a seven-branched candlestick, a seven-branched stalk of corn[14] and

---

[11] Revelation 17 and 18.
[12] *Centuries* II:30; II:97; and X:86.
[13] Revelation 1:12; Exodus 25:31-40; and Genesis 1:1-2:4.
[14] Genesis 41:4.

seven years of plenty predates Karnak, where seven-branched candlesticks occur, for Joseph would have served an earlier dynasty, and the candlestick symbol may thus originally have been a celebration of the seven years of plenty in Egypt. Whether this is correct or not, Nostradamus's mind seems to have readily associated the seven 'branches' with two consecutive periods of seven years. During the first of these (1552-1559), France would be defended against the Turks by Admiral Gaspard de Coligny in a time of relative safety and prosperity during the reign of Henri II. Then, subsequent to Henri's death in 1559, his widow, Catherine, would mourn his death for a further period of seven years (1559-1566). As these two periods are amongst the few occurrences of seven-year periods in the Centuries and as they are consequent, a 'lean' period following a 'prosperous' one, it seems clear that, long before the discoveries at Karnak, Nostradamus was aware of the association between the seven-branched candlestick and the Joseph story.

One of the earliest references to the 'House of Seven' (the seven children of Henri II) is to be found in the Presages: 'The House of Seven by a "suit" of death will die'.[15] The seven children were Francis (François) II, married later to Mary Stuart of Scotland; Elizabeth, who would marry Philip II of Spain just before Henri II's death; the Duchess of Lorraine, who would die within about ten years; Charles IX, who would reign under the guidance of his mother; Henri III, who would be recalled from the crown of Poland to become king under the direction of Catherine; Francois, duke of Alençon, and King of the Netherlands, and Marguerite, who would marry Henri of Navarre, the future Henri IV and founder of the new Bourbon dynasty. Nostradamus rightly perceived that they would all die, and that the dynasty of Valois would die with them. However, perhaps to please his patron, he wrongly predicted that they would all rule.

References to the seven branches recur later in the writings of Nostradamus, particularly in the Centuries, but we now turn to the two periods of seven years each. The first of these relates to Gaspard de Coligny, who as Admiral protected French interests against the Turks during the last seven years of Henri II's reign, but resigned at Henri's death in 1559 to

---

[15] Presages 40: line 1.

place himself as chief of the Huguenots.

> *The great Pilot will be summoned by the King*
> *to leave the fleet for a higher command*
> *but seven years later he will be in revolt*
> *and Venice will be afraid of the barbarian army*[16]

During Henri's reign and Gaspard's captaincy, France would feel safe against the 'barbarians' for seven years. When Henri died seven years later, Gaspard would rebel, and begin the wars of religion, and France would be less secure in the east against the Turks. This was particularly true of the next seven years until the death of Suliman the Magnificent in 1566, after which the threat retreated, particularly after the Battle of Lepanto in 1571, though the Turks captured Cyprus in 1570. During those 'lean years', to coin Chesterton's words about the Sultan: 'the inmost sea of all the earth' was 'shaken with his ships'.[17]

During those 'lean years', Catherine would mourn the death of her husband, as Nostradamus foretold elsewhere:

> *Seven years she will be weeping with distress*
> *Then she will live long, for the welfare of the Kingdom*[18]

Note that both predictions come from Century VI, which did not occur in the first published set of Nostradamus's predictions in 1555, and that the prediction about Catherine's grief occurs just before that of Gaspard's command, whereas historically it occurred after the command was resigned.

We can begin to reflect on the validity of the predictions we have so far examined. Though there is a preoccupation with the number seven and though the two seven-year periods can be historically identified, nothing is beyond rational explanation. Nostradamus used an historical model to anticipate the end of the Valois dynasty;[15] the prediction of Gaspard is dated (at the earliest) 1555,[16] three years inside the seven-year period (1552-1559), though in the future tense, and could have been added afterwards; while the prophecy of seven years mourning by Catherine[18] could have been

---

[16] Centuries VI:75.
[17] G. K. Chesterton, 'Lepanto'.
[18] Centuries VI:63.

deliberately fulfilled by her (participant fulfilment) since she was a devotee of Nostradamus.

At this stage the predictions can therefore be explained, and their quality is somewhat reduced by the fact that Nostradamus calls the volatile Catherine, who was partly responsible for the massacre of the Huguenots, the 'sainted widow'. To some readers the theory that Nostradamus used the two consecutive seven-year periods of the biblical 'Joseph' as a model for *his* two seven-year periods may seem highly imaginative, unless it is appreciated that Nostradamus may have used Joseph himself as a 'model'. Like Daniel, the biblical 'Joseph' was reputed to have risen to prominence at a royal court as one who held true religion, but who yet realized the worth of some occult sciences. An early dream that he had interpreted used astrological symbols and he also had a reputation for practising divination.[19] He could have provided Nostradamus with yet another excuse (or precedent) for compromising his position with French royalty. Nostradamus died in 1566, the very year that Catherine ceased mourning. This can be regarded as coincidence; even if Nostradamus had predicted his death to have occurred at that time, he was then old, and, as stated in the previous chapter, it is not difficult to predict that a 'given' year will probably be the year of death of an old man.

His death is important, however, for it provides further evidence that Nostradamus saw himself fulfilling a role similar to the 'Joseph' model. Of Joseph, it is said that he: 'gave commandment concerning his bones'.[20] In imitation of his 'Joseph' model, Nostradamus did exactly the same thing. He predicted evil for the man who found his tomb and did not shut it immediately.

> *The man who opens the monument, when it is found . . .*
> *and who does not shut it promptly,*
> *evil will come upon him*[21]

There is a similar prophecy[22] about a treasure, which has

---

[19] Genesis 37:8-11 and 44:5 and 15.
[20] Hebrews 11:22.
[21] Centuries IX:7.
[22] Centuries I:27.

been misread as a prediction about Nostradamus's bones. I shall deal with this later. The real prediction about his bones sounds almost like an Egyptian curse, of the sort actually fulfilled on the discoverers of the tomb of Tutankhamun in 1922, thus confirming the connection with Joseph.

Paradoxically, however, Joseph's 'testament' was written to avoid burial in Egypt. His bones were taken out of Egypt three generations (i.e. two hundred years) later to be reburied in Israel. There is no evidence that Nostradamus's 'Egyptian' curse was ever carried out on those who disturbed his corpse; but by a curious parallel, it lay in the church of Salon (where he died) for about two hundred years, and when the church was destroyed during the French Revolution, the bones were transferred and reburied at Notre-Dame de St Laurent, where a permanent epitaph is inscribed on a marble monument. This parallel at least partly justifies the theory that Nostradamus used Joseph's seven-year prophecies as a model for the period from 1552 to his own death in 1566.

Let us continue with the image of the seven-branched candlestick (the Jewish 'menorah'). In the Apocalypse of John,[23] it introduces a whole series of sevens, a seven-sealed scroll, seven trumpets, seven 'bowls' of wrath,[24] and so on. Nostradamus would have noticed that each of these are divided in the ratio 4:3, for the first four of each are special: four horsemen, four trumpets on the 'cosmos' — earth, sea, subterranean waters, and heaven — and four 'bowls' poured on the same 'divisions' of the 'universe' of the ancient world.

This 4:3 division is studiously copied in some of the Centuries for no apparent reason, and if we were not aware of the 4:3 division in John's Apocalypse, the references would be curious and obscure indeed. There are a few references to the 'seven', some of which also concern a remaining 'three' branches, thus presupposing a 4:3 division in the heirs of house of Valois.

Let us examine them in turn.

> *The seven, reduced to three, will be in agreement,*
> *to subjugate the Apennine Alps —*
> *but the tempest and the cowardly Ligurian* [Genevan league]
> *will soon throw them down into ruin*[25]

---

[23] Revelation 1:12-20.
[24] See consecutively Revelation 6:1-8; 8:1-13, and 16:1-8.
[25] *Centuries* III:39.

This seems to be a prophecy of a time when three of the seven children of Henri II are left. There are some ambiguities, for 'reduced to three' is, in French, *en trois seront mis*,[26] but instead of this, Cheetham[27] reads *en trois mois*, which means 'in three months', rendering the whole line: 'The seven shall be in agreement for three months'. If so, the prophecy 'failed' for there were no 'seven' at the time. However, we can be confident about the earlier reading, not only because of the 'apocalypse' model, but because it appears elsewhere, and without ambiguity in Nostradamus's writings. For example:

> *The seven branches will be reduced to three,*
> *the oldest ones will have been surprised by death.*
> *The two will be seduced to fratricide . . .*[28]

The contents of the two quatrains are similar, and appear to refer to a time when Catherine de Medici's seven children would be reduced to three in 1575, when only Henri III, Francois d'Alençon and Marguerite would be alive, and when the Ligurians (Genevan leaguers) would plot conspiracy against Henri III.[29] The importance of both these passages does not simply lie in the fact that they appear to relate to the same time in history, but in the 'apocalyptic' division of seven into two series of four and three. Nostradamus is, in effect, saying 'four will have gone, and three will be left'. The division is not only symbolic but poetic. The most common verse-form of the period, the sonnet, consisted of seven couplets divided into two stanzas — one of four couplets, and the other of three.

Though the fulfilment is surprisingly accurate, some of it could have been foreseen. Unless two children died at the same time, there would have to be a time when four children were dead and the other three survived. Further, Nostradamus, as the court physician, would have known the

---

[26] J. Laver, *Nostradamus*, p. 82.
[27] E. Cheetham, *Nostradamus*, p. 137.
[28] Centuries VI: 11.
[29] I have adopted a possible Genevan interpretation here (see Cheetham, p. 137, 27 *supra*), even though the term 'League', which does not occur in the stanza but sounds like 'Ligure', would obviously be a reference to the opposing Catholic (Holy) League.

children's affections and disaffections for each other and may even have been aware of their likelihood of survival. Participant fulfilment is unlikely, for two became attracted to Protestantism (hence the mention of the Ligurians, or Genevan leaguers), and as Protestants would not have been sympathetic to Nostradamus's reputation as an astrologer. In the first of these prophecies there is some 'interpretational fudge', as we have seen, depending on the reading of *mis* as *mois*, and there is always the chance of a few words of the stanza having been altered after the event, to suit the fulfilment. There is also some interpretational 'fudge' in the stanza itself, for there is no evidence that a literal 'tempest' (storm) occurred, to fulfil the line: 'but the *tempest* and the cowardly league'.

The line has to be interpreted, but when words are taken to be symbolic they are laid open to a whole range of possible fulfilments. Yet, despite all these elements of caution, this stanza must be regarded as the most perceptive of Nostradamus's predictions about the period. There is no chance of pleading that the prediction was written after the event, for it appears in the first and incomplete edition of 1555.[30] Let us note it as one of the unexplained 'core' of Nostradamus's unexplained but relatively accurate predictions, with a time horizon of at least twenty-one years (1576–1555).

Are there other references to the seven-branch candlestick? Earlier in the centuries is the following stanza:

> *New, and sudden unexpected rain*
> *will prevent the two armies* [from battle]. *From heaven* —
> *Stones and fire will make a stony sea*
> *The death of the seven suddenly, by land and sea!*[31]

It does, at first glance, look like a very convincing prediction of an intended battle between one league (opposed to Henri III) and Henri. Even the term, 'league' is ambiguous in predictions of the period, for it may refer to a Protestant league of Germans and Swiss Calvinists sympathetic to Henri of Navarre, who was later to renounce his Protestantism and

---

[30] *Les Propheties de Michel Nostradamus* (Bonhomme, Lyons 1555).
[31] Centuries II:18.

become Henri IV; or it may mean the Catholic 'league' of the Duc de Guise, who opposed the German invasion. By 1583, both were antagonistic to Henri III, and Jacques Clement, who was involved with the latter faction, was to cause uproar in Paris six years later, kill Henri III and hold a besieged Paris against the forces of Henri of Navarre. Thus, the two opposing armies were 'leagues' and the earlier stanza (Centuries III:39) has been variously interpreted to mean both of them. The reference to a 'league' would be clear and mean the Catholic 'Holy League' if not for the subtle similarity between 'league' and 'Liguria'.

However, a battle, due to be fought between 36,000 German and Swiss troops and the Duc de Guise (on behalf of the Holy League), was prevented by a thunderstorm. This could not have been a fulfilment of the 'tempest' passage of the later stanza (VI:11) which has already been discussed, for it did not produce ruin but simply prevented the battle. There is no recorded evidence of the 'fire from heaven' (lightning) of II:18, and the last line has been severely distorted by commentators to give it an accuracy that it does not have. For example 'by land and sea' is read by Laver to mean 'the man of earth and sea', and thought to mean Brissac, who headed the Parisian revolt of 1588-9 against Henri III. Henri was reputed to have told Brissac that he was 'good for nothing on earth or sea', hence a subtle reference that 'earth and sea' meant (a) a *man* of earth and sea, and (b) therefore meant Brissac, who was clearly told that he was *not* a 'man of earth and sea'. There is no evidence of prediction, in this case, for not only is the line distorted, but Henri III may have known of the stanza, and was, in effect, telling Brissac that he was *not* the fulfilment!

A second example of inaccuracy in the line is the phrase: 'the death of the seven' (VI:11), which is interpreted to mean the death of Henri III by assassination in Paris in 1589 two years later than the inhibited battle of Montargis. The line literally means that the 'seven' will die suddenly (all together) by land and sea. It is generally understood to mean the death of Henri III, who is assumed to be the last (remaining heir) of the seven children of Catherine de'Medici. But this is faulty interpretation, since he was not the last to die. The last survivor of the seven was Marguerite of France, first wife of Henri IV (Navarre), who did not die until 27 March 1615.

Two possible references to the 'seven' remain to be considered, before I discuss the three remaining Valois kings individually. These are:

> When the head of Perouse will not risk his robe
> — without cover, stripping himself naked
> seven aristocrat [princes] will be taken
> father and son dead because of throat wound[32]

and

> A serpent [= 'shroud' or 'coffin'] is placed in the vault of iron
> where the seven children of the king are held;
> the ancestors and fathers will come out from the depths of hell
> mourning to see the last of their line, like dead fruit[33]

Both these stanzas are inaccurate, but show some perceptiveness on the part of the prophet.

The robed 'head' of Perouse (Perugia) is taken to mean the Pope, *chef* in the line being similar to *clef* meaning 'key' (hence, the 'keys' of St Peter). The reference to a 'robe' cannot be taken literally, but means the papal office and title (hence the English 'defrocked'). The Pope had excommunicated Henri of Navarre when he returned to Huguenot belief after having become a Catholic to avoid death during the massacre of the Huguenots in 1572. If he also excommunicated Henri III for defection, the papacy (Sixtus V) would become powerless (disrobed). All this seems like 'interpretation' but is based on Nostradamus's knowledge of the Bible, and of John's Apocalypse in particular: 'Happy is he, who watches and keeps his robes lest he walk naked'.[34]

However, as I have already shown, 'the seven [aristocrat] princes' were *not* taken, for Marguerite of Navarre did not die for nearly twenty-six years, and if the prediction refers, as is supposed, to the fact that both Henri II and Henri III would be stabbed to death, the details of the prediction are hopelessly inaccurate. Henri II died in 1559 from a duelling wound while Nostradamus was alive, four years after the publication of the first edition of the Centuries, which does

---

[32] Centuries V:67.
[33] Centuries I:10.
[34] Revelation 16:15.

not contain the stanza in question (V:67). Henri III was assassinated by a Dominican, Jacques Clement, who, like the biblical Ehud[35] made his way to the king's personal apartment on the pretext of giving a message, found him (just like Ehud) in the embarrassing act of relieving himself, and stabbed him in the belly. The similarity to the biblical account of Ehud and Eglon is remarkable, but the events of Henri III's assassination are quite unlike those of his father. Henri II died from a throat wound, in a rather 'loose' sense, for it was facial, but it was the result of a jousting accident in public. His son Henri III died from a belly wound, administered by an assassin in secret. When it is considered that Nostradamus may have written the prediction after the death of Henri III — unlike another reference to his death: 'In cage of gold, he will pierce his eyes — its inaccurate comparison deprives it of useful predictive value.

The other stanza is not at all complimentary to Catherine's seven children or to their ancestors. The word 'hell' is *l'enfer* in French. It is not the biblical word for the grave, but for a place of punishment, and as such the stanza is simply a poetic prophecy that all of Catherine's seven children would die, and could expect little happiness in the afterlife. The reference to a vault of iron could refer to the final resting place of Henri III, Catherine de'Medici and Henri IV in St Denis, after Henri III had been temporarily buried from 1589 to 1610. But even this prediction was not literally fulfilled, for in 1610, one of the seven, Marguerite of Navarre, was still alive, and the reference to iron vault was to a tomb that already had been in existence centuries before Nostradamus's time. Previous kings of France had been buried there, and it required little guesswork to predict that some of the seven children of Catherine would finally be interred there.

So much for the seven branches of the Valois candlestick. There is one remarkable unexplained prophecy, but quite a few others the details of which are obscure and whose words have been 'fudged' and distorted by over-zealous interpreters. There is little doubt that Nostradamus role-played the parts of the biblical Daniel and Joseph; that he adopted biblical symbolism to motivate, pattern and structure some of his predictions. Sometimes he could be hopelessly

---

[35] Judges 3:15-30.

inaccurate, but he was astonishingly correct in one stanza on several points of detail. We can discard the failures, and shall do later; but how did he manage, on a few occasions, to see the future so clearly? This question has to be left until the end of the book. Let us now turn to the three Valois kings, examine the prophecies concerning the Huguenots, and analyze some of Nostradamus's more accurate predictions about the Bourbon dynasty.

Three Kings

Of Catherine's seven children, only three became sovereigns. These were: Francis II (1559-1560), Charles IX (1560-1574) and Henri III (1574-1589). Very little in the Centuries can be seen to refer to the first of these. The only reference comes late in the prophecies and could be an interpolation:

> The first son, [with a] *widow, unfortunate marriage;*
> *without children, two islands in discord,*
> *Before eighteen* [and therefore a minor], *of incapable age;*
> *the betrothal of the other one will be even lower*[36]

Francis II married Mary Queen of Scots, and died before achieving majority on 5 December 1560, a few weeks before his eighteenth birthday. Mary was a childless widow, and returned to Britain to an unwelcome fate shortly afterwards. Francis was married before Nostradamus's death, and thus the first line of the stanza would cause no problem, nor would the prediction that Mary would die childless, though this occurred five years later than the incomplete publication of the Centuries in 1555. The statement that Mary would place the Isles in discord is technically inexact, though Nostradamus may have intended it that way, for the two islands would be Britain and Ireland, and the two kingdoms thrown into discord were England and Scotland, both on the 'mainland' of the larger isle. The amount of discord was not particularly great, and resulted from the attitude of Elizabeth I to Mary Stuart. During her short reign in France, Mary, though a daughter of Mary of Lorraine, of the Catholic Guise family, was known to have adopted a tolerant attitude to

---

[36] Centuries X:39.

Protestantism, while Mary I of England was a bigoted Catholic. So, if the stanza is early, it would have meant that a Protestant would have been regarded by a Catholic queen as disruptive. The reverse occurred. Elizabeth I, a Protestant, became Queen of England in 1558, and Mary of Scots became a Catholic, though Elizabeth's antagonism to her was political, rather than religious. The fulfilment resulted from a peculiar 'trick' of history and reversal of roles, though Mary of Scots did not, of herself, place the 'two Isles' in discord, even if the phrase is liberally interpreted. Catholic-Protestant discord in France, England and Scotland, and elsewhere in Western Europe was a common phenomenon of the sixteenth century, and it did not require Nostradamus to foresee it.

The most likely 'predictive' line in the quatrain concerns the other betrothal (Fr. *l'accord*) of Charles to Elizabeth of Austria in 1561 when he was only eleven; but there is evidence from Michieli, a Venetian ambassador, that the stanza was well known at the time and Catherine, who was a devotee of Nostradamus, could have arranged the betrothal with the prediction in mind. It would not only have been a case of participant fulfilment, but of hereditary necessity, though Charles IX did not actually marry Elizabeth until 1570, when he was twenty.

Let us now see if we can find clear predictions about the second of these kings, Charles IX, who succeeded his brother when he was only ten years old and reigned for fourteen years until 1574, his reign spanning the infamous massacre of the Huguenots in 1572. I shall be dealing with Nostradamus's predictions about the Huguenots in the next part of this chapter. It is sufficient, at this stage, to say that the whole affair resulted from a 'trick' to which Charles IX, who was both sadistic and insane, ignorantly succumbed. During his reign, the royal family's loyalties were torn between the Catholic house of Guise and the influence of a number of outstanding Protestants, including Coligny, who, as we have already seen, resigned on Henri II's death from being admiral of the French fleet after seven years of success to head the Huguenot community. Charles, who was suspicious of his mother and brother Anjou (the future Henri III), tried in 1570, when a Catholic-Protestant war had ended with the Peace of St Germain, to re-establish dialogue with the

Protestants. This meant coming to terms with Coligny, who
became his chief advisor, in place of his mother and brother.

Catherine first grasped the opportunity of using Coligny
to arrange a marriage between Charles's sister Marguerite
and Henri of Navarre, the future Henri IV, on 17 August
1572, but the effect was to strengthen Protestant influence
over the king and make the Guise family even more jealous,
particularly as Coligny had advised the king to disregard his
mother's advice and make Anjou King of Poland. The Guises
thus plotted the murder of Coligny with an arquebus on 22
August, and when this failed, Charles's mother and Anjou
took credit for the attempted murder, saying that they had
done so to save the king.

It was Charles's response, that if they were to get rid of
Coligny, they would have to get rid of all the Huguenots,
that fired the massacre. The conspirators, who also realized
that Coligny's death would throw the country into the worst
possible war of discord at the hands of the now influential
Huguenots, first murdered Coligny in his bed, and then
ordered provincial governors to sanction massacres simul-
taneously. Charles, who was endowed with a sadistic streak
of insanity, when his friend and advisor was dead, had no
alternative but to side with his mother and brother, and
throw his strength into making the massacre as successful as
possible.

This is all that need be said about the massacre at present. It
is mentioned because it is the subject of the only one of
Nostradamus's quatrains that actually concerns Charles IX:

> When the fierce [black] king [noir = roi] will have tried
> his blood-drenched hand through fire, sword and bent bow
> all the people will be afraid to see
> the great ones hanging by their neck and feet[37]

This looks like a clear prophecy of the massacre of the
Huguenots, an event that occurred six years after Nostradamus's death. But let us not be too enthusiastic, for the
following reasons.

First, Protestant expositors of the Apocalypse of John,
had, as we shall see later, been forecasting massacres of

---

[37] Centuries IV:47.

Protestants throughout this period on the strength of their understanding of the prophecies of that book. Secondly, massacres of Huguenots had previously occurred, resulting from the edicts of the *chambre ardente* of Henri II (1547-59), and a miniature massacre occurred a while before Nostradamus's death, when the congregation at Vassy were mass-murdered in March 1562. Thirdly, the stanza mentions a 'bent-bow', but Charles IX used an arquebus. It cannot be argued that Nostradamus would not have known about the invention of the arquebus and used 'bent-bow' instead, for it had in fact been invented a century earlier. Fourthly, the practice of hanging bodies 'by neck and feet' was also common in France at the time. Finally, the word *noir* is not necessarily an anagram of *roi*, and the evidence of its use in this way post-dates (rather than precedes) Nostradamus. In other words, the anagram has *become* acceptable because of the quatrain, and without the word *noir* there is no suggestion of a king. The stanza could just as easily be an apocalyptic summary, combining some of the elements of the 'seals' sequence such as a 'black horse',[38] a 'bent bow',[39] a sword,[40] 'blood',[41] and persecution,[42] a matter that, at this stage, needs to be reserved for a discussion of Nostradamus's use of the Bible in Chapter Seven.

The stanza is thus almost, but not completely, explained. The word *Noir* does appear with a capital 'N' and looks like a reference to the king, and though some details are inaccurate, Coligny was hanged by his feet from a gibbet at Montfaucon. So, though Nostradamus is not reliable, he foretells enough to make people, at least, uncomfortable, about his predictive powers!

Before moving from Charles IX to Henri III, it is appropriate to discuss the only other assumed prediction of an event that occurred during Charles's reign, the Battle of Lepanto. It was mentioned earlier in this chapter, as the culmination of the second of Nostradamus's seven-year periods. The quatrain that is assumed to deal with this battle is found early in the Centuries and reads:

---

[38] Revelation 6:5.
[39] Revelation 6:2.
[40] Revelation 6:4.
[41] Revelation 6:10
[42] Revelation 6:9.

> *On the fields of Media, Arabia and Armenia*
> *two great 'copies' [= 'armics', Latin copiae] will meet three*
>   *times*
> *by the river-bank of Araxes, the household*
> *of Suliman the Great will tumble to the ground!*[43]

It is Laver,[44] in particular, who suggests that this quatrain is a prediction of the battle of Lepanto (1571), but only by ignoring the first two lines. Others have suggested that, despite the use of a future tense, these lines refer to battles between the Turks and their opponents in Media and Armenia (but not Arabia) before the peace of 1555, which could even include the Battle of Araxes in 1514. But the tense is future, and must therefore have been intended to mean something future to 1555, when the quatrain was first published.

The suggestion that it means Lepanto is based on the premise that 'Araxes' should be 'Araxum', another name for Cape Papa where the naval battle of Lepanto was fought. In this case *rivage* (river bank) could mean 'shore' — hence 'Cape Araxum'. To anyone who doubts Nostradamus's predictive powers the allusion is uncomfortably correct; but, again, in this stanza there is inaccuracy and interpretational 'fudge'. Consider the following. First, battles had been occurring in the very area mentioned by Nostradamus, at the very time when he was writing, between Suliman I and his opponents in Iraq (1534) and around Lake Van (1548), so that it was a 'good gamble' for Nostradamus to want to say something about them. Yet, by a trick of fate against Nostradamus, as soon as the Centuries were published in 1555 they came to an end! Secondly, the text says 'Araxes' *not* 'Araxum'. The Araxes is an important river in the area of Armenia and Media previously mentioned. The word *rivage* suggests a river bank or boundary, though it can mean a coast (but not a cape); but in context it suggests the bank of Araxes, or a boundary, and Araxes has, for much of its history been a boundary, as it is today, for most of its length, between the USSR, and Turkey and Iran. Further, Lepanto did not involve Suliman I, who died on 5 September 1566, and who was the 'grand Soliman' (Suliman the Great) of the

43 Centuries III:31.
44 Laver, *Nostradamus*, p. 63.

fourth line. The forces that 'fell to the ground' at Lepanto were those of his son Selim II. So, the prophecy now looks like a failure, that anyone, writing in Nostradamus's time, would have been tempted to produce.

We can now dispense with the reign of Charles IX, but I shall return to the problem of the Huguenots later in this chapter and briefly consider the reign of Henri III (Anjou). The inaccuracy of the prophecies of his death have already been considered when discussing the seven-branched candlestick. Were there any other notable prophecies about this king? If the interpreters are correct, he is the man of Blois — so-called because he was descended from the counts of Blois — who appears in several stanzas. But the connection is a weak one, for he was no more a descendant of them than any of the other children of Henri II and Catherine of Medici. The relevant stanzas are:

> *The King of Blois will rule in Avignon*
> *— again the people drink blood*
> *In the Rhone, by the walls, he will make them swim*
> *until five — the last one near Nolle*[45]

> *The King of Blois to rule in Avignon*
> *— from Ambois, and Seme [= Seine] shall come the length of*
>   *Lyndra*
> *claws at Poitiers holy wings, brought to ruin*
> *before Boni . . .*[46]

> *When a king is chosen against his own*
> *— a native of Blois will subdue the Ligures [Genevan or 'holy'*
>   *Catholic league]*
> *Mammel, Cordoba and the Dalmatians*
> *Of the seven then a shadow to the King.*
> *— 'estrennes' and 'lemures' [spirits of the dead]*[47]

If Henri III is the 'native of Blois', the three stanzas (when written in full) appear to contain very little that is historically accurate. Henri III did not actually rule from Avignon; the last line of the second stanza has been mutilated because it

---

[45] Centuries VIII:38.
[46] Centuries VIII:52.
[47] Centuries X:44.

may have been anti-Papal, for Boni could be a mutilated version of 'Boniface'. Henri III did not 'subdue' the 'Ligures', if they are the Protestants, but passed an edict of toleration in 1577 to try to compensate for the harm done them five years earlier, nor did he subdue the 'leaguers', if they are the Catholic 'holy' league, but was finally murdered by one of their sympathizers because of his toleration of Protestants. In fact, the edict of toleration provides the only 'silver lining' in this cloudy trio of stanzas for it was enacted at Poitiers, hence the line: 'claws at Poitiers, holy wings [the papal eagle] brought to ruin'. It did not ruin the papal eagle, but simply provided some toleration of Protestant assemblies. A second supposed prediction of the Edict of Poitiers, need not have been successful, for it reads:

> For the pleasure of an edict of voluptuousness
> poison will be mingled with law
> Venus will be in Court, and so virtuous
> that all the glory of the Sun will be obscured[48]

Laver's suggestion[49] that this was a prediction of the Edict of Poitiers is neither critical nor scholarly, but unimaginatively follows an existing tradition, running back to Nostradamus's early expositors, and one that has never been changed. The Edict of Poitiers was not voluptuous, but merely tolerated Huguenot worship. The references to voluptuousness and Venus clearly predict another kind of edict sanctioning immorality, of which those of the French Revolution would be a better fulfilment, but by then the French Court had been exterminated, leaving little chance of an accurate fulfilment. But all this does not entirely denigrate Nostradamus, who may never have intended the prophecy to refer to a literal edict, nor (as commonly held) a prediction of the Edict of Poitiers. It is a picture of a morning star (Venus) holding power in the sky, so that the Sun could not appear. He lived long enough to know that the seven children of Catherine, and particularly the future Henri III were immoral — Henri III was homosexual also. His perceptiveness and the biblical model discussed earlier in this chapter told him that such a 'Venus' dynasty could never last. It was obscuring, and

---

[48] Centuries V:72.
[49] Laver, p. 81.

would ultimately be replaced by, a new dynasty, the Bourbons, which included the 'Sun King'. But he was not perceptive enough, for the Bourbon dynasty would ultimately share a similar fate! The symbolism is perceptive also. It seems to be astrological and Nostradamus may have intended it that way; but it is soundly based on the 'Lucifer' prophecy of Isaiah against Babylon:

> *How are you fallen from heaven*
> *— O Morning Star [a male Venus], son of Dawn!*
> *How are you cut down[50] to the ground —*
> *— you who weakened nations[51]*

I have shown earlier in the chapter that Nostradamus looked on Paris as a model counterpart of the biblical Babylon. Readers need only examine the rest of Isaiah's passage[52] to see that the remainder of it, especially the reference to hell, is captured elsewhere in Nostradamus's predictions of the Valois dynasty. He used a clear biblical-historical model, which he knew would repeat itself.

This small series almost exhausts Nostradamus's assumed predictions of the reign of Henri III (Anjou), and we can see that they are not impressive. There are those referring to his assassination, which have already been considered in the study of the seven-branched candlestick. Some of these predictions, as we have seen, were read to fit the circumstances, such as the attempt to make the '[man of] earth and sea' mean Brissac, when Henri III himself told him that he was not. This is an interesting case of distortion, for if 'man of earth and sea' means anyone in Nostradamus's prophecies, it means the Pope (or the papacy) and is used, in that context, elsewhere, as I shall show, because of Catholic expositors' interpretation of the 'angel of earth and sea'[53] in John's Apocalypse.

The Huguenots

We shall shortly spend a little time on Nostradamus's

---

[50] A reference to last 'eligible' 'branch' of the seven branches.
[51] Isaiah 14:12.
[52] Isaiah 14:12-21.
[53] Revelation 10:1-2. See also Luther's exposition.

prophecies of the Bourbon dynasty (1589-1789), but before doing so, it is well to examine the claims that he predicted the sufferings of the Huguenots. It would not have been difficult for him to have done so, for the Huguenots had themselves attempted to interpret John's Apocalypse, in common with other contemporary Protestants, and they believed themselves to be the 'Holy City' and the Roman Catholic Church to have been 'Babylon the Great'.[54] Such an interpretation was imperfect and inadequate, as I have shown elsewhere;[55] but at least, because of the cyclical processes of history, the Apocalyptic model would have been quite useful for predictive purposes, and goes a long way to explain the accuracy, if any, of some of Nostradamus's predictions.

The Huguenots were Calvinists who had been influenced by Luther's writings in 1517, and were persecuted from 1523 onwards after the first French Lutheran martyr had been burned at the stake. In October 1534, their protests against the Mass drew widespread persecution and John Calvin fled from France. Persecutions reached a first climax during the reign of Henri II (1547-1559) when large numbers were imprisoned, but at his death in 1559 the community began to organize itself under Coligny and Condé, and drew up a confession of faith. Wars of religion commenced in 1562, and the attempted murder (and subsequent murder) of Coligny in 1572 — as we have seen — provoked the infamous massacre of the Huguenots on 23 August 1572, when thousands were killed throughout France. The Edict of Poitiers (enacted by Henri III) removed some of their disabilities and later Henri IV, a Protestant, became a Catholic (July 1593) but restored the religious and political freedom of the community in the Edict of Nantes (1598). During the Bourbon times, persecution was resumed under Louis XIII in the 1620s, and some of their privileges were again restored at the Peace of Alais in 1629, but they no longer had separate political rights, though their religious rights were confirmed by a declaration in 1643. The French clergy agitated for the removal of their other rights, and on 18 October 1685, Louis XIV revoked the Edict of Nantes, after which hundreds of thousands of Protestants fled the country or died, and the remainder

---

[54] Contrast the symbols of Revelation 21-22 with those of Revelation 17-18.
[55] D. Pitt Francis, *The Most Amazing Message Ever Written* (Castle Books, 1983).

suffered because of a thirty-year campaign until 1715. Another, short period of persecution lasted for about ten years (1745-1754), but after the French Revolution (1789) the National Assembly proclaimed complete freedom to the community.

This background is common knowledge, but it is not as commonly known that throughout the period Bible students were trying to fit an Apocalyptic biblical model to the historical details of persecution. The best of these wrote little. Nostradamus's friend J. C. Scaliger[56] is reputed to have said of John Calvin: *Calvinus sapit, quod in Apocalypsin non scripsit* ('Calvin was wise, because he wrote not on the Apocalypse'), yet made comments about the Apocalypse himself.[57]

The bulk of these commentators, which included people like Joseph Mede and Sir Isaac Newton in later times, believed that the 1260-day witnessing period of Apocalypse 11[58] represented 1,260 years from the accession of Constantine, and the union of Church and State, to the year 1572, when the Huguenots were massacred. They imagined that there would be a period of 3½ years (i.e. 3½ days in the prophecy)[59] in which Protestantism would lie dead, and considered the restoration of liberties by treaty with Henri III in May 1576, 3½ years later, to mean the resurrection of the 'witnesses'. When persecution was renewed, Protestant expositors tried, like the interpreters of Nostradamus, to find some other meaning to the Apocalyptic vision.[60] Jurieu,[61] a Dutch Huguenot, over a hundred years later was to conceive the fantastic notion that the 3½ days were to be dated from the revocation of the Edict of Nantes (1685) because of the temporary respite that came 3½ years later by an edict on 4 June 1690. But this was again disproved, because persecution continued and, because the Apocalyptic prophecy of the two witnesses (Revelation 11:3) was being misinterpreted, Biblical commentators strained the text to make it fit with history. One desperate attempt employed by later commentators was to stretch the period of '3½ days' to make it read

---

[56] Scaliger II:41.　　　　[57] Scaliger I:13.　　　　[58] Revelation 11.3.
[59] Revelation 11:9.　　　　[60] Revelation 11:1-4.
[61] P. Jurieu, *Accomplishment of the Prophecies* (Rotterdam: 1687), II,12/13. Jurieu was of French descent, but lived (and wrote) in French Holland.

3½ × 30 years (or 104/5 years) from the revocation of the Edict of Nantes in 1685 to the French Revolution in 1789.[62] I mention these details not simply to show that the interpreters of John's Apocalypse have been guilty of the same kind of 'interpretational fudge', or 'distortion' to fit historical events, as those of Nostradamus, but also to show that there was, during these centuries, a strong body of Protestant opinion that believed on Scriptural grounds that there would be a period of intense persecution of Protestants in the sixteenth and seventeenth centuries, and that Nostradamus would have been aware of this opinion, through his friendship with Scaliger.

Osiander (1544),[63] Bale (1553),[64] Chytraeus (1571),[65] Aretius (1574).[66] Foxe, the famous martyrologist (1586),[67] Brightman (1600),[68] Joseph Mede (1627),[69] and later Vitringa (1755)[70] and Sir Isaac Newton (1733)[71] (who was both a Hebraist and a scientist), all believed that the apocalyptic vision of the persecution of witnesses (Revelation 11:3,9) related to the persecution of Protestants. Whether they did so wrongly is not of much account: it is more important to realize that they thought in terms of an historical model in which some participant fulfilment was involved, in which some Protestants would behave in such a way as to bring persecution on themselves in fulfilment of their expectations. It is even more appropriate to realize that one of these Biblical commentators, Chytraeus, who wrote in 1571, actually

---

[62] Bicheno, *The Signs of the Times* (Newbury, 1793), reported in J. Thomas, *Eureka*, vol. II, p. 657 (New York, 1866/Birmingham, 1875).

[63] Osiander, *Conjecturae de Ultimus Temporibus ac de Fine Mundi* (Nurenburg, 1544).

[64] Bale, *The Images of Both Churches* (1553) reported in E. Elliott, *Horae Apocalyptae* (London, 1866 edition).

[65] Chytraeus, *Explicatio Apocalypsi* (Wittemberg, 1571).

[66] Aretius (Berne, 1574), also reported by Elliott (note 64 above).

[67] Foxe, *Eicasmi in Apocalypsin* (1586); (see note 64 above, vol. IV for summary).

[68] Brightman, *Commentary on the Apocalypse* (see note 64, vol. IV).

[69] J. Mede, *Clavis Apocalyptica* (London, 1627).

[70] Vitringa, *Anacrisis Apocalypsis* (Froneker, 1705).

[71] Newton, Apocalyptic Commentary appended to *Treatise on the Prophecies of Daniel* (London, 1733).

believed that the 'witnessing period' would end in 1572 and was expecting something like the massacre of the Huguenots to happen! The more notable Protestants, such as Luther[72] were much more vague and non-committal in interpreting Biblical prophecy, but their expectations were similar. If Nostradamus had expected Huguenot persecutions, he would have had reasonable premises for doing so and, as a Catholic, would have had less sympathy with the persecuted than any of the above commentators. With this model in mind, we now need to examine those quatrains that are claimed to relate to the persecution of the Huguenots.

In historical order, the first of these stanzas refers to an incident that occurred in 1560 in Lyons. It did not appear in the earliest 1555 edition of the Centuries, so needs little explanation.

> *In Lyons, twenty-five of one breath,*
> *Five citizens, Germans, Bressans, Latins,*
> *They will conduct a long train under a noble*
> *— and are discovered by the barking of the 'mornings'*
> [watch-dogs][73]

The incident to which this is supposed to relate occurred in September 1560, when five citizens of Lyons and twenty others tried to betray the city to the Huguenots but were discovered by guards. The prediction needs a little comment, for it is not accurate; the sense of what happened is inverted in the first two lines, and it could easily have been rewritten after the incident occurred.

The second relevant stanza relates to Louis de Condé, one of the Huguenot chiefs:

> *The hunchback will be chosen by the council,*
> *— a more hideous monster was never seen on earth!*
> *a flying shot will pierce his eye,*
> *— the traitor whom the King received as faithful![74]*

This stanza was published before the death of Condé, for he

---

[72] Luther, Preface to the Apocalypse in his German Translation of the Bible (1517).
[73] Centuries X:59.
[74] Centuries III:41.

was shot as a prisoner by Montesquiou after the battle of
Jarnac on 13 March 1569, fourteen years after the first edition
of the Centuries was published. The prediction is not
completely accurate, for Condé was not the most hideous
monster, either physically or morally; but it contains
sufficient to be classified as unexplained. Nostradamus may
have been able to predict logically, that it was likely that
Condé would be chosen by the Huguenot assembly, and that
he would occasionally try to betray Charles IX; but his death
could not have been so easily predicted. The suggestion that
Montesquiou knew the prophecy by Nostradamus, and
literally carried it out, is useful, but improbable. Let us for
the time being, classify it as unexplained.

Next come those predictions of the massacre of the
Huguenots on St Bartholomew's Day 1572. The most
important of these is, as we have seen, quite inaccurate, and
was considered when we examined predictions of the reign
of Charles IX. Having considered evidence that some of
Nostradamus's religious contemporaries were expecting
something like the massacre of the Huguenots to occur in
1572, we need not be further concerned about it. A further
prediction occurs in the sixains, and says that

> at the festival of St Bartholomew . . .
> Nimes, La Rochelle, Geneva and Montpellier
> Castres, Lyons will be [places of] civil strife
> . . . all by the orders of a Lady[75]

But this is not unexplained. The sixains were not published
until after Nostradamus's death, when the memory of the
massacre was well-established. Further, the prediction is
sufficiently obscure and inaccurate to be of little help as a
reliable statement, for the massacre of the Huguenots did not
extend to Geneva. It has only become noticeable because of
its mention of St Bartholomew; but it would, at least, have
been mentioned earlier than at its somewhat delayed time of
publication. It is not impressive, either as an original
prediction, or as an accurate one.

The fourth stanza in supposed historical order is assumed
to relate to the Edict of Poitiers (1577) and has also been

---

[75] Sixain 52.

considered when studying the predictions of the reign of Henri III. I have shown that, in context, this has hardly anything to do with the Huguenots whatsoever but refers to a 'voluptuous' (= 'venereal') edict, and is patterned on a 'morning star' (= 'male Venus') prophecy of Isaiah against Babylon (Isaiah 14:12).

Later prophecies of the Huguenot wars are even more obscure and we must look in vain for real accuracy. For example, Laver suggests that a siege of the Protestant stronghold of La Rochelle,[76] after the revocation of the Edict of Nantes in 1685, is predicted in the stanza:

> The entry at Blaye for La Rochelle,
> — and the English will pass the great Aemathien
> Not far from Agen, the Gaul will wait
> Help from Narbonne misled by conversation[77]

Yet, the details are obscure, and the interpretation of the four lines depends on the meaning of Aemathien. If, as Laver supposes, Aemathien is the 'Sun King', Louis XIV, then there is a vague reference to a siege by Louis XIV of La Rochelle. Not all interpreters agree on this meaning, though it is probable, and will be discussed below when examining predictions relating to the Bourbon dynasty. Cheetham[78] thinks that Aemathien means Macedonia. But even if it is correct, Laver thinks that the last two lines refer to the Protestant 'War of the Camisards' (1702-4), which occurred fifteen years later. La Rochelle was a Protestant stronghold in Nostradamus's time, and there is nothing in the stanza that he could not have reasonably foreseen.

The Bourbons

Nostradamus's identifiable predictions of the Bourbon dynasty (1589-1789) relate to important historical events, and these are, on the whole, occasions when interest in his predictions was more intense than others. There are many references to Henri IV (Navarre) under a number of different names, such as 'Hadrian' and 'Light of Love'. If Henri is Hadrian,

---

[76] Laver, *Nostradamus*, p. 108.
[77] Centuries IX:38.
[78] Cheetham, p. 365, footnote 2.

then the six-month siege of Paris by him, after which the new dynasty commenced, is predicted in the lines:

> *How often will you be taken, city of the sun?*
> *You are changing laws, barbaric and vain!*
> *A bad one approaches, you will suffer more tribulation,*
> *Great Hadrian will revive your veins!*[79]

Something of the siege of Paris was foreseen, but the details are sufficiently vague and contradictory to reduce their reliability. Nostradamus calls Henri IV *ton mal* ('bad one') yet implies that he has the virtues of Hadrian, the Roman emperor. Interpreters assume that Nostradamus calls him 'bad' because of his Protestantism, which in fact he renounced; but the Hadrian reference has little reason in it, except that the details of the stanza fit the six-months' siege of Paris (April to September 1590).

Nor, alternatively, does there seem to be much good reason for using Hadrian's name, at all, except that Hadrian, like Henri IV, was rather a libertine with a fondness for culture and that he also put down a revolt, — the final Bar-Cochba revolt of Israel in the second century AD — by means of a siege.

Henri was reputed to have 'revived the veins' of Paris by letting in food supplies, and finally had to abandon the siege at the advance of Palma, Philip II's general, from Flanders. Here another piece of 'fudge' occurs in the standard interpretation of the next quatrain:

> *From the east will come an African* [Punic = Carthaginian]
> *— to disturb Hadrian and the heirs of Romulus*
> *Accompanied by the Libyan fleet*
> *Maltese temples and nearby isles shall be deserted*[80]

If this is taken to predict the raising of the siege of Paris by Henri IV in 1590, then one is in for some disappointment. The first two lines have that meaning, but nothing similar to the second two lines happened *after* the siege of Malta some

---

[79] Centuries I:8.
[80] Centuries I:9.

fifteen years earlier (1565), and the 'prophet' is not only seen to jump backwards in time, but interpreters actually distort the sense of the stanza, for 'Punic' (line 1) and 'Libyan' (line 3) are obviously identical; if the Libyans are the Turks associated with Malta in line 3, then Henri IV would have to have been forced to raise the siege of Paris by a Turk, which he was not. So, although Nostradamus showed some insight in anticipating Henri's raising the siege of Paris, the two stanzas in context may not have meant anything like that at all, reflecting instead Nostradamus's expectation of an eastern (Turkish) antichrist — a matter that will be discussed in a later chapter.

The only other significant Hadrian reference to Henri IV is in the words:

> *In the conflict the great one, of little worth*
> *will, at his last, perform a marvellous deed*
> *while Hadrian sees what is needed*
> *during a banquet he stabs the proud*[81]

This is, perhaps, a little more convincing, and is thought to refer to the way in which the rule of the Sixteen (*seize*) who had 'seized' power in Paris ended. The Duke of Mayenne (the great one of little worth) made away with (or stabbed) the proud (the *'seize'* leaders) on behalf of the Guise family and the Catholic league, hoping to become King himself. At that stage Henri IV renounced his Protestantism, 'seeing what is needed', and became acceptable to the League and master of Paris. Given that Henri IV had now been accepted by interpreters of Nostradamus as 'Hadrian', the whole quatrain reads like an accurate prediction, and one that we must relegate to the unexplained 'hardcore' with one reservation — that Henri would have known this prophecy of Nostradamus, and to some extent fulfilled it willingly!

Prophecies of Henri IV would be convincing if there were only one cipher (e.g. Hadrian), but there are more. He is called 'Light of Love',[82] presumably because he carried on two affairs with (i) Gabrielle d'Estrees and (ii) a leading woman citizen of Cambrai, in a stanza that is assumed to

---

[81] Centuries II:55.
[82] Centuries X:38, line 1.

mention his raising the siege of Paris, not (as was historically the case) for fear of the Duke of Flanders (1590), nor, as wrongly predicted earlier, because of the 'Punique', but because of *Grisons*,[83] Swiss mercenaries. To make things less credible, the figure of Hadrian, used earlier, as we have seen, for Henri IV, is used in this stanza[84] in a completely different context. Apart from the mention of its subject as a 'converted barbarian' (that is, a 'Protestant converted to Catholic') the stanza has very little detail to convince us of its predictive value.

Henri is also perhaps referred to as 'The Gay Gascon'[85] — if some interpreters, like Laver[86] be believed; but Laver only makes the prediction sound convincing by leaving out sufficient detail from the relevant quatrain, one that is so confusing that few interpretations have been clearly suggested.

The most appropriate title used by Nostradamus is, of course, Navarre[87] and with detail that is more difficult to explain, for the stanza lines:

> *The shadow of the kingdom of Navarre is not true*
> *it will make the life of a strong one illegitimate*
> *The uncertain promised vow of Cambrai*

all *seem* to be a prophecy of a future king (Henri of Navarre) who would lead an irregular life with one of his mistresses, the wife of Cambrai's governor, *until* it is realized that this is no prophecy at all; that Nostradamus was actually referring to the uncertain claim (illegal = *illegitime* = illegitimate) of Henri of Navarre, as a Protestant, to the French throne. Even the 'Cambrai' reference in the third line relates to the Peace of Cambrai (1529), the conclusion of a Protestant/Catholic war into which Francis I of France had been provoked by a German Protestant invasion of Italy. The last line of the stanza: 'the king at Orleans will give a lawful "wall"' has never made much sense, and does not seem to have the wealth of meaning with which subsequent historical events

---

[83] Centuries X:38, line 4.
[84] Centuries X:38, line 3.
[85] Centuries IX:39.
[86] Laver, *Nostradamus*, p. 93.
[87] Centuries X:45.

have loaded the other three lines.

At this stage, readers may perhaps think that all Nostradamus's quatrains can be explained in much the same way, as historical references that interpreters tried to fit into subsequent history, or that French royalty tried to fulfil. But some stanzas defy such explanation. One cipher describes Henri as 'the son of Mammon', or perhaps as 'the son of Hamon [Haman]'.[88] It occurs in an amazing flash of insight about the final confirmation of Henri's power:

> *The house of Lorraine* [the Guises] *will give place to Vendôme*
> — *the high will be abased and the low exalted*
> — *the son of Hamon* [Mammon] *will be elected in Rome*
> *and two great ones* [the dukes of Guise and Mayenne] *will be set aside*[89]

Some of this can be explained. Nostradamus would sensibly foresee that Henri would become king, and that he would need to become Catholic to be confirmed as king by the Papacy. The 'Vendôme' reference is also easy to explain for that was yet another of Henri IV's titles (Duke of Vendôme); but two dukes were set aside in the process, just as predicted. Again, we have isolated another element in that 'unexplained hardcore' to be discussed at the end of this book — and along with it another biblical reference, for Nostradamus has lifted his second line from the biblical book of Isaiah.[90]

The 'Vendôme' cipher occurs elsewhere as an anagram:

> *Mendosus will shortly come to his exalted reign*
> *Putting the Nolaris behind him.*
> — *the pale red* [man], *the man in the interregnum*
> — *the frightened young one, and the fear of barbarians*[91]

The anagrams (Mendosus = Vendôme, and Nolaris = Lorraine), obtained by inverting essential letters, were neither ingenious nor required much insight on the part of

---

[88] Centuries X:18, line 3.
[89] Centuries X:18.
[90] Curiously Isaiah 40:4, in a series of prophecies about the fall of Babylon and the Jewish return from exile. See the model given earlier in this chapter.
[91] Centuries IX:50.

Nostradamus, for he was familiar with both names, and using the Babylon model explained earlier in this chapter would have sensed the drift of history. But the last two lines contain four people who *can* be historically identified: (i) the pale red man (the Cardinal of Bourbon, who was declared Charles X but died shortly afterwards); (ii) the man in the interregnum (the duke of Mayenne); (iii) the frightened young one (the duke of Guise) and (iv) the 'fear of barbarians' (Philip II of Spain — a 'fear' to the English, and another claimant to the throne). Before he died, Nostradamus would have recognized three of the four as likely claimants, but these lines defy total explanation. Yet, again, lest Nostradamus be presumed too successful, it should be stated that his other Mendosus reference falls flat on its face as a prediction:

> *Great Mendosus will attain his 'Empire'*
> *— far from his court he will have countermanded*
> *Piedmont, Picardy, Paris, and at worst, Tuscany*[92]

It presupposes great conquests in Italy, along earlier French lines, but Henri IV did no such thing: Piedmont belonged to the dukes of Savoy.

After the crisis of Henri of Navarre's ascent to power, there is a wide gap to the next epoch of supposed fulfilments and of interest in Nostradamus. A number of sixains (six-line stanzas)[93] were published in 1605 after the events to which they were supposed to relate, and need not be considered. One quatrain[94] actually mentions 1607 as a date for the legal suppression of astrology. Prejudiced commentators state that this happened at a supposed 'Council of Malines' in 1607, but there are no records that such a council ever took place.[95] Nostradamus seems to have sensed (as a Jew) the exclusion of the Jews from Spain in 1610[96] but would have had Bible prophecy to help him.[97] He mentions 'Cordova' as one who

---

[92] Centuries IX:45.
[93] See particularly sixains 6 and 18, the former referring to a traitor Robin (= Biron) who would be apprehended and brought to justice.
[94] Centuries VIII:71.
[95] Cheetham, *Nostradamus* , p. 335.
[96] Centuries III:20.
[97] Deuteronomy 28:65, and many other references.

would 'betray' the last safe Jewish haven in Spain, but incorrectly, for the person that commentaries identify as 'the man from Cordova' (Fernandez de Cordova) helped to negotiate the treaty of Grenada, not to break it.

Henri IV was assassinated on 14 May 1610. Of the two supposed prophecies of his assassination, one[98] is hopelessly inappropriate, apart from mentioning 'Hadrian succumbing' (line 4), and a sword (line 3), although Henri was killed by a dagger. It does not mention assassination and has a host of details, such as aerial warfare, the cutting of a sacred branch, pestilence and thunder, that are either apocalyptic or suggestive of modern warfare. The second[99] could refer to any assassination around Easter — based on the model of the crucifixion. Though it was convincingly applied by Laver to Henri IV, Cheetham speculated that it may refer to the murder of a third Kennedy. Statistically, it can be applied to the assassination of about a twelfth of all kings murdered from Nostradamus's time to our own.

Henri was succeeded by Louis XIII (1610–1642), of whom Nostradamus is reputed to have written only one quatrain:

> *The Dauphin lily will be carried into Nancy*
> *— as far as Flanders, the elector of the Empire*
> *— a new prison for the great Montmorency*
> *— to the usual place, delivered to clear punishment*[100]

At first it seems to dazzle us with brilliant accuracy. Even if we disregard commentators who make 'to clear punishment' read 'Clerepeyne', the supposed (but unproved) executioner of Montmorency, the lines all suggest events that coincided in 1633. Louis XIII (the first Bourbon to bear lilies in his arms, and the first to take the title of Dauphin) *did* visit Nancy then. His kingdom included Treves (Trier in Germany), taken by the Elector of the German Empire in 1632 and occupied, but abandoned to the French because he was captured and taken to Flanders by the Spanish in 1633. At the same time, a rebel, Montmorency, was captured in southern France, imprisoned and beheaded. Thus three events coincide.

---

[98] Centuries III:11.
[99] Centuries IX:36.
[100] Centuries IX:18.

But let us not be overdazzled by this brilliance. The German Emperor had given up claims to Flanders at the Treaty of Cambrai (1529), and it was 'Anne' of Montmorency (one of the rebel's ancestors) who had negotiated that treaty and was a leading figure during Nostradamus's lifetime as governor of Southern France. There is still some 'dazzle' left, but, at least, it is clear that Nostradamus was speculating on topical events of his lifetime and on some future time when the 1529 treaty would fail, Montmorency would be dishonoured, and there would be renewed activity on the previously disputed north-east Franco-German border, Flanders, and Lyons, and other areas. It explains the prophecy, but not the historical coincidence, and the strange way in which it could later be interpreted.

Louis XIII was, of course, overshadowed by Cardinal Richelieu, and it is claimed that one of the quatrains was fulfilled by him:

> *Old Cardinal, by young one deceived —*
> *he will find himself disarmed and dispositioned.*
> *— Do not show Arles that double is perceived*
> *— and Liqueduct and the Prince embalmed*[101]

In 1642, he was dispositioned by Cinq Mars, to whom he had previously assigned the work of spying on the king. But Cinq Mars tried to plot the downfall of King and Cardinal by arranging, together with Orleans, the King's brother, a treaty with Spain. At Arles a copy ('double') of the treaty fell into Richelieu's hands, and he informed the King of the treachery. That year Richelieu was carried to Paris by water (hence 'Liqueduct' — an appropriate Latin description), and both Cardinal and King died and were embalmed.

The details of this stanza are so accurate that it also has to be included for future consideration in the 'hardcore' of unexplained prophecies. The statistical chance of all five elements occurring in one year is small, and King and Cardinal could not will themselves to die the same year, simply to fulfil one of Nostradamus's prophecies.

Louis XIII was succeeded by the 'Sun King' (Louis XIV), and Richelieu by Cardinal Mazarin. The age was one of

---

[101] Centuries VIII:68.

indolence and speculation and of considerable interest in Nostradamus's predictions. We may suspect forgeries of quatrains and attempts to fulfil them, and indeed we find many of both. The Frondeurs, who resisted the Cardinal, forged and inserted two in a 1649 edition, based on a faulty 1605 edition, in patent support of their activities. The 1605 edition itself contained a forgery, a quaint reference to six half-bodies and six open scissors, which Laver, by reading *demy corps* (half-bodies) as *demy cors* (half-horns), tries, with some verbal gymnastics, to read as a reference to the year 1660, when Louis XIV broke free of Mazarin's influence. But the date is speculative and inaccurate. Mazarin did not die until 9 March 1661.

Phrases such as 'Sun King' and 'City of the Sun' provide us with a useful study of participant fulfilment. Nostradamus used (or suggested) them but did not necessarily foresee them. Earlier in this chapter I showed that the reference to a future 'Sun' in France, obscured by a 'morning star', is based on a Biblical model, and 'City of the Sun'[79] is simply an extension of the model. The term 'Aemathien' (based on the Greek myth of the child of dawn) may or may not have been intended by Nostradamus in the same context. It is more appropriate to realize that Louis XIV was an admirer of Nostradamus, visited his tomb in 1660, and would have liked to role-play his 'Sun King' description. Nostradamus's 'City of the Sun' was a double allusion. It was in common use because of Spanish accounts of conquests of South America during the period. Campanella (1568-1639) would also use the Inca-based dream to construct an imaginary utopia. But Louis XIV's Paris would be quite different from that: it would not be Campanella's communist utopia, but was to sow the seeds both of reaction and revolution.

The first apparent fulfilment of a Nostradamus prophecy in Louis XIV's reign seems to span the whole eighteen years from 1642 to 1660, and is therefore not as dazzlingly perceptive as it seems:

> *At a time of mourning, the 'felin' monarch*
> *will make war on young Aemathien.*
> *Gaul [France] will shake, and the 'barque' [papacy] endangered*
> *Phossens to be attempted — a treaty in the West*[102]

---

[102] Centuries X:58.

At any time of death and mourning there are always likely rival successors, so, without much perceptive effort on Nostradamus's part, Philip IV of Spain fitted the bill in 1642 quite easily. With Greek and Biblical models of history in mind, Nostradamus perceived that France's 'sun-splendour' was being inhibited while the seven branches of the Valois family were alive, and Louis XIV, the first to be born after the death of the last of them,[103] saw himself as a willing accomplice. Line 3 is obscure: France has shaken and the papacy been endangered intermittently on numerous occasions in the past four centuries. Line 4 is a curious case of textual distortion *and* participant fulfilment. The text reads 'Phossens' from *phos,* the Greek word for 'light', an obvious extension of the 'Aemathien' (child of dawn) figure; by this Nostradamus would simply have meant that the 'dawn-king' will extend his brilliance. But by Louis XIV's time 'Phossens' had become distorted to 'Phocens' (Phoceans), the ancient builders of Marseilles (in 600 BC) — and therefore Marseilles itself. So Louis, armed with a distorted prophecy and interpretation, successfully besieged Marseilles, which had always maintained some independence and had supported the Fronde rebellion (1649–53), having already entered into a treaty with Spain in the west in 1659. Most of this distorted, extended (eighteen years) and historically disordered prediction would have been an easy matter for Louis XIV to fulfil.

In the same Century, Aemathien occurs in a more obscure reference, in which Nostradamus seems to suggest that he would invade Britain 'by wine and salt':

> *The great fight that they will prepare at Nancy*
> *Aemathien will say, I conquer all —*
> *The British Isle, by wine and salt is troubled*
> *Hem me two Phi, Metz will not hold long*[104]

There was no great conflict at Nancy, but it, together with

---

[103] The morning star heralds but inhibits the sun, hence the Lucifer reference in Isaiah's prophecies of Babylon, which Nostradamus borrows as a model of Paris. Like a willing patient, Louis XIV became the Sun King by faith in Nostradamus's predictions. However, the 'Aemathien' reference is not always clear. See comment in note 77.

[104] Centuries X:7.

Metz, was incorporated into France during Louis XIV's reign and fulfilment would again have been an easy matter for him. If lines 2 and 3 are read together sensibly, Nostradamus suggests that the 'dawn-king' would also invade Britain, or trouble it 'by wine and salt'. He found he had no need to do so, for interpreters ingeniously took 'wine and salt' to mean taxation during his reign, and British taxation troubles culminated in the execution of Charles I in 1649. But this is misinterpretation in a stanza which is clearly about France and French involvement with Britain; the same applies to the gymnastic attempts to explain 'Hem me two Phi', which stretch the Greek letter to several Philips, who were obscurely connected with Metz. So the stanza is explained by assuming participant fulfilment and some obscure interpreta-tion, but *not* by such verbal distortion as 'Phossens' in the previous case (X:58).

But another supposed prediction *is* explained by partici-pant fulfilment and verbal distortion:

> *The enemies — from the strong one —are well distanced*
> *By chariots the bastion is carried*
> *Above the crumbled walls of Bourges*
> *When Hercules strikes* [battra] *Aemathion*[105]

In context, the strong one is clearly Hercules, who in Greek mythology was famed for his strength; 'striking' Aemathion could not also be Louis XIV. None of Hercules's twelve labours involved building, but his historical equivalent, Alexander the Great, used the bastion of the crumbled ruins of coastal Tyre to destroy maritime Tyre in fulfilment of Bible prophecy (4th century BC)[106] while battling with the 'sun-kingdom' of Persia.[107] Using the model tabulated earlier it anticipates the *end* of Bourbon rule, and a new Alexander (= Napoleon). But by Louis XIV's time *battra* was cleverly altered to *bastira* (shall fortify) to make the 'strong one' Louis XIV and remove the contradiction. Though there were many 'Hercules' cities throughout Europe — cities named 'Herac-lea' exist in Lucania, Italy, Sicily, Greece and several in

---

[105] Centuries IX:93.
[106] Ezekiel 26:12-14.
[107] See the analogy between the 200-year Persian dynasty and the period of Bourbon rule (1589-1789) in my table on p. 35.

Turkey — Louis took account of Nostradamus's easy and obvious prediction of the decay of Bruges (an old Roman town) and set about constructing the Languedoc canal at a cost of thirty-five million francs. Its connection with Hercules is secondary and vague: it replaced the 'Pillars of Hercules' (Gibraltar) as a link between Atlantic and Mediterranean. It was constructed in the Bruges (Aquitaine) area. But the (participant) fulfilment only becomes sensible when an essential word of the last line has been altered.

This is the last of the predictions relating to Louis XIV, and most of them can be explained. The prediction of the sinking of a French fleet near Corsica in 1655[108] is undated and therefore easy to identify with other historical tragedies in that area in the past four centuries. Louis XIV later invaded Spain in apparent fulfilment of several of the quatrains: 'The fleet will embark, and an army will cross the Pyrenees';[109] and 'Aemathion will pass across the Pyrenees',[110] but it is impossible to believe that he did not do so without actively trying to fulfil Nostradamus's prophecies. Eight editions of Nostradamus's Centuries were produced between 1643 and 1698, together with a host of commentaries, and a concordance in 1709. Even the mention of 'greatest ladies brought to France' (IV:2) is not as perceptive as it seems, though the details fit the events of the War of Spanish Succession (1701-1713), for invasions in Nostradamus's times frequently resulted in treaties and marriages!

Louis XIV died in 1715 and little of Nostradamus's work has ever been applied to his successor, Louis XV. The most obvious reference is 'Through death a child will rule over France',[111] which must stand as one of the very few 'unexplainably perceptive' predictions of a regency and a long reign, lasting from 1715 (when Louis was only five years old) to 1774. But the prophecy is undated, and so it is not beyond the bounds of chance-fulfilment. We may take little account of the suggestion of Elisée de Vignois[112] that stanzas numbered 14, 15, 16 and 17 in each Century refer to

[108] Centuries III:87.
[109] Centuries IV:2.
[110] Centuries IX:64.
[111] Centuries III:15.
[112] Elisée du Vignois, *Notre histoire racontée à l'avance par Nostradamus* (Paris 1910).

Louis XIV, XV, XVI and XVII respectively, for most of them have been assigned different meanings since his time.

Louis XV was debauched, depraved and for a long while under the influence of a regent, Cardinal Dubois. The alleged prophecy of Dubois (*'de bois'*)[113] is scarcely worth mentioning, for Cheetham assigns it a period shortly after the French Revolution. Nor is the reference to the failure of the Sallic Law (by which women were not allowed to succeed to the French throne)[114] appropriate, for though it describes the debauchery of Louis XV with Madame Pompadour and Louis XVI (1774-1789) with Marie Antoinette, it is inaccurate: the Sallic Law did not fail. The reigns of Louis XV and Louis XVI present us with very few outstanding accomplishments of Nostradamus's prophecies, perhaps because they were weak kings who were not easily able to fulfil them.

This chapter has traversed a minefield of supposed predictions and bizarre fulfilments. It has been suggested that Nostradamus saw himself as a kind of 'Daniel' in a decadent and immoral Babylon, waiting for a dynasty to end, and the armies of a better enemy to read the 'writing on the wall' and establish a superior dynasty. Some of his predictions can be explained simply by reference to that model. Some were speculations about contemporary history that failed, and were distorted by later commentators to mean quite different things. In many cases, French royalty was powerful enough to fulfil Nostradamus's predictions (or distorted versions of them), and clearly did so. In other cases predictions were actually forged to match contemporary events, and I have illustrated at least two instances of participant fulfilment and textual distortion. A statistical tabular analysis of this chapter appears in Chapter Six.

Much of Nostradamus can therefore be explained one way or another, and he should certainly not be regarded as an infallibly accurate prophet. But a few unexplained cases are left, and these are almost incredible. These disturb the most scientific of analysts, and at least give the impression that in an uncontrolled way Nostradamus's mind could on occasion scan one or two future events with glaring and uncomfortable accuracy.

---

[113] Centuries IX:27; but see Cheetham, p. 360.
[114] Centuries V:38.

3
Nostradamus and Revolution

In Chapter One, I showed that Nostradamus borrowed and used the Apocalyptic style of biblical and other Hebrew writers, and I produced a table showing the parallels between one of his sequences and a corresponding sequence from John's Revelation. He was not alone in doing so. Other apocalyptic literature written since the Bible, such as the Qur'an and the Book of Mormon, also seems, in places, to borrow the apocalyptic style of Biblical literature. Apocalypses patently describe political disturbances and revolutions, though I have shown elsewhere[1] that John's Apocalypse, correctly interpreted, is an exception. Armed with the interpretations of the Apocalypse that were current in his time, Nostradamus would naturally have been moved to 'lace' the Centuries with predictions of political upheavals, for if Jesus' words about war and revolution — 'this must take place but the end is not yet'[2] — are to be believed, anyone who stakes his reputation on the probability of future political upheavals is likely to have backed a winner!

This chapter commences, as far as French history is concerned, at a point where the weight of explanation of Nostradamus's predictive powers changes somewhat. Chapter Two has shown that the French monarchy respected the words of Nostradamus, and that its more powerful members attempted to fulfil many of his predictions. The explanation for some of them resulted from calculated model-building involving the repetition of biblical history; others have been verbally distorted and fitted by interpreters to events

---
[1] D. Pitt Francis, *The Most Amazing Book Ever Written* (Castle Books, 1983).
[2] Matthew 24:6.

contemporary with themselves; a few are so accurate and perceptive that they baffle the most sceptical mind. But after 1789 we are in completely different terrain. No longer is there a French monarchy eager to quote and fulfil the Centuries, and Nostradamus's writings are now officially banned to Catholics, having been placed on the Index of prohibited books a few years earlier. But where participative fulfilment fails, the doomsday messages begin to pay dividends, even though, to quote Jesus again, 'the end was not yet'. Every major revolution would now send secret admirers of Nostradamus to their bookshelves, to clothe the more blood-curdling of his messages with fresh meaning. Nostradamus would still be adored by French patriots, including the revolutionaries, many of whom, not being Catholics, were free to quote his writings; and, as though in willing fulfilment of the quatrains, France would experience more revolutions than most European countries and have more interpreters to fit the details of Nostradamus's predictions to those revolutions.

So much for France, with its troubled nineteenth-century history. But during the stable two-hundred-year rule of the Bourbons, some of the seer's French admirers had already tried to fit one or two of his revolutionary predictions to the rule of the 'Seize' (1589/90), and he also accumulated English enthusiasts, who assumed that the rise of Cromwell and the subsequent Glorious Revolution matched some of his other ideas. This chapter therefore considers the extent to which Nostradamus successfully predicted the following, simply by regurgitating Biblical-style prophecies of revolution:

1. Cromwell and the Long Parliament
2. The Glorious Revolution
3. The First French Revolution, 1789.
4. Napoleon I
5. The Second and Third French Revolutions, 1830 and 1848.

It is perhaps significant that, because of the eagerness of interpreters to fit the details of these events to the predictions of Nostradamus, other, much greater, happenings — such as the Russian Revolution of 1917 and the Chinese Revolution of 1949, which involved immensely greater numbers of people

— rarely appear in any interpretations of his writings.

Cromwell and the Long Parliament

Apart from a small apparent reference to Mary, Queen of Scots, which was mentioned in the previous chapter, Nostradamus seems to have had little to say about English affairs until English interpreters began to appear. Though his Centuries and medical works were published in England in 1559, the first English commentary on the quatrains did not appear until 1672,[3] and so would have been written just after the period of Cromwell's interregnum. I showed, when dealing with the life of Louis XIV in Chapter Two, that there is an isolated line about Britain being troubled by 'wine and salt' in a stanza that apparently suggests that Louis would conquer Britain;[4] but by interpreting 'wine and salt' to mean taxation, and showing that the beheading of Charles I in 1649 came within the years of French history described in the rest of the stanza, Nostradamus was saved from the embarrassment of having predicted an invasion of Britain that never occurred, and the line was isolated to read as a prediction of British affairs that were, indeed, contemporary with Louis XIV's reign. This explanation may sound mundane to many, and there are perhaps good reasons for not emphasizing it, for it is matched by a similar stanza that is much clearer and unexplainably perceptive:

> *Ghent and Brussels will march against Antwerp*
> *— the Senate in London will put their king to death*
> *— the salt and wine will oppose him.*
> *Because of them, he will have the Kingdom in disorder*[5]

Here, Nostradamus seems to have got things absolutely right, and this is one of the very few cases of clear perception in the Centuries. We need not labour the point that this stanza is numbered IX:49, and that it was in the forty-ninth year of the seventeenth century (1649) that the events

---

[3] Nostradamus, *Almanacke for 1559* ; Nostradamus, *An excellent Treatise on Contagious Infirmities* (London, 1559); T. Garencieres, *A Commentary on the Prophecies of Nostradamus* (London, 1672).
[4] Centuries X:7.
[5] Centuries IX:49.

happened. The statistical chance of this kind of coincidence happening somewhere or other in Nostradamus's writings is quite high, and it does not, in fact, happen very often. It gives us some ground for interpreting 'salt and wine' as taxation (taxable things) and for the somewhat isolated reference to Britain in one line of the Louis XIV stanza mentioned earlier.

Statistics help us with the next set of references. In Chapter One we saw that as time passes the chances of a more accurate fulfilment of some of Nostradamus's writing increase. This is verified in two 'Cromwell' stanzas. Laver wrote his explanation of Nostradamus's predictions in 1942, when the abdication of Edward VIII was fresh in memory. Hitler had some respect for the Duke of Windsor, and may have reinstated him if England had been successfully invaded. Thus, despite the abdication, Laver 'played safe' with a standard Cromwellian interpretation of two stanzas, but suggested a later application to Edward VIII:

> *The young one born to the Kingdom of Britain*
> *which his dying father had recommended to him*
> *—once he is dead Lonole will dispute with him*
> *and the Kingdom will be demanded from his son*[6]

> *Not wanting to agree to the divorce*
> *which will afterwards be realized as unworthy*
> *the King of the Islands will be forced into flight*
> *— and one put in his place who has no sign of Kingship*[7]

The first two lines of the first stanza could be applied to any succession by a young king on the death of his father, within the history of Britain, and 'Lonole' could be any disputant to the throne. Until Edward VIII's abdication, the standard interpretation won, because Lonole could be taken as a distorted anagram of Cromwell's first name 'Oliver'. The process of identification is somewhat desperate. 'Lonole' is an anagram of 'olleon' (Greek: destroyer): and 'Ole Nol' (a supposedly French nickname for Oliver); Oliver Cromwell did not dispute with Charles I, once the dying father (James I)

---

[6] Centuries X:40.
[7] Centuries X:22.

was dead. So the prophecy cannot accurately match the
events that occurred when the 'Senate in London' (Parliament) put their king (Charles) to death in 1649, and when
Parliament ruled beyond Cromwell's death in 1658 to the
Restoration of 1660. But it was a good try. By Cheetham's
time in 1970, the abdication of Edward VIII was irreversible
history, so she makes the dying king, George V, the 'young
one', Edward VIII (older than George VI, so scarcely
accurate), and identifies Lonole as 'London' by a very
imperfect anagram. But London did not dispute with
Edward VIII as soon as George V died, not until it recovered
from the shock of his impending marriage with Mrs Simpson
— a divorcee.

The second stanza in this pair also provides the uncritical
enthusiasts of Nostradamus with some similar problems.
Laver makes the 'divorce' entirely symbolic (a figurative
divorce between King and Parliament, which would at the
time of the Restoration have been regarded as unworthy —
line 2). Charles II, the future King of the Islands, was forced
to flight, and Cromwell, who had no sign of kingship, was
proclaimed as Lord Protector. The interpretation is tenuous.
Apart from the reference to the 'Isles' it need not even refer to
Britain, and it becomes a description of the events of the
Commonwealth only by stretching the meaning of the word
'divorce'. History seems to have found a better 'niche' for
this prophecy at the time of Edward VIII; but is it even
accurate as a picture of Edward's abdication? There was no
question of 'agreeing to the divorce' of Mrs Simpson. The
real point at issue was Edward's marriage to her. The couple
did not regard their relationship as unworthy. The King *was*
'forced to flee', but Albert (who became George VI) had, in
fact, every sign of kingship, and was more than a worthy
successor to his brother. The events of 1936 seem to provide
interpreters with a much clearer and more detailed fulfilment
than those of 1649, but in neither case is there a set of events
that fully and accurately matches the predictions.

This does not exhaust prophecies of Charles I and
Cromwell, however. Early in the quatrains are the words:

From the Kingdom of England, the unworthy man is chased
— the counsellor will be burnt through indignation
His followers will stoop so low
that the pretender [batard] will almost be received.[8]

Charles, of course, was not chased from his kingdom, but his
son, Charles II, fled abroad. Archbishop Laud was beheaded
for treason, but other counsellors were not, and the stake was
a common method of punishment in those days. The Scots
betrayed Charles I, and the 'pretender' is assumed to be
Cromwell. But the term was rarely used of him, and much
more used of the Jacobite pretenders of the following
century. In fact, much of this stanza can, in turn, be applied
to the Old and Young Pretenders of 1715 and 1745 also, but
this is never done because the traditional interpretation has
'stuck'. Then there is a description of Cromwell, much later:

More of a macelin [= meat-basket] than a king of England
Of doubtful rank he will gain empire through force.
Coward without faith, without law, he will 'bleed' the earth
His time comes so near that I sigh.[9]

There is almost enough here to match the details of
Cromwell. But he was not of entirely 'doubtful' (or obscure)
origin. He came from a well-established Huntingdonshire
family. He did not 'bleed' the country any more than Charles I
before him. He was not without faith, certainly not without
law, and was a model of tolerance compared with many of
the bigoted independents of his time. So, is the application to
Cromwell another strained interpretation of the quatrains to
make them fit history, or has Nostradamus simply been
coloured by his own prejudices against Protestants? The time
was 'at hand', only a century away, so although inaccurate,
the prediction is, to say the least, remarkable.

Two words add weight to another, and more accurate,
prediction of Cromwell:

---

[8] Centuries III:80.
[9] Centuries VIII:76.

> *The great crier, shameless and audacious,*
> *will be chosen governor of the army*
> *The brazenness of his contention —*
> *A broken bridge, a city faint from fear.*[10]

This could be a prediction of any army takeover, except for its mention of the broken bridge (Latin: Pontefract), and the fact that the stanza comes next to one also assumed to be about Charles I and Cromwell. The first is, if anything, a late interpretation, which appeared in Laver's writings. Pontefract held out for Charles I and endured two sieges. But it was one of many cities in England that suffered the same fate. Further, the fact that the previous stanza has a Cromwellian interpretation need not worry us unduly. Most quatrains are historically disarranged. Finally, there is an obscure reference to Cromwell's successes in Scotland:

> *The feeble band will occupy the land*
> *Those from high places will make horrible cries*
> *The large troupe will be troubled in this coin* [= in a pound].
> *Near to D. nebro, discovered the writings.*[11]

Charles II landed in Scotland in 1650 and was supported by the 'highlanders', who were numerous, but the 'feeble band' (that of Cromwell) succeeded at the battle of Dunbar (east of Edinburgh). If there is genius in this quatrain it is in the word D.nebro, which is a quaint conflation of the words Dunbar and Edinburgh. The battle was fought at Dunbar, but the 'writings' (papers of the Scottish War Office) fell into Cromwell's hands at Edinburgh.

Some Cromwellian interpretations are late, but others were influenced by British attempts to interpret Nostradamus. Of the eight that I have given, one is coincidental, two have been reapplied to Edward VIII, and nearly all have an element of inaccuracy. But we have seen that, occasionally, extraordinary insight reveals itself. Century VIII:76 is about the best example of this, and the reference to D.nebro.

---

[10] Centuries III:81.
[11] Centuries VIII:56.

The Glorious Revolution 1688-9

The restoration of 1660 did not involve a popular uprising, but simply ended a Civil War. Charles II had some Catholic sympathies, and his brother, James II, was clearly Catholic. The subsequent upheaval of 1688/89 involved a miniature civil war, but was comparatively bloodless, and so there is little in Nostradamus's writings interpreters have found to be appropriate to it. Yet, a few things in the events of that time deserve some mention, if only because past commentators on Nostradamus have seen them as appropriate pegs on which to hang some of his prophecies. For example, there are the words:

> *Of the eagle* [north] *the efforts will be great*
> *Over the ocean a gate* [way] *will be open*
> *The rule on the island will be re-established*
> *London will be afraid of the fleet when discovered.*[12]

This could refer to every threatened invasion of England, and 'island' (isle) rarely means anything but the mainland of Britain in interpretations of the quatrains elsewhere. This is not a brilliant prediction of William III (Orange) and the period 1688/90, except if one makes the 'island' mean 'Ireland', thereby reading the stanza in the context of James II's attempt to use Ireland as a 'Kingdom in exile'. Its only strength as an interpretation comes from the position of the stanza, next to another one thought to be of William of Orange, who is described as a 'blond one'.[13] But 20 per cent of Europeans are blonde, so millions of others could fit the bill!

The picture of 'brother contending with brother' (Nostradamus's use of a biblical figure) has also been variously applied to this period, but does not fit it very well:

> *A Kingdom divided between battling brothers,*
> *— taking arms and the name of Britain*
> *The Anglican title will be advised to keep watch*
> *Surprised by night, led to Gallic* [i.e. French] *air.*[14]

---

[12] Centuries II:68.
[13] Centuries II:67.
[14] Centuries VIII:58.

William of Orange and James II were not brothers; the former was the latter's son-in-law, and the stanza had been even applied to Charles II's flight to France earlier. The chance event that made the quatrain appropriate to the 'Orange' affair was the matter of Anglican or Catholic succession. Nostradamus would have used 'Anglique' to mean English, but by William III's time it had acquired a new ecclesiastical meaning. In the same Century is another quatrain that seems appropriate:

> *The blood of the Just, by Taur and La Daurade*
> *In order to avenge himself against Saturnines*
> *In the new lake they will immerse the band,*
> *then they will march against Alba.*[15]

Laver's interpretation is ingenious, but wrong. 'Taur' is understood to mean 'Torah', the Hebrew word for Law (establishment), and thence the Tory party in England, who associated themselves with James II. There were those, identified with both the Stewart and Protestant claims to the English throne, who marched against Alba (if this means England) in 1659/60, 1689/90 and in 1715 and 1745, so that any application to Charles II or William of Orange is doubtful. Nor is the quatrain some vague astrological reference to Taurus and Saturn. In context, it is a clear reference to two churches: (i) St Saturnin du Taur and (ii) Ste Marie de la Daurade in Toulouse. Nostradamus was condemning the ambiguous religious position of that city's inhabitants in his day, and suggesting that, in possible future French conquests in Alba — in Italy — Toulouse would be 'in the way' and so come directly under the influence of the French throne. It is a strange twist in interpretation that makes it have everything to do with England and the Stewarts at all.

Yet, elsewhere, two 'blood of the Just' references seem to be clearly associated with London, and are among the few inexplicably perceptive Nostradamus predictions:

---

[15] Centuries VIII:40.

> *The blood of the Just will be demanded of London*
> *— burnt by fire of twenty-three, the six[16]*

and shortly afterwards:

> *The great plague in the maritime city*
> *— will not stop until death is avenged,*
> *the price of 'blood of the just' taken and condemned without crime*
> *— the 'great lady' is outraged by pretence.[17]*

But let us not be overwhelmed by the fact that they come close together, and that the fire of London (1666) and the great plague (1665) also came close together historically. The phrase 'twenty-three, the six' (literally), from *'vingt-trois les six'*, can be interpreted to mean 'twenty times three plus six', sixty-six, and so 1666; but there are many other mathematical solutions that would fit the words, e.g. (i) $23 + 6 = 29$; (ii) $20 \times (3 + 6) = 180$; (iii) $20 \times 3 \times 6 = 360$ — the latter being a common Babylonian measure of time, and thus more probably what Nostradamus intended. It seems more than a mathematical fluke that the Fire and Plague of London not only came together, but are mentioned by Nostradamus in close proximity with each other, although the fire is mentioned before the plague, when, in fact, the plague came before the fire. Also, can it really be considered to have been a punishment for the 'blood of the Just' (Charles I) for these events to have occurred in the reign of his son Charles II? Given Nostradamus's dislike of Protestants, should they not have occurred during Cromwell's interregnum? Does one punish the just for the 'blood of the Just'? Even if the 'great lady' means St Paul's Cathedral, as has been suggested by some — the old cathedral was burned during the fire — the punishment does not seem to fit the crime of executing someone who was hardly 'without crime' himself — to use Nostradamus's ill-suited words.

There are a few other supposed prophecies of the Restoration (1660) and the Glorious Revolution (1689/90), including two from Century IV. The first is reasonably perceptive for it says that:

---

[16] Centuries II:51.
[17] Centuries II:53.

Thirty Londoners will secretly conspire against their King . . .
— A King elected fair, native of Friesland[18]

but between these first and last lines, which seem accurately
to describe the London conspiracy against James II and the
accession of the Dutch King William III, is a reference to a
'bridge' that has never been clearly identified, and the last line
does not make it too clear whether the king is identical with
or different from the one in the first line. This vagueness is
enough to make interpreters fudge the issue slightly, and
apply the most appropriate line to William III without
bothering too much about the problem of doing so.

The second of these stanzas is hopelessly inaccurate:

> *The elder sister of the British isle*
> *will be born fifteen years later before her brother.*
> *Because his promise will prove to be true,*
> *she will succeed to the Kingdom of the balance.*[19]

Mary, the wife of William III was in fact twenty-six, not
fifteen, years older than her brother James, who never came
to the throne, and the attempts to make 'balance' (= Libra)
mean England are all tenuous. Before moving on to the
French Revolution, I should state that both the Restoration
and the Glorious Revolution are often assumed to be
mentioned indirectly in yet one other quatrain:

> *Seven times you will see the British nation change —*
> *— dyed in blood for 290 years.*
> *Not entirely free, for German support*
> *Aries doubts for Bastarnian [= Polish?] support.*[20]

I shall show later in the book that Nostradamus adopted a
millennarian world view and thought that the world would
end in the twentieth century. Allowing about a century for
upheavals, he would assume 300 years as the longest time
(1950 − 1555 − 100) for British greatness, and this fitted with

---

[18] Centuries IV:89.
[19] Centuries IV:96.
[20] Centuries III:57.

'seven times' (7 × 40) or 280 — giving a pseudo-accurate 'guess' of 290 years. At the very end of the Centuries is a rounder reference to the same thing, which I will discuss later:

> *A great empire will be for England*
> *The pempotam [= all-powerful] for more than 300 years.*[21]

What has all this to do with the Restoration and the Glorious Revolution? The answer is 'Not much', except indirectly by the reference to 'seven times'. Nostradamus, of course, took this phrase from the Bible: 'I will chasten you seven times for your sins'[22] and 'Seven times shall pass over you',[23] but expositors naturally disagree both about the time-period and the seven changes, resulting in at least three time periods of 290 years, and at least ten changes. Only three upheavals are indisputably placed in all commentators' lists: 1660, 1689 and 1714/5. But this curious stanza was to form the basis of an absurd yet self-fulfilling interpretation about Hitler, with which I shall deal in Chapter Four.

The First French Revolution, 1789

Nostradamus's 'apocalyptic' style of writing is such that, statistically, large quantities of his material could be made to fit the French Revolution; as he never gave dates in clear style, it has been easy for interpreters to match much of his material to specific events. It is surprising that he could not have been clearer. Some interpreters of the Revelation of John were to take his prophecies of 1,260 days' tribulation of the Church to mean 1,260 years, and some were to speculate that they may be counted from the Edict of Justinian (AD 530) until 1789/90, so that something notable would be expected that year. Laver gives some evidence that others, [24] including d'Ailly (1414) and Turrel (d. 1531), expected a French crisis in 1789, but their speculations happened to be correct. Those of

---

[21] Centuries X:100.
[22] Leviticus 26:18.
[23] Daniel 4:25, 3:19.
[24] See J. Laver, *Nostradamus, The Future Foretold*, pp. 138-142, for these references. Laver's mathematics are unconvincing.

many others did not. Laver's attempts to prove that Nostradamus expected 'le Commun Advenement' about that time are inaccurate, for if he believed the Creation to have been dated 4173 BC his date for the end of the sixth millennium would have been AD 1827 (4173 + 1827 = 6,000); and in his 'Epistle to Henri II', the seer was reputed to have dated the 'Advent of the Commons' (if it means the French Revolution) at the beginning of the seventh millennium – even later than AD 1827. Not until the revolutionary period itself was the phrase 'le Commun Advenement' assumed to refer to the Revolution: it had previously been understood to refer to the Seize's rule of Paris in 1589/90; in context it means neither of these. Its most obvious meaning is the 'Common Advent', and the most commonly termed 'Advent' of all is the Second Advent of Christ, which Nostradamus along with all Biblical expositors of the time thought would happen at the beginning of the seventh millennium, the biblical 'millennium'.[25] Even Nostradamus's clearest prediction of the French Revolution has some other, more obvious and more acceptable, meaning.

But the Apocalypse of John had anticipated the coming of an Antichrist shortly before the end of the sixth millennium, and Nostradamus's Antichrist would have been anti-Catholic and anti-ecclesiastical. Clerics of the time expected him, using Daniel, to 'change times and laws',[26] and whatever the words may mean in context, Nostradamus, as we have seen, had a great respect for Daniel and for the Catholic clergy. How then would he use (or abuse) these Biblical prophecies?

> How shall we see a great people disturbed
> and the holy law in total ruin?
> By other laws Christianity will be governed
> When a new source of gold and silver is discovered.[27]

Of course it all happened when the French clergy was disestablished in 1790, but if the 'Antichrist' that he had read into the various prophecies of Daniel was to be universal, he would have to rule France and change its laws. Law-

---

[25] Revelation 20:2, 5 and 6. See particularly Centuries X:74.
[26] Daniel 7:25 (translations vary from 'the law' to 'laws').
[27] Centuries I:53.

changing would not be successful without first suppressing the clergy and using its wealth. Nostradamus would have known the recent history of Henry VIII's dissolution of the monasteries in England, and regarded the seizure of ecclesiastical wealth by the State as a hallmark of the universal Antichrist when he came. So it would have to happen in France. It was coincidental, not ingenious, that it happened during the French Revolution.

The first of Nostradamus's quatrains savours slightly of the French Revolution, but only because it uses the phrases 'new republic' and talks of 'reds' and 'whites'.[28] It seems to us a glimmer of anticipation in the right direction, but only because we use 'red' and 'white' to mean revolutionary and reactionary respectively, as with Russia after the 1917 revolution. To talk of a republic involved very little ingenuity, for Graeco-Roman ideas of the Republic were common currency and formed a basis of Utopian writings common to the period. Another very early stanza[29] blandly describes 'Princes, and a Lord [Seigneur] in prison', while divine prayers are said by 'headless idiots'. 'Headless' would mean 'mindless' and the term fits most *unreasonable* revolutions, and 'mindless' suppression of them. Even if 'headless' were to be taken literally, it would still not be an ingenious prediction of the French Revolution, for decapitation was one of the most common methods of execution during Nostradamus's times.

Of course, Nostradamus foresaw the suppression of clergy (by Antichrist) some time or other in France, shortly before the end of the world. But if he thought, as I suggested earlier, in terms of the English model (Henry VIII) it would be done at the instigation of a king, not by the people. It is significant that commentators generally suppress two lines of one quatrain assumed to be fulfilled when the French clergy were abolished in 1790:

> *Eyes closed, open to ancient fantasy*
> *— the habit of priests will be abolished.*
> *The great monarch will chastise their frenzy*
> *robbing temples of the treasure in front of them.*[30]

---

[28] Centuries I:3.
[29] Centuries I:14.
[30] Centuries II:12.

To Nostradamus and his time, Antichrist, like Antiochus IV, the villain of Daniel's prophecies, would 'rob temples' and 'persecute priests'. But no great monarch ever did so, after Henry VIII. So the lines are ignored in context, in fact, and uncritically applied to the *popular* plundering of temples during the revolutionary era. Sometimes the 'great monarch' is assumed to be Napoleon I; but he simply used wealth robbed from temples *before* being acclaimed emperor, and made his peace with the papacy to be appointed emperor. Napoleon, therefore, could never have literally fulfilled the prophecy.

The abolition of laws in France (in the manner expected of Antichrist) is a common theme of other quatrains. One[31] specifically mentions Paris under the anagram of Rapis, but is vague and could mean any popular uprising and change of law in France; it could even be applied to the surrender of the French Government to the Nazis in 1940 by Petain.

A much more perceptive account of revolutionary France occurs late:

> *Topography will be falsely changed.*
> *The urns of monuments will be opened.*
> *Sects will flourish: holy philosophy.*
> *Black for white, and green for ancient.*[32]

Every detail surprisingly seems to fit, and there is none of the vagueness that could be applied to a series of incidents. But is this because Nostradamus used a biblical model? Nearly every detail of the stanza is encompassed in one chapter of John's Apocalypse,[33] 'mountains and islands being moved from their places', the dead crying for vengeance because of violation, ecclesiastical battles, and even three of the four colours of the apocalyptic horsemen ('pale'[34] meaning 'green'). Further, he expected that 'Antichrist' would desecrate tombs, hence his own 'curse' in respect of his remains. Topography was changed by a division of France into 'departments' in a way that he would not have expected. At St Denis, the sepulchres of the Kings of France were

---

[31] Centuries VI:23.
[32] Centuries VII:14.
[33] Revelation 6.
[34] Revelation 6:7.

desecrated by the revolutionaries. The rest is almost inevitable. False philosophies and religious sectarianism flourished in his own day, and it required very little reasoning on his part to predict that they would be much more prominent if the Church should ever be suppressed.

Against this reasoned prediction is one that seems to have little reason about it, but which was fulfilled, almost to the letter, by Louis XVI:

> *By night will come through the forest of Reines*
> *two parts [partners] roundabout, Herne, the white stone.*
> *The black monk arrayed in grey at Varennes*
> *Elected cap. causes tempest, fire and slicing blood*[35]

Some interpretation of anagrams is necessary to give this its full meaning, and it is wrong in at least one detail: there is no 'forest of Reines', and to make the word 'forest' into *fores* (Latin: door), through which a queen would escape, is to do violence to the text. Nor is there a patent reason why 'cap.' on this occasion should mean 'capet' (elected king), or that *noir* should be an anagram for 'king' (*roi*) when 'black monk' is a perfectly sensible reading — or that 'Herne' should be (by a slightly distorted anagram) *reine* (= queen). But, even if these inaccuracies and uses of 'interpretational fudge' are allowed, the historical incident to which it is supposed to relate matches quite remarkably. In 1791 Louis XVI, who was 'elected king' by assembly, fled with his partner (wife) Marie Antoinette, who is graphically described as a 'white stone' because she wore white. He was disguised in a monastic robe (according to some accounts), and shortly afterwards faced the 'slicing blood' (guillotine), but in contradiction of the line did not 'cause' it. Given that one of the details as interpreted at the time, 'elected cap.', seemed to fit, Louis XVI could, even in a state of flight have voluntarily fulfilled *some* of the details of the account, but for losing his way — 'roundabout' (route) — and the fact that Varennes is specifically mentioned, this being the little town at which, having lost his way, Louis XVI finally arrived. Of course there were no fires or tempests, and to identify Marie Antoinette with the 'white stone', when Nostradamus was

---

[35] Centuries IX:20.

probably using a well-known biblical phrase,[36] is unwarranted; but I have said sufficient to show that, despite its inaccuracies, the prediction is, at least, remarkable.

Century IX, from which the above stanza is taken, contains a whole series of casual lines that contemporary interpreters applied to the period after the French Revolution. Shortly after, there is assumed to be a picture of Louis XVI's son playing in a garden, with Louis himself in a tower looking on; but this is not what the text actually says:

> *The younger son playing outside under the arbour*
> *— the top of the roof on the middle of his head.*[37]

This suggests a calamity in which the roof falls on the child's head whilst the father remains a helpless onlooker; but this did not occur, nor did the king (imprisoned inside) sacrifice: interpretations about sacrificing to the Revolution are somewhat fanciful.

Between these two quatrains is an even weaker reference that detracts from the suggestion that the 'temple' reference applies to the place of Louis XVI's imprisonment:

> *King and court in place of much speaking,*
> *— within the temple opposite the palace.*[38]

The picture is not of solitary imprisonment, but of a large number of people talking, and of a king who sacrifices. Yet, what has happened in the process of interpretation? Interpreters have found one remarkably perceptive stanza (IX:20) and looked for other contemporary fulfilments in stanzas near to it (IX:22, 23).

Some ten stanzas further on, much the same process has taken place:

> *The solitary married partner will be 'mitred'*
> *Return conflict will pass over 'thuille'*
> *By five hundred a traitor will be 'titled'*
> *Narbonne and Sauce for knives will have oil.*[39]

---

[36] Revelation 2:17.
[37] Centuries IX:23.
[38] Centuries IX:22.
[39] Centuries IX:34.

Historically, the interpretation of this stanza is assumed to begin with the Varennes incident mentioned earlier, when Louis XVI and Marie Antoinette, in 1791, spent the night at the house of a man called Saulce. 'Mitred' is interpreted as 'capped', and taken to mean, not a bishop's mitre, but the 'cap' of the revolutionaries. 'Thuille' is interpreted as the Tuileries palace near the Louvre. But Nostradamus would have known of the palace, for it was commissioned by Catherine de'Medici during his lifetime and was not stormed until 1792; the 'oil for knives' line is usually taken as a reference to the guillotine, but this did not come into use until later, during the Terror. But it is only this line that contains the name 'Sauce', and though there is evidence that Saulce, who accommodated the king and queen at Varennes, afterwards betrayed them (along with Narbonne), it is both circumstancial and tenuous. His intentions are assumed, because of the effect of Nostradamus's writings. There is no hard evidence. Saulce was said to have been awarded 20,000 livres by the National Assembly for having prevented the King's flight, but could hardly have done otherwise. There was a 'Narbonne' at the time, both person and town, but they had little, if anything, to do with the king's betrayal. Though historians, familiar with Nostradamus, have mentioned 'five hundred' people involved in the betrayal, real evidence has always been missing. Only the name Saulce (for Sauce) and the betrayal reference are of real value in correlating the prediction with its assumed fulfilment. Yet, there is interpretational fudge again, with a degree of possible (but inaccurate) perceptiveness on the part of Nostradamus. Century IX has not yet been exhausted by revolutionary interpreters, except that on this occasion they have hit a more successful match between prediction and history:

> *The kingdom taken, the King will make advances*
> *the lady taken* [will be condemned] *to death by those sworn by lot.*
> *Life to the Queen's son they will refuse*
> *and the pellix* [mistress?] *suffers the same fate as the wife.*[40]

The drift of the quatrain clearly correlates with the events of

---

[40] Centuries IX:77.

the Revolution. Louis XVI was executed in January 1793, and his wife Marie Antoinette condemned to death by a balloted jury. Louis XVII, though, was not denied life, but his kingdom; and it was the mistress of Louis XV (not Louis XVI), Mme du Barry, who was imprisoned, but not executed. There is therefore perceptiveness of an upheaval in France in this quatrain, but events did not work out exactly as Nostradamus foretold.

And yet, Century IX is not exhausted, for a generalized revolutionary passage earlier assumed to mean the French Revolution:

> *Against the red ones, sects will unite . . .*
> *fire, water, iron, rope, by peace will weaken.*[41]

This has acquired a richer interpretation this century because 'red ones' (cardinals) now signifies communists, and the line seems to refer to underground religious organizations. But it is more easily explained by reference to Nostradamus's interpretation of Biblical prophecies of Antichrist, as I shall show later.

A few apparent references to the revolutionary period will complete the picture. These are scattered through the Centuries. There is assumed to be a reference to the execution of Louis XVI on 21 January 1793. It depicts a trumpet sounding and a face anointed with milk and honey lying on the ground in blood.[42] The trumpet reference is obscure, and it could describe any execution. The only quasi-significant link between prediction and event is the reference to 'milk and honey' and the fact that the office of St Agnes' Day on which Louis XVI was executed contains references to milk and honey. A later supposed reference to the 'third estate' (*tiers*) states uncharacteristically for Nostradamus, that France will become a 'barbarian empire'.[43] It also states that 'the greater part' (i.e. over half) of its people will be put to death (the French Revolution did not go so far as this) and that the 'fourth man' (assumed to be Napoleon) will be struck dead. Napoleon died in exile, probably by slow poisoning.[43]

---

[41] Centuries IX:51.
[42] Centuries I:57.
[43] Centuries III:59. Recent research indicates arsenic poisoning.

By contrast, the atrocities that occurred at Nantes in 1793 as a reprisal against counter-revolutionary activities are described with amazing accuracy:

> *Males are sliced, unhappy confusion* . . .
> [men and women bound together naked?]
> *Cries and shrieks at Nantes, pitiable to see.*[44]

We have obtained one amazingly accurate prediction, to be discussed later in the book, but only by treading through a wilderness of poor matches. A supposed reference to the execution of Louis XVI in a later Century[45] looks accurate when 'face' is read as 'fax' and made to mean the lime powder in which the severed head of the king was burned, but meaningless when it predicts: 'A *city* put to the sword, consumed with face powder'[45] — a line that has little real connection with the head of the King in the next line.

In Century VIII there are a few apparent references to the French Revolution, but they are not clustered, and the opportunity for biased interpretation to make the references fit the events of history is less than in Century IX. But the references are weak. A stanza describing 'support' for 'Cappe' and reds fighting reds has been variously interpreted: Cappe can mean (i) the papacy; (ii) a word for 'elected King' (Laver) or (iii) the Capulet (French Royal) family line.[46] Another passage describes the massacre of innocents, widows and virgins and the desecration of churches by 'the Great Red One' (Nostradamus's preconception of the biblical Antichrist) but fits nearly every anti-religious revolution in the past four centuries, while a supposed reference to the betrayal of Louis XVI is even vaguer.[47] But when we leave Century IX, with its mass of revolutionary interpretations, we come at last to a graphic account of the labours of Marie Antoinette in prison and her daughter's impeded marriage to Angoulême, to whom she was betrothed:

---

[44] Centuries V:33.
[45] Centuries VI:92.
[46] Centuries VIII:19.
[47] Centuries VIII:80.

The working [imprisoned] queen seeing her pale daughter
because of unhappiness in the stomach enclosed
Lamentable cries will come from Angoulême
and marriage to the cousin greatly impeded.[48]

This is an unexplained gem, and so it will require discussion in Chapter Eight.

There is just one flaw. *Ergaste* also means 'sterile' and the reference to an 'enclosed' (locked) stomach confirms this interpretation. But Marie Antoinette was not sterile, so even here there is brilliant perception of the future with one characteristic piece of inaccuracy and unreliability. Madame Royale (the daughter), however, *was* sterile.

Apart from a supposed reference[49] to the 'framing' of Marie Antoinette in the necklace affair, which is even weaker, this section has exhausted the references to the French Revolution in the Centuries. A pattern emerges that is similar to Nostradamus's prophecies of British history. Some predictions have an obvious revolutionary flavour and are written in an apocalyptic style because Nostradamus believed in an Antichrist who would arise shortly before the end of the world. Most of these 'general' prophecies can match the French Revolution easily. Others have odd words that have been 'fudged' by interpreters to fit incidents in an almost opposite way from what Nostradamus meant. Finally, there is the inevitably inexplicable hardcore of a few passages that show amazing insight, though none is absolutely accurate.

Nostradamus and Napoleon I

In Chapter Two I suggested an historical model from which Nostradamus may have worked. Paris under the decadent Valois dynasty was similar in many respects to Babylon. The Bourbon dynasty of Henri IV (who, like Cyrus, changed his religion to suit popular opinion[50]) would last for about two hundred years, just like the Persian empire, then suffer

---

[48] Centuries X:17.
[49] Centuries X:43.
[50] Cyrus became (though an Elamite) a worshipper of Bel-Marduk.

upheaval and come under the power of another Alexander the Great — Napoleon I. If this is assumed, some of Nostradamus's predictions about Napoleon I can easily be explained. Further, he believed the millennarian theory that the world would end some 6,000 years after the creation, before which an Antichrist would arise. It is almost inevitable that some of his predictions about the Antichrist would match the actions of a dictator and conqueror such as Napoleon.

Nostradamus played safe, and provided a number of options about the birth place of this dictator/Antichrist; by the rules of probability, one of these options must have fitted:

> *In the profoundest part of the West of Europe*
> *— a child will be born of poor family*
> *By his speech he will seduce a great company,*
> *greater in reputation than in the Kingdom of the East.*[51]

But, though Laver says the 'child' is Napoleon, he did not come from 'the West of Europe' (to quote Nostradamus literally); neither did Hitler (as Cheetham suggests). Franco partly matches the bill, but the *West* has been ruled out by history.

What about the 'North'? In Chapter Two, I showed that Nostradamus speculated about the equivalent of a biblical Cyrus, who might come from the North[52] to conquer the 'Babylon' of Paris under the Valois Kings:

> *The king of Europe will come like a griffin*
> *accompanied by those from the 'north'*
> *He will lead a great army of red and white ones*
> *and they will go against the King of Babylon.*[53]

But Napoleon did not come from the north either, though the stanza is sometimes used to mean those allied forces that came *against* Napoleon in 1815, but there was not one 'king of Europe' who joined forces to depose Napoleon, but several. If anything, this was a speculation about what would

---

[51] Centuries III:35.
[52] See particularly Isaiah 41:25: 'I stirred up one from the north' — to conquer Babylon.
[53] Centuries X:86.

happen to the 'Babylon' of Valois Paris, 200 years before the
Napoleonic era. Nostradamus may have had his mind on
Henri of Navarre, but, using Bible prophecies, have
speculated about the north as well, with a stanza vague
enough to refer both to Antichrist and to Valois Paris.

As for the East, the model was Alexander the Great, hence
a Greek reference:

> *The leader who will conduct infinite people*
> *far from their skies to foreign customs and language*
> *Five thousand in Crete and Thessaly are finished*
> *— the leader flees into a maritime barn.*[54]

Though the model is Alexander the Great, some of the details
remarkably match Napoleon's attempted invasion of Egypt
in 1789/99, if 'maritime barn' is understood to mean 'wooden
ship'. The speculation about an eastern Antichrist also
involved Nostradamus' taking 'pot-luck' with biblical
prophecy of the fall of Babylon, 'calling a ravenous bird from
the east',[55] so he writes:

> *The man from the East will leave his seat*
> *— and cross the Apenines into France.*[56]

The details may fit Khomeini and others, as I shall show;
Laver unsuccessfully tries to match them with Napoleon's
return, but it is simply one more of Nostradamus's
speculations about the origin of the Antichrist.

Finally, the South.

> *An Emperor will be born near Italy*
> *— who will cost the Empire very dearly.*[57]

The remainder of the quatrain could apply to any dictator.
By offering options on every direction — west, north, east
and south — Nostradamus has at last scored a hit with regard
to Napoleon, who was a Corsican. Of course, he 'cost the

---

[54] Centuries I:98.
[55] Isaiah 46:11.
[56] Centuries II:29.
[57] Centuries I:60.

Empire very dearly', but it was largely the empire he had built up himself by military conquest.

Speculation that Nostradamus predicted the name of Napoleon does not merit serious consideration. It uses the line: 'This man will be called by a barbaric [*farouche*] name'[58]. But the word *farouche* can mean anything from 'barbaric' and 'wild' to 'shy'. It does not mean 'destroyer', and to make things worse, neither does the name 'Napoleon'. The suggestion that it means 'Yes. Destroyer', from the Greek *Nai (Yes)* and *Apollyon* (Destroyer) takes some believing, for it requires two L's in the spelling, and only Nostradamus's most uncritical followers have spelt the name in that way. 'Napoleon', of course, means 'inhabitant of Napoli' (or Naples) in Italy.

There are no clear prophecies of a Neapolitan or of a Corsican, but Nostradamus talks of one who has an unfamilar name:

> *Of a name never held by a French King*
> *never was there a thunderbolt so afraid*
> *Tremble — will Italy, Spain and the English*
> *He will be greatly attentive to foreign ladies.*[59]

This is the first 'perceptive' stanza in this section of the chapter, for clearly some details fit those of Napoleon. He was a 'King' with a name not previously held by a French ruler, but so was Francis II who was *craintif* (afraid) and who married a foreign woman, Mary Queen of Scots, and thus was 'attentive' to foreign ladies. Napoleon was fearsome rather than fearful, but was, of course, attentive to foreign ladies — Josephine the Creole, Marie Louise of Austria and his Polish mistress, Marie Walewska. We have finally found some brilliance, but with one clear error of fact. There is also participant-fulfilment, as I shall show.

Laver argues[60] unsuccessfully that the nickname 'shaven head' in some quatrains means Napoleon, but 'shaven head' means other things elsewhere.

---

[58] Centuries I:76.
[59] Centuries IV:54.
[60] Laver, p. 167 and 181.

> *Divine wrath overtakes the great Prince*
> *a short while before he will marry*
> *Both support and credit will suddenly be minimized.*
> *Counsel. He will die by a shaven head.*[61]

In context, 'shaven head' probably means 'shaven-off head' (i.e., decapitated); in any case, commoners would have had shorter hair than the cavalier kings of France. It is symptomatic of commentators that they make much out of a little.[62] Thus, Cheetham applies the quatrain to Charles I's 'incurring wrath', marrying Henrietta Maria of France and granting tolerance to Catholics in 1625, so becoming bankrupt, after which he was executed by a 'shaved head' ('roundhead' = Cromwell). But was not Nostradamus elsewhere supposed to have called Charles I 'the Just One' and would he have disapproved of an edict of Catholic toleration? Laver, conversely, makes 'shaven head' mean Napoleon, who was reputed to have lost his credit and friends after abandoning Josephine. But he did not die because of a shaven head, so the stanza's details do not fit either case perfectly, but are generally typical of most executions.

Another 'shaven head' passage occurs later in the stanzas. It speculates about a 'shaven head' (= commoner or executioner) coming from a maritime city to take up a 'satrapy' (= regional *not* universal government), chasing away 'sordid ones' and being a tyrant for fourteen years.[63] This was a speculative prophecy, not without a biblical model of fourteen years' supremacy, followed by an uprising. Napoleon was a believer in Nostradamus's capabilities, and Theodore Bouys in 1805 was to recast and reinterpret many of Nostradamus's writings and apply them to Napoleon, for whom he foresaw brilliant destiny. How

---

[61] Centuries I:88. See Cheetham p. 63.

[62] Nostradamus *did* anticipate that an anti-Papal Antichrist would be a commoner (with shorter hair than cavalier royalty), so his generalization partly fits both Cromwell and Napoleon. He states that a simple soldier would rise to empire and vex the clergy (Centuries VIII:57) — a prophecy of most modern dictators.

[63] Genesis 14:4 and 5. This is the first biblical account of a Babylonian (Shinar) war, and also involved Elam, hence the use of 'satrap'.

would Napoleon have reacted to such interpretations? He would, of course, identify himself with the 'shaven head'. He had already taken the naval town of Toulon from the British in 1793. He had not risen to 'satrap' (a Persian term for a provincial governor) but to emperor, so would assume that his imperial rule would last fourteen years, after which, if he gave Nostradamus any credence, he would, at least, be weakened by the effect of the prophecy on him. His power, in fact, lasted for fifteen years, from 1799 to 1814, after which, apart from the Hundred Days in 1815 between the exiles of Elba and St Helena, he was to live, powerless, until his death in 1821. So the prophecy, based on what Nostradamus imagined to be the Genesis model of the first Babylonian war in history, affected Napoleon's behaviour, and was thus successful. The remaining details are fudged in interpretation. For example, the 'sordid ones' in the passage have been variously interpreted as (i) the Directorate (of France), and (ii) the English. But Napoleon did not become Emperor until 1804.

So much for the directions from which 'the great King' was supposed to come, and the names given by Nostradamus, and applied to, or assumed by Napoleon I. Some, as we have seen, have been affected by Nostradamus's biblical expectations of Antichrist. As a Catholic, he would assume Antichrist to be anti-papal, so a few prophecies of papal sufferings would not be out of place. There is a vague prediction of a sack of Rome, and an attack on a 'Bridge' (Fr. *Pont* = Pontiff),[64] but earlier we saw that 'bridge' could mean anything from Parliament to Pontefract. There is also a vague prediction[65] about 'Paul the celibate' dying three leagues from the Rhone (but Rosne could also be a misspelling for Rome) and it would seem to have been fulfilled when Pius VI died near Lyons in 1799 after imprisonment by the revolutionaries. But it is so vague that it has been applied to events in modern times.

In contrast is a brilliant stanza describing a war against Sext (= Sextus) the Celibate, in which the opposition is said to come from 'Mont Gaulfier' *and* the Aventine.[66] Opposition

---

[64] Centuries V:30.
[65] Centuries VIII:46.
[66] Centuries V:57.

did not come from the Aventine, but the success of the
revolutionaries was (in 1794) partly attributable to the fact
that the Montgolfier brothers invented the hot air balloon. A
'Sextus' (or 'Sixth'), if it means Pius VI (who was captured
by Napoleon), was involved, but the Aventine suffered
attack, rather than being its source. Again, there is, as with
all other inexplicably perceptive quatrains, an Achilles' heel
— a weak spot to show that Nostradamus is rarely 100 per
cent reliable.

At the end of Century II are two other of these
ecclesiastical prophecies, inspired by a contemporary view of
Christendom's future sufferings under Antichrist:

> *Roman Pontiff, beware of approaching*
> *a city watered by two rivers.*
> *You will spit blood in the place.*
> *You and yours, when the rose blooms.*[67]

With his vision of Babylon, Nostradamus would have
associated the two-rivered city with Paris (watered by Seine
and Marne) as Babylon was by the Tigris and Euphrates.
Somehow, France would be associated with anti-papal
hostility and blood-letting. But the Napoleonic period was to
see some of its detail fulfilled. Pius VI was not assassinated,
but he did die near Lyons, another city watered by two rivers,
the Rhône and the Saône. He died vomiting (but not
necessarily spitting blood), and those referred to in the word
'yours' (the thirty-two priests imprisoned with him) neither
spat blood nor died at that time. Again, some of the description matches the events of Napoleon's time, but not all
of it.

The second of these prophecies again expresses the fear
that, if Paris was 'Babylon', then the anti-papal Antichrist
might arise there:

> *Roman land that the Augur interprets*
> *will be greatly molested by the Gaulish* [French] *nation*
> *But the Celtic nation will dread the hour*
> *Boreas, fleet, too far having driven.*[68]

---

[67] Centuries II:97.
[68] Centuries II:99.

Armed with such a prophecy, and without any patent suggestion of an Antichrist in the passage, Napoleon did invade the Papal States, before adopting Catholicism and obtaining papal blessing from a subsequent pontiff. But the rest is vague, and does not match history, for it suggests maritime disaster by a north wind (Boreas), and Boreas is usually and necessarily interpreted to mean Napoleon's Russian (1812) defeat, which, of course, was entirely on land; his only significant naval defeat occurred at Trafalgar in the south-west.

Pius VII, the successor Pope, chosen by cardinals in hiding, crowned Napoleon in 1804 but was taken prisoner by the French in 1808. These details are wrongly assumed to fit another quatrain based on Nostradamus's anticipation of the papacy:

> *While sailing, the Great Pontiff will be captured.*
> *Great preparations by disturbed clerics fail.*
> *Second elected absent, his power fails,*
> *his favourite bastard put to death.*[69]

The details are inexact, if applied to the events surrounding Pius VII, for the only preparations by disturbed clerics were those of the election in 1804 four years before Pius was taken prisoner. Though the second pope with whom Napoleon was concerned, he was not the 'second elected absent', but the first, and the 'favourite bastard' could not have been Napoleon (as often suggested), nor was Napoleon put to death. It is sufficient to say, in explanation, that Napoleon believed in his involvement in fulfilling this quatrain, and partly performed it.

But Nostradamus was preoccupied with Antichrist, whom he thought would have a short life, during which he would trouble the papacy, as one of his earliest stanzas shows:

> *Over the universe, there will be a monarch*
> *Whose peace and life will not be long*
> *At this time the fisher-ship* [the papacy] *will be lost*
> *— governed in its greatest detriment.*[70]

---

[69] Centuries V:15.
[70] Centuries I:4.

This is almost a 'crib' from Malachy's prophecy [71] of Peter the fisherman, his 'motto' of the final pope. But torn from context and applied to Napoleon (whose kingdom was not universal) it does little more than describe his attack on the papacy. Further, it is not accurate. Napoleon lived into his fifties, the normal expectation of life for the time.

This leaves us with few cases in the arid wilderness of speculation; some indicate participant fulfilment on the part of Napoleon, and others that 'sixth sense' that sometimes shows itself — a striking combination of events, with just one weak inaccuracy to show Nostradamus never to be completely reliable.

Napoleon invaded Milan, in fulfilment of the words:

> *Milan, prince of* [or captured by] *the Eagle,*
> *is deceived by ambush*
> *Its ancient walls are breached by cannon.* [72]

As if to ensure that he was fulfilling the prophecy, Napoleon captured Milan twice (15 May 1796 and 2 June 1800), but identified himself as the 'Eagle' whereas the prophecy, using Moses' prediction of the Roman invasion of Israel, [73] identified Milan (as a Roman city) with the Eagle.

Predictions of the sacrifice of an eagle may also have been used by Napoleon as an inspiration for his Northern Italian campaign (1795-7) or at least as propaganda:

> *The bird of prey offers himself to heaven . . .*
> *Cremona and Mantua will come to suffer great hardships.* [74]

In fact, Cremona and Mantua were only two (rather obvious) cities among many. He may have tried to fulfil the words:

---

[71] The prophecies of Malachy, Bishop of Armagh, mentioned earlier.
[72] Centuries III:37.
[73] Deuteronomy 28:49.
[74] Centuries I:24.

Great Pau [= Po, in North Italy] *from a Gaul, great harm will receive.*
Vain terror to maritime Lyons [interpreted as 'Lion', and so Britain']
Large numbers of people across the sea will pass.
There shall not escape, a quarter of a million.[75]

For, having succeeded in the Po area (Italy) Napoleon's next ambition was to invade Egypt, armed with a Delphic oracle about crossing the sea. But like the ambiguous oracle of Delphi, when consulted by Xerxes about invading Greece, the quatrain does not say that 250,000 of Napoleon's own men would not return, or that he would need a large army with which to do battle. The prediction is remarkable, but not inexplicable. For Napoleon's contemporaries, who believed that Daniel 11 was being fulfilled in their day,[76] would have been tempted to urge Napoleon on in his ambition, believing that a European conquest of Egypt at that time had been foretold by the Bible: 'He shall stretch out his hand against the countries — and the land of Egypt *shall not escape*'.[77]

It is doubtful whether Napoleon would have used Nostradamus's prophecy of an invasion of Malta as propaganda for his invasion of the island en route to Egypt, for despite the wishful thinking of interpreters the (non-relevant) quatrain.[78] is of a *Libyan* leader who would invade Spain and Malta (held even in Nostradamus's time, by the knights of Rhodes: anagram = Herodde) or of a Muslim Antichrist, accepting another of Nostradamus's alternative speculations. Napoleon was, in fact, doing the reverse. During his invasion of Egypt, he was, despite poor relations with the papacy, carrying on a Christian crusade against the Turks in the minds of many.

A vague quatrain seemed to provide a precedent for the attempted invasion of England: 'In Bolognia, he will want to wash away his faults',[79] but only by reading 'Bolongne' as 'Boulogne', one of the seaports for the invasion. There were other precedents for an invasion, including a quatrain that is

[75] Centuries II:94.
[76] As, for example, Sir Isaac Newton's *Observations on the Prophecies of Daniel*.
[77] Daniel 11:42.
[78] Centuries V:14.
[79] Centuries VIII:53.

clearly used elsewhere to mean James II's invasion of Ireland; Laver uses this for both occasions.[80] The first round of the conflict with Britain ended on 21 October 1805, with the battle of Trafalgar; again, Napoleon's admirers may have tried to strike a silver vein. Nostradamus had written a vague quatrain based on Greek mythology about a king waiting on a rock for a sign of conquest, dismayed when a black sail mistakenly appeared. The details seemed to fit Gibraltar, but the quatrain did not state that Napoleon would lose the battle:

> *Between two seas a promontory stands*
> *who later will die by the bit of a horse.*
> *For his own* [or for a sign] *Neptune will release a black sail.*
> *By Calpe, and the fleet near to Rocheval* [to rhyme with *cheval*
> = 'horse'].[81]

There is a cape (Calpe) and a rock (Roche) at Gibraltar, where two seas meet. With some knowledge of Nostradamus a French admiral on the run would have regarded it as an auspicious place to fight and win. There is no clear evidence that this admiral (Villeneuve) died of a horse 'bit' (*mords*). He was strangled, but not necessarily by a horse 'bridle' (*mors*) as the text is mistakenly read. But in curious fulfilment, the English fleet did raise a black sail, though victorious, for its admiral, Nelson, was mortally wounded. Thus, in this incident participant fulfilment could have been at work; but the trick of history in Nostradamus's favour is the black sail. As in the Greek legend, the victors hoisted it, not by mistake, but because of the loss that it signified.

A supposed picture of Napoleon's retreat from Moscow after his attempted invasion of Russia[82] (1812/13) is unconvincing. It describes a 'destroyer' (*L'Olestant*), an army coming from (but not necessarily retreating from) Slavonia (i.e. Russia) and a burning city. The picture seems to derive from the Apocalypse of John: 'Apollyon — the Destroyer',[83] an army from beyond Euphrates,[84] and the 'smoke of a great

---

[80] Centuries II:68. See also his use (p. 176) of Centuries VIII:37, which most commentators apply to the time of Charles I.
[81] Centuries I:77.
[82] Centuries IV:82.
[83] Revelation 9:11.
[84] Revelation 9:14-16.

furnace'.[85] Contemporary commentators on John's Apocalypse had applied the prophecy to the Mongol invasions of Europe, in which cities were burned to the ground; further, the stanza paints a picture of *invasion*, not *retreat*. 'Apollyon', of course, does sound like 'Napoleon', but I have already shown that this identification is mistaken, though some contemporaries would have been excused for using the Apocalypse rather than Nostradamus to speculate about Napoleon's future. But by a trick of history the stanza has come to be regarded as a prophecy of Napoleon's retreat from Moscow. Did Napoleon use it as an inspiration for invading Russia, or has history simply been kind to Nostradamus?

Prophecies of eagles are applied to this period,[86] but eagles featured in the symbolism of most European nations. Laver tried to find in the phrase *haute velle* (high valley) the name of Wellington.[87] A prediction of 'five strangers' in a temple is read by some interpreters[88] as a description of five European nations in France, though Nostradamus does not elsewhere use a temple as a symbol for France. Then came the first expulsion to Elba. Louis XVIII was proclaimed King, a little earlier. The only town faithful to Napoleon was Nice, which some interpreters have found in the words 'Nisse',[89] 'Antibe' (from the old Greek name for Nice — Antipolis)[90] and even 'Antipolles',[91] which Laver[92] also takes to be a punning reference to St Helena in the *antipodes*, though the St Helena expulsion came later. Napoleon had a last 'fling' of a hundred days, culminating in Waterloo, before his second and final exile. The only attempt to find the Hundred Days in the words 'in the third month' (a hundred days ends in a fourth month) is unsuccessful,[93] and the only apparent reference to the battle is a symbolic fight of animals using a leopard, not a lion, as a symbol for Britain; there are no verbal references that match Waterloo at all.

---

[85] Revelation 9:2.
[86] Centuries II:44.
[87] Centuries I:89.
[88] Centuries III:45.
[89] Centuries X:87.
[90] Centuries X:23.
[91] Centuries X:87.
[92] Laver, *Nostradamus*, p. 186.
[93] Centuries I:23.

The Revolutions of 1830 and 1848

By 1830 much of Nostradamus's revolutionary writing had already been used by his interpreteres to signify earlier events. But there was still scope for ingenuity, and for new expositors to strain new meanings from Nostradamus's words, just as the interpretation of biblical prophecy underwent reappraisal in the nineteenth century. Curiously, the period of 1260 years (the 1260 days of Daniel 12 and Revelation 11 and 12) had been thought by some to run from AD 529, when an edict of Justinian gave authority to the papacy, to 1790/2, when Pius VI suffered imprisonment under the revolutionaries. Such an interpretation necessarily revealed a Protestant bias. With his knowledge of the Babylonian time measurement of 360 days, Nostradamus was probably able to perceive that the biblical 1260 day-years could mean either 1260 calendar years, or 1260 Babylonian 360-day periods, and so 1242 years (i.e. 1260 × 360/365.25); that there would (or could) be a gap of about 17/18 years between two fulfilments and, therefore, between two revolutions. This would become useful information, as we shall see.

Despite the efforts of Le Pelletier,[94] and of Laver, who largely follows him, little that Nostradamus wrote can be positively matched with the reign of Louis XVIII, Napoleon's successor.

The 'long-haired' one[95] could have meant any Bourbon king, and the reference to Aquitaine in the same stanza concerned is positively misleading. A reference to a 'German prince'[96] is wrongly identified with Louis XVIII by Laver, and two stanzas used by him[97,98] are also vague, including one (X:90) which Cheetham applies to Napoleon. There are also a series of obscure references to Italy[99] that have been identified with Louis XVIII's Italian connections[100] but only

---

[94] Anatole Le Pelletier, *Les Oracles de Michel de Nostredame* (Paris, 1867).
[95] Centuries III:83.
[96] Centuries II:87.
[97] Centuries X:10.
[98] Centuries X:90.
[99] Centuries V:39.
[100] Centuries III:96.

one event during Louis XVIII's reign of fifteen years merits real attention as a serious prediction of unexplained perceptiveness, and that has an Achilles' heel, a set of flaws which, as shown earlier in this chapter, are characteristic of those striking prophecies of Nostradamus in which everything else apparently seems to fit. It is about a February 13th and a 'Chef de Fossan' who will have his throat cut by a Republican (Tarpeian) who is in charge of bloodhounds and greyhounds. Fossan(o) had associations with the Savoy family and Kings of Sardinia (as rulers of non-Habsburg Piedmont) and the Duc de Berry (who was a maternal grandson of a King of Sardinia, but a potential heir to the French throne as a son of the future Charles X) was stabbed on 13 February 1820. His throat was not cut but his attacker was an employee in the royal stables. Despite the comments of some Nostradamus expositors, the reference to 'Saturn in Leo' is no more than a veiled reference to astrological symbols. We shall consider this stanza again in Chapter Eight.

In 1830 came a change of government that resulted in the exile of Louis XVIII and the ascent of Louis-Philippe to the French throne. There was, during his reign, a fresh interest in Nostradamus, whose work had not been interpreted since 1806, when both Bouys[101] and Belland[102] had written books for the benefit and advice of Napoleon. Now, it was to be Eugene Bareste,[103] and this should tell us something about participant-fulfilment, for it signals top-level interest in Nostradamus and the probability that a King is being advised by people who are familiar with his writings. Does anything about the reign of Louis-Philippe suggest a participant-fulfilment? There are unlikely puns about Orleans (*dort leans*),[104] and there is the usual clutch of vague statements,[105] given new meaning. But there is detailed fulfilment too. Louis-Philippe, identifying himself with the Philip of one of Nostradamus's quatrains (based probably on the model of Joseph's seven years of prosperity, was to be encouraged by it to wage a prosperous Arab campaign:

---

[101] Theodore Bouys, *Nouvelles Considerations . . . sur Nostradamus* (Paris, 1806).
[102] M. Belland, *Napoléon, premier Empereur des Français, prédit par Nostradamus* (Paris, 1806).
[103] E. Bareste, *Nostradamus* (Paris, 1840).
[104] Centuries VIII:42. The word 'Orleans' is explicit. The pun is not needed.
[105] Centuries VI:84; VIII:38; V:7; V:6.

> *Seven years shall Philip's fortune prosper.*
> *He will overcome the Arabs.*[106]

He did not do so completely, and seven years from his accession brings us to the Mehemet Ali trouble with which he was involved. He was to have trouble from an Ognion, who has been variously identified with Mehemet Ali, a French coin (!), the New Republic that opposed him, and Napoleon III — the French coin being illustrative of the 'Republic' of the period. After his success against the Arabs had ebbed and he had tried to subdue Africa, adopting the new French tricolour in possible part-fulfilment of Nostradamus's prophecy:

> *unfurling a flag of gold,* [not white] *blue and red,*
> *— he will subdue Africa.*[107]

Philippe was to become less popular, and would finally be deposed and replaced by Napoleon III. With the possibility of a seventeen-year gap between revolutions in mind, using the calculations that I have given earlier, Nostradamus would have had little difficulty in predicting that, sooner or later, there would be a king who would reign for seventeen years and then be deposed:

> *After the throne has been held for seventeen years*
> *. . . one will be elected at that time,*
> *who will not conform to the Romans.*[108]

Did the Directory have the prophecy of Nostradamus in mind when they deposed Louis-Philippe and elected Napoleon III, after the former had reigned for seventeen years? It matters little, for with Napoleon III a whole spate of expositors was to arise who would read many of his actions into Nostradamus's writings and try to find obscure references to Louis Napoleon. Biblical commentators were to do the same thing, taking the decree of Phocas (about the papacy) in AD 610 and successfully predicting the end of the

---

[106] Centuries IX:89.
[107] Centuries V:69.
[108] Centuries V:92.

temporal power of the papacy in 1870, 1260 years later. But Nostradamus was to help the process along, by predicting, as some later expositors were to understand, that Napoleon III would not be sympathetic to the Romans (i.e. the papacy).

4
Nostradamus and the Second World War

The Great Divide

I have dealt in the previous chapters at length with the application of Nostradamus's predictions to the French monarchy and to the Revolutionary and Napoleonic periods, because the 'classical' commentators on Nostradamus's prophecies have generally been able to fit some of the stanzas easily to events during these periods. At this point a yawning chasm appears in most interpretations, because of the difficulty that some interpreters have in matching used quatrains to contemporary events. It should be a rule of interpretation that no 'prophecy' is used twice when other 'prophecies' are still unused unmatched by historical events. For when a quatrain can have more than one application it must, by the rules of probability, be easy to fit other events in subsequent history, and thus it must describe a comparatively common occurrence.

Victorian biblical commentators who favoured what was known as the 'historical' school of the interpretation of John's Apocalypse had much the same difficulty, except that the Apocalypse is a systematic prophecy, for its visions are known not to be jumbled. Yet they treated it as though its symbols had been drawn on a wide piece of elastic, which was stretched more and more to fit the march of history. Even when there appear to be systematic interpretations that match the prophecy to sequential history, wide gaps have to be created because events are left out as the prophecy is reinterpreted and applied to more modern events. If this can happen with systematic Biblical prophecy,[1] how much more

---

[1] See D. Pitt Francis, *The Most Amazing Message Ever Written* (Castle Books, 1983), Chapter 1.

likely is it to have happened with a set of predictions that are generally agreed to be jumbled!

Thus, apart from a few common modern interpretations, those stanzas that were known not to have been identified before 1870 have been matched with different events by subsequent interpreters. For example, Elisée du Vignois produced[2] some incredible applications of Nostradamus's quatrains to the period from 1870 to 1910, when his book was written and from them James Laver rescued a few applications of Nostradamus's prophecies, though they are in themselves quite unconvincing. An unidentifiable quatrain[3] about a child who refuses to listen to a foreign mother and the loss of five hundred men was applied by Laver to the Prince Imperial of the late nineteenth century but by Cheetham to an event in the life of Louis XIII, long before the end of the nineteenth century.

Another stretch of interpretation renders the 'bearded star in Cancer' as the 'long-haired star'[4] in a passage that does not specifically mention a comet. Laver takes interpretation one stage further by assuming the accompanying details of the quatrain to apply to the death of Pius XI and the accession of Leo XIII. The only possible precedent for doing so is the prophecy of Malachy, which calls Leo XIII *'lumen in caelo'*. But he was possibly elected for that precise reason, for his family arms include a comet (i.e. a hairy star). However, Nostradamus's quatrain is correctly translated:

> *He shall appear towards the Septentrion* [north]
> *— not far from the bearded star in Cancer.*
> *Susa, Siena, Boetias, Eretria,*
> *The great mass of Rome will die and the night disappear!*[4]

Literally, the reference is not to a 'Great One' (supposedly Pius XI) but to a 'great mass' of people in Rome; and 'he' (whoever he may be) is 'near to', but therefore *not* 'identifiable with', the bearded star — a star assumed to have a fixed position in Cancer. The result of the appearance of

---

[2] Elisée du Vignois, *Notre histoire racontée à l'avance par Nostradamus* (Paris, 1910).
[3] *Centuries* VII:11.
[4] *Centuries* VI:6.

'he' is that many people will die in Rome, so that whatever appears is not the 'bearded star', even if either 'he' or the 'bearded star' be a comet. There is in Cancer a cluster known as the Praesepe (the beehive) to which Nostradamus may have been referring. But even if the reference is to a literal comet, it would be in the north, near the Pole star, and an attempt to make 'Septentrion' mean a town in Italy north of Rome, and 'great mass' mean 'Great One' (i.e. Pius XI) is ludicrous. Perhaps Nostradamus was talking literally about the Second Advent coming, as astronomers of those days with fixed views about heaven may have thought, from the 'Cancer' region of the galaxy. Perhaps he was referring to a celestial plague that would cause death to many people. What is certain is that he *does* refer to the death of a mass of people, *not* to the death of a previous Pope.

I have cited this case as an example of how difficult it is to find clear predictions by Nostradamus that are specific to the period 1870-1914 and that cannot be applied to any other time in the intervening history between his time and our own. Erika Cheetham tried to update the prophecies of Nostradamus as much as any interpreter, but her analysis presents us with a great void during the period, largely because she tried to recast some of Elisée du Vignois's interpretations to fit such modern events as the assassination of two of the Kennedy brothers. There is little with which she fills this void. She attempts to make Century I:7, with its mention of Dreyfus's opponent 'Rousseau', fit the Dreyfus affair of 1894-1906, in which a French Jew was accused of selling military secrets to the Germans; but the evidence for this 'fulfilment' is slender. Take away the reference to Rousseau and the quatrain is quite ambiguous. Along with Laver, she makes Century II:43 fit the Triple Alliance of 1881, but only by reference to the Malachy prediction of the contemporary Pope as *Lumen in Caelo* and by assuming that the bearded star referred to the contemporary papacy.

Few of Nostradamus's quatrains have ever been applied to the First World War, 1914-18. There is a passage[5] about British attacks on Aquitaine, after which attempts to take a 'Port Selin' would be made; but 'Selin' has a host of meanings:

Against Aquitaine by British assaults [or perhaps 'islands']
and by the same, great incursions
Frosty rain will make the land unsafe.
Port-Selin will make strong invasions.[5]

This has been interpreted to refer to the assault on the Dardanelles in 1915, when France (Aquitaine) and Britain were making little headway against their opponents (the German Empire and Turkey) and attempted an assault on the Dardanelles (Port Selin — Istanbul) instead. The problem with this interpretation is that the stanza explicitly states that British assaults would be *against* Aquitaine (taken to mean 'France'), whereas in the First World War Britain and France were allies against Germany and the Ottoman Empire. So, though this has been 'slotted' as a World War I quatrain in the writings of several interpreters, it is logically impossible to do so without (i) interpreting Aquitaine to mean France and then (ii) depriving the first line of its real meaning.

Although some of the events of the French Revolution seem to have been chronicled in advance by Nostradamus, there is scarcely an unambiguous reference to the Russian Revolution of 1917. The nearest that Cheetham gets in applying Nostradamus to this revolution is her interpretation of one of the later stanzas:

Innocents' blood, widow and virgin
— such evils committed by means of the great Red One
Holy images placed on burning candles.
Terrified by fear, none will be seen that moves.[6]

The details fit both French and Russian Revolutions. The reference to the 'Red One' seems to make the quatrain a little more appropriate to the Russian Revolution; but when it is appreciated that the colour red is often associated by Nostradamus with ecclesiastics and clerics, and that the whole quatrain could thus be read as an account of an ecclesiastical rather than a revolutionary massacre, any clear application to the Russian Revolution is lost.

[5] Centuries II:1.
[6] Centuries VIII:80.

The only remaining stanza that can be identified as having anything to do with the twentieth century up to the rise of Hitler in February 1933 is a passage about an epidemic:

> *The horrible war, that in the West is prepared*
> *— the following year will come the pestilence*
> *So horrible that neither young, old nor beast* [will endure it]
> *Blood, fire, Mercury, Mars, Jupiter in France.*[7]

In general, apart from the uncharacteristically clear astrological reference in the fourth line, it is just one more of Nostradmus's patent borrowings from John's Apocalypse. War is often followed by pestilence, as the apocalyptic 'seal' sequence[8] makes clear. The specific stanza is usually understood to mean the First World War, which was followed by an influenza epidemic at a time when Mercury, Mars and Jupiter were in conjunction. But two things are wrong. In the first place, the epidemic did not follow the war: it raged before the armistice of 1918. Secondly, it did not kill in the large proportions envisaged by Nostradamus. Other (subsequent) epidemics would have been much worse, had it not been for medical developments.

Thus, we have detected a massive void in the fulfilments of Nostradamus's prophecies. If we disregard, for the most part, Elisé du Vignois's spurious applications, it seems to stretch over two-thirds of a century, from 1870 to Hitler's rise to power in 1933. Even C. A. Ward's lucid work in 1891 (see Bibliography) had been little more than a re-hash of previous explanations, including a large section on the life of Nostradamus. Was this some blind spot in Nostradamus's vision, or was he daydreaming, or is there some other reason for so few fulfilments? Could it be that this increasingly materialistic age was one in which fewer people took Nostradamus's writings seriously, and that consequently there were fewer people to participate in voluntary fulfilments and events or (even more likely, as we have seen) fit his prophecies to contemporary history? During this period Nostradamus was relatively silent, after over three hundred years of turbulent reminders of his writings, even though the years 1870-1933 produced a far greater number of world-shattering events than the preceding three centuries.

---

[7] Centuries IX:55.
[8] Revelation 6:1-8.

But soon, a few years before 1933, Nostradamus was to be roused once more, to help *produce* one of the greatest holocausts against his own race in the history of mankind.

Calling the Tune

Throughout this book I have shown that participant-fulfilment can (and does) explain much of Nostradamus's success as a prophet, that the Bourbon kings and Napoleon were believers in Nostradamus and either consciously or unconsciously (as in Napoleon's invasion of Russia) carried out current interpretations of some of his stanzas to the very letter. More often than not, the details did not depend on Nostradamus, but on his interpreters. Thus, even if an interpretation were wrong, but yet believed, it could influence a devotee of Nostradamus to carry out the faulty interpretation. The age of materialist rationalist extremes, which produced few interpreters that were politically credible, culminated in the advance of a materialistic socialism and the Russian Revolution of 1917. But in one place in Western Europe, astrology was to become respectable, and with it the gaunt, nebulous and perhaps unwilling image of Nostradamus. He was not to call the tune, nor to know how faulty the interpretations of his writings would be. But a tune would be called, on an entirely wrong note. And in two decades it would send the German armies blundering into Poland, and lead to one of the greatest conflicts in the history of mankind.

The error was not Nostradamus's fault: it resulted from the faulty interpretation of one of his stanzas and was first voiced by C. Loog, a Berlin postal official. In 1921, he first published his *Die Weissagungen des Nostradamus* (The Prophecies of Nostradamus), and, to provide that element of mystery that always enhances popularity, disclosed, under secrecy, a 'code word' to his publisher. This 'code word' was the 'final key' to the prophecies. It was disclosed on 22 December 1920, and accompanied by an affidavit about its discovery a few weeks afterwards.

The book was extremely successful and ran into five editions. The series of interpretations it contained were important because they were read by Frau Goebbels, and became a 'basis' for action by several members of the hierarchy of the Third Reich, and, for a short time, by the Führer himself. If the theory of participant-fulfilment is to be applied to Hitler, this book, rather than the prophecies themselves, requires particular attention.

In Chapter Three (p. 51) I considered the 290-year prophecy of Nostradamus:

> *Seven times you will see the British nation change*
> *— dyed in blood for 290 years*
> *Not entirely free, for German support.*
> *Aries doubts for Bastarnian [= Polish?] support.*[9]

I showed that, in context, it was an attempted prophecy *against* Britain rather than a prediction of greatness lasting for three centuries, and that the mention of 'seven times' may have been borrowed from biblical prophecy.[10]

The problems in the text include the word 'Bastarnian', and the dating of the 290 years. The second is the more difficult, for the 290-year period is as flexible as it can be, and interpreters have differed as much about it as about the *termini a quo,* and *ad quem* of biblical time periods. Three well-known interpreters identified at least ten upheavals that could fit the 'seven times' prophecy, over a period from 1501 to 1939, a total of 438 years; the only common points seem to be the years 1660, 1689 and 1714. Le Pelletier[11] took 1501 as his starting point, and arrived at 1791, which he identified as the final year of the French Revolution. Of course, the British monarchy did not change at the French Revolution. In fact, neither of the years 1501 or 1791 seems to fit a 'seven times' prophecy of Britain's changes of dynasty, nor do they specifically fit prophecies of Britain's greatness. Britain's rise to empire could arbitrarily be dated from 1501, though this dating has been generally discarded in favour of better starting points; but Le Pelletier's interpretations produced an interpretive element that Loog was to use. It was the identification of 'Bastarnian' with the Polish people. In fact, the Bastarnae were a German tribe, while the Poles are Slavs. But during the time of Tacitus, when they were first

---

[9] Centuries III:57.
[10] Daniel 3:19, 4:25 and Leviticus 26:18.
[11] Le Pelletier, *Les Oracles de Michel de Nostradame* (Paris, 1867).

mentioned, the Bastarnae occupied an area east of the Vistula, identifiable with modern Poland. By an interpretational 'hash', Le Pelletier identified the tribe with Poland. Loog in his 1921 interpretation was to do the same.

Secondly, Loog took a later date as his 290-year *terminus a quo,* acknowledging that Britain had been great during the nineteenth century. The Abbé Charles Nicoullaud had also experimented with later starting points. In his work[12] on the subject, he mentioned two. The first was the date of James I's accession (1603), but the addition of 290 years to that date produced 1893, a year in which nothing eventful happened; the second was 1649, the date of Charles I's execution, which gave a termination date of 1939.

Combining Le Pelletier's wrong identification of Bastarnae (a German tribe) with Poland (for no more than geographical reasons) and the twentieth-century fulfilment date, Loog concluded that Britain's greatness would be on the wane after 1939 because of a crisis involving the royal family. The relevant paragraph may be translated:

> In 1939 there will be the last important change of dynasty in Britain. 'Aries doubts for his Bastarnian protectorate'. In the era of Tactius, the German 'Bastarnae' tribe was across the Vistula . . . Nostradamus clearly shows that in 1939 there will be a critical set of events in the rejuvenated state of Poland along with Britain's final greatest crisis.[13]

Loog wrote for an anti-British German public with a keen interest in the occult sciences and in astrology. When Hitler later adopted Nostradamus as his guide in the late 1930s, many expected Loog's fulfilment in 1939. When a crisis occurred involving the abdication of Edward VIII, it looked as though Loog would be right. Just one stroke would be necessary to topple the British dynasty. Loog had also said that the British dynasty would be intertwined with the destiny of Poland. Britain had a military treaty with Poland. Therefore, to implement the prophecy, Germany should

---

[12] Abbé Charles Nicoullaud, *Nostradamus, ses prophéties* (Paris, 1914).
[13] C. Loog, *Die Weissagungen des Nostradamus* (Berlin, 1921).

invade Poland, involve Britain, and end British supremacy
for ever. The hierarchy of the Third Reich had over six years
to plan the 1939 invasion of Poland, using Loog as their
guide. The invasion was no credit either to Nostradamus or
to Loog, whose interpretation was a first-rate blunder, and
did not, as he predicted, bring about 'Britain's final greatest
crisis'. Instead, Loog's interpretation was a direct cause of
one of the most devastating wars in the history of mankind.

The Failure of Peace and the Rise of Hitler

Loog had now called the tune, and the yawning empty void
of apparent non-fulfilment would soon close in the next
decade, with a flurry of renewed interest in the French seer.
Quatrains would soon be twisted out of context, and many
stanzas retranslated to make them read like direct predictions
of the Second World War. Even when the war was over,
serious students such as Cheetham were to find the war in
over 6 per cent of Nostradamus's writings, a staggering
contrast to the near-absence of fulfilments for over two-
thirds of a century. To find between fifty and sixty of
Nostradamus's quatrains to be relevant to less than ten years
is truly astounding. At such a rate the whole of the Centuries
could have been fulfilled in less than two centuries. But this
was not all. As we shall see later, a Swiss astrologer, Karl
Ernst Krafft, was to be given the task of retranslating the
Centuries to apply them to the progress of the German
Reich, and of forging other quatrains for propaganda
purposes, while on the British side, Louis de Wohl (later a
novelist), would be preparing counter-propaganda along the
same lines. But first, the believers of Nostradamus would
have to find material to predict the failure of world peace, for
the war of 1914-18 had ended with pledges on all sides and
the formation of a League of Nations. They could have
consulted the Bible: 'When they shall say "Peace and
security" — then sudden destruction will come upon them as
travail comes upon a woman with child and they shall not
escape'.[14] But the Bible is never too popular among the
world's more unscrupulous politicians, except when they use
it for their own advancement. Somewhere, something had to
be found in Nostradamus.

---

[14] 1 Thessalonians 5:3.

Two quatrains are relevant. Both are used by Cheetham, and the first is used by Laver:

> *Of Lake Leman, the sermons will be angered*
> *— the days are drawn to weeks,*
> *— then month[s], then year[s], then all will fail.*
> *The 'magistrates' will 'damn' their useless powers.*[15]

The stanza is perceptive because it identifies Geneva (Lake Leman) as the location of the League of Nations in 1920, but the league failed to prevent Hitler's war: it became ineffective in 1939, and was finally replaced by the United Nations Organization (and then the United Nations Association) after 1947, as this quatrain seems to indicate. Further, Geneva has retained some of its importance as a city associated with world (peace) organizations. But the stanza does not talk specifically about a peace organization at all, although Geneva has, for most of its history, been a peaceful city. It is about 'sermons' emanating from Geneva. In context, it was probably inspired by Nostradamus's acrimony towards Calvinism and the ineffectiveness of French authorities to deal with the Calvinist scourge, which issued from Geneva, where Calvin, though French, spent most of his later years. There was no brilliance in his assumption of Geneva as a place of protest. It was outside French general jurisdiction, and became associated, as the smallest of Swiss cantons, with Switzerland quite late, in 1815. Nostradamus's anti–Calvinist and his anti–Genevan attitude is shown in the other supposed League of Nations quatrain:

> *By the Sueves* [Swiss] *and the areas around*
> *— they will make war because of the clouds*
> *A swarm* [field] *of marine locusts and gnats.*
> *The faults of Leman will be exposed.*[16]

Again, if this is read in the context of the League of Nations' failure and of Hitler's War, it may seem partly applicable. But the prediction describes a war in the clouds, and in the areas around Switzerland, i.e. in areas of high altitude, and if

---

[15] Centuries I:47.
[16] Centuries V:85.

read correctly presages an invasion of Switzerland. When the stanza was first applied to World War II, Krafft, a disillusioned, Swiss-born German astrologer, may have wanted to think of the stanza as a prophecy of a German invasion of his native Switzerland. But this never happened. Nostradamus was perceptive in describing the breach of something involving Switzerland. But he was not perceptive enough.

Hitler's actions will receive fuller treatment later in this chapter; let us now consider some of the supposed predictions of his rise to power. The best known is the 'Hister' prophecy:

> *Beasts wild with hunger will swim across [tranner] rivers,*
> *The greatest part of the 'field' will oppose 'Hister'*
> *In a cage of iron he will drag the leader*
> *when German offspring knows no law.*[17]

If ever a verse sets the scene for participant-fulfilment, this is it. Cheetham admits in her book [18] that Hitler recognized himself in this quatrain as early as the mid-1930s and that Goebbels made great use of it for propaganda purposes, though her reference to Ellic Howe's book should be treated with some caution, for he places[19] most of the Nostradamus propaganda in the years subsequent to 1939, *not* before it. There is sufficient evidence in his earlier publication to show that Hitler did regard himself as 'Hister' long before the Second World War. But surely, he would not have been flattered by the last line? The answer is that he did not have to be, for the French *rein* could be a pun on 'Rhine'. The quatrain commences with a mention of 'river'. Le Pelletier had already identified 'Hister' with the Latin 'Ister' meaning the Danube, and with the Etruscan word meaning a clown. Most commentators before 1933 agreed with the former meaning. Hence, as far as Hitler was concerned 'Hister', though a reference to himself, was a play on the

---

[17] Centuries II:24.
[18] Cheetham, *Nostradamus*, p. 82. Her reference to Ellic Howe's *Nostradamus and the Nazis* relates to evidence that is best obtained from Howe's *Astrology and the Third Reich* (Aquarian Press, 1984), formerly titled *Urania's Children*.
[19] E. Howe, ibid.

word for Danube, and *rein* a play on the word Rhine. The reference to lawlessness, in any case, may not be an accurate translation of the last line, which can be literally translated 'observes a trifle [*rein*]'.

Clearly, Hitler's identification of himself with 'Hister' was nothing more than a figment of imagination, and yet he was able to play the lawless role that Nostradamus had prescribed. There is no anagram that can make Hister into Hitler, and the fact that Hister clearly means the Danube in Nostradamus's writings is shown by its link with the Rhine in a later stanza:

> *At a nearby place, not far from Venice* [Venus]
> *— the two greatest ones of Asia and Africa*
> *From Rhine and Danube* [Hister] *will be said to have come* [Fr. *venus*]
> *Cries, tears from Malta — and the coast of Liguria.*[20]

The Rhine and the Danube were boundaries of the ancient Roman Empire and linked by Nostradamus for this reason alone. To many Germans they have for centuries also been regarded as the western and southern boundaries respectively of Germany. The quatrain is sufficiently vague to apply to any invasion involving these two natural boundaries between Germany and the Roman Empire. It was an imperfect attempt at fulfilment by Hitler and Mussolini, who would have regarded the Rhine and Danube as their mutual boundaries, and the 'two great ones' as themselves. That the two leaders were guided to invade Malta shortly afterwards by their reading of the stanza is of little importance. Again, most of the detail is not valid prediction but attempted fulfilment.

I have had to discuss the tripartite pact between Germany, Italy and Japan, and so move out of the 1930s in order to prove that 'Hister' was not originally Hitler but clearly signified the Danube to Nostradamus. Let us now return to Hitler's rise in the 1930s. Paradoxically, a prediction of the concordat indicating the supremacy of Axis Germany over Axis Italy had already been found by some contemporary interpreters of Nostradamus:

---

[20] Centuries IV:68.

> *Roman power will be entirely abased*
> *— following [imitating] the 'vestiges' of its great neighbour.*[21]

Interpreters have made much of the fact that Musolini means 'muslin maker' generally regarded as a base craft in Italy, and of the mention of *bouffons* (= buffoons = Hitler and Mussolini) later in the stanza. In fact reverting to the model discussed in Chapter Two, the verse is a 'vague' prediction of a decline in Catholic power because of the Protestant factions Nostradamus overtly despised. It has nothing to do with Hitler or Mussolini.

We can couple mention of Hitler's association with Mussolini in the 1930's with Hitler's attitude to the Vatican, in particular to Mussolini's 'concordat' with the papacy:

> *Of freedom, there will be no recovery*
> *It will be occupied by a black, proud, wicked villain.*
> *When the matter of the bridge shall be opened,*
> *— of Hister [the Danube]. the republic of Venice will be vexed.*[22]

There are so many puns in the passage that it could appear to be a prophecy of the concordat. 'Black' (*noir*) is usually understood by Nostradamus enthusiasts as an anagram for 'king' (*roi*); but here, strangely, the details do not fit. Neither Hitler nor Mussolini was an hereditary king, so the usual anagram is discarded and the words are taken as a reference to the blackshirts of Mussolini's fascists. *Pont . . . d'Hister* would, to a critical non-obscurantist reader, mean a bridge over the Danube. But in this interpretation *pont* has to mean the papacy because it is supposed to be a cipher for the papacy elsewhere in Nostradamus's works, even though *pont* can refer to other things — for example, Parliament — and though the papacy is also signified by the word 'ship'. 'Hister' is taken as Hitler, even though he had not risen to power when Mussolini first drew up his concordat with the Vatican in 1928. Of course, some of the details 'fit' — but only by spoiling a sensible passage about a bridge over the Danube.

---

[21] Centuries III:63.
[22] Centuries V:29.

Finally, two closely occurring stanzas are both used by Cheetham and Laver in connection with Hitler and Mussolini. One talks (quite generally) of a 'cruel wicked man',[23] interpreted as Mussolini. They are in Century VIII. The first fruits of his power in Venice will be 'the Prince of Peschiera' (Victor Emmanuel III), so called because at Peschiera he was thought to have performed the most 'manly' act of his reign — he stood his ground and fought when he could have surrendered. Venice had its association with Mussolini, who lost his popularity there; but unfortunately for Nostradamus the 'wicked one' of the passage was to be led to evil by the younger 'Celin' (or 'Selin'), an Islamic name. Even Cheetham admits that this prophecy failed. Mussolini never was converted to Islam, and indeed offended many Islamic neighbours when he invaded Libya and Ethiopia. Hence the prophecy is not the significant one that it seems to be on first sight. Nearby is another stanza, supposed to refer to Mussolini because it calls him the one 'bearing an unworthy name', the name Mussolini (= muslin-maker) representing a debased trade. This is all that it has to offer us, and in a 'potted' explanation of its greatness,[24] Cheetham (without acknowledgement) borrows a whole sentence, almost word for word, from Laver: 'Mussolini [which literally] means [the] muslin maker. The vengeance [which] he desires[d] was against those powers who [which] frustrated his [imperial aims] [dream] of Mare Nostrum'.[25]

The words in brackets are peculiar to either Cheetham or Laver. The sentences are so near to each other in content to show us that, although Cheetham is usually much more critical of Nostradamus than Laver, in this case she has used Laver without much concern for thinking through the meaning of his interpretation. This joint explanation says very little about the value of the quatrain. The description would fit many with 'disreputable names' besides Mussolini.

---

[23] Centuries VIII:31.
[24] Centuries VIII:33.
[25] Compare Cheetham, p. 319 with Laver, p. 227.

Two Preludes to War

We shall return to Hitler and Mussolini later, but a double prelude has to be played before we do so. Two events were to reinforce Hitler's enthusiasm for world power. The fascists were to rise to power by means of a civil war in Spain, and Edward VIII was to abdicate, giving the impression that Loog's interpretation of Nostradamus, presaging the collapse of the British monarchy in 1939, was correct. Let us consider these two events in turn.

One quatrain[26] talks of a 'great man' fleeing (*fuira*) to Spain, of Spain bleeding from a wound, of devastation by troops (hence a military dictatorship) and of a 'reign' of peace. Except for 'fleeing', the quatrain is an exceptionally accurate description of Franco's rise to power; it resembles a few of the 'French monarchy' quatrains, which are accurate except for one 'Achilles' heel'. Laver[27] tried to surmount the problem by making *fuira* mean 'fly' (i.e. by air), but this is an inaccurate translation. A further stanza is less conclusive:

> *People without leaders of Spain and Italy,*
> *— dead and overcome in the Peninsula*
> *Their leader betrayed by stupid folly.*
> *Blood will flow all around at the crossroads.*[28]

The stanza may be a good description of Italy at Mussolini's execution. Indeed, the word *traverse*, which may mean 'crossroads', is appropriate, for Nostradamus may be referring to the gibbet on which Mussolini was hanged. But that one accurate detail covers a large flaw. Spain was never leaderless. Franco died an old man, and his death signalled the restoration of the Spanish monarchy.

Against these two faulty stanzas, one has to balance a much more positive reference to Spain under Franco, one which cannot be attributed to interpretational fudge or participant-fulfilment:

---

[26] Century III:54.
[27] Laver, p. 223.
[28] Centuries III:68.

From Spain [castel] Franco will bring out the assembly
— the ambassadors not pleasing [or agreeing] will cause schism
The people of Ribier will be in the crowd,
and the great man will be denied entry to the gulf.[29]

At last we may have found an explicit reference to Franco, and the quatrain has none of the flaws of the two previous cases. It says that Franco will (or would) bring out the Spanish Government, and that there would be schism (or war) in Spain. It mentions his people as the people of Ribier (Rivera), or of De Riviera, the name of the dictator who preceded Francisco Franco, and then Franco's exile to Morocco (his being denied entry to the Spanish gulf). Its only flaw is its chronology: the war in Spain will precede the exile to Morocco. Historically, the reverse occurred: Franco returned from exile in Morocco to bring about the 'assembly' and the 'schism' (war) in Spain.

Finally, we move from this shining coincidence, with its clear mention of the names of both Franco and De Riviera, to a real 'low' in Nostradamus's predictive ability:

From the depths of Spain, banners
— coming from the corners and borders of Europe . . .[30]

There is, at least, the suggestion that, if this really means the Spanish Civil War, it would lead to a Spanish invasion of Europe. The fire of fascism spread via Spain, but Franco's government was largely neutral during the Second World War and Spain made no attempt to invade Europe. Later lines in the quatrain contain an obscure reference to 'Laigne', identified by some interpreters with events at the end of the Second World War and having nothing to do with Franco whatsoever.

What of the second prelude to the War — the abdication of Edward VIII? I have already shown that Loog (1921) in interpreting Nostradamus expected an 'end' to the British monarchy in 1939, and that Britain's downfall would be associated with Poland. The Third Reich knew of the prediction and were looking for 'cracks' in the British

---

[29] Centuries IX:16.
[30] Centuries X:48.

monarchy before involving Britain in her expected downfall
by invading Poland. A much-wanted 'crack' appeared in
1936/7 — the abdication of Edward VIII; but despite the
expectation of an end to the British dynasty in 1939 not much
in Nostradamus could be used to fit Edward's abdication. A
supposed prophecy of Cromwell was now to be clothed with
new meaning:

> *The young one born to the British realm*
> *Which his dying father had 'recommended' to him*
> *When he is dead Lonole will dispute with him*
> *— and the kingdom will be demanded from the son.*[31]

In Chapter Three I showed the weakness of an application to
Cromwell. This application held until 1940 and occurs in
Laver, who adds the Edward VIII application as an
afterthought,[32] having taken it hurriedly, in an unpolished
form, from a current second edition of a work by Dr E.
Fontbrune.[33] Unlike previous commentators who made
Lonole mean 'old Nole', and thus 'Oliver' (Cromwell),
Fontbrune suggested that 'Lonole' was simply the English
word 'lonely' in imperfect form, and meant the 'lonely' king
(Edward). But with whom would he have disputed, other
than his dead father, in some figurative sense? Surely this was
carrying both prophetic and poetic licence much too far. It
was left to Cheetham much later to decide that 'Lonole' was
simply an error for London, and that the prophecy meant
that London would dispute with Edward VIII. But London
did not demand his kingdom. He chose to marry, and to
abdicate. With as many as three possible interpretations, and
with no mention either of Edward or of abdication, the
stanza was weak, but the interpretation was formulated just
in time to be used as propaganda by the Third Reich,
together with Loog's prediction of 1921.

Clearly, any mention of divorce in Nostradamus's
writings would provide further fuel for a view that he
foresaw Edward's abdication and the supposed impending

---

[31] Centuries X:40.
[32] Laver, p. 222.
[33] Dr M. de Fontbrune, *Les Propheties de Maistre Michel Nostradamus*
(2nd edition, Sarlat, 1939). Compare with Cheetham, p. 405.

end of the British monarchy. Though he was not a Nazi, Fontbrune had discovered such a prediction:

> *Not wanting to consent to the divorce,*
> *which afterwards will be considered unworthy*
> *The King of the Isles will flee by force*
> *and one put in his place who has no token [sign] of kingship.*[34]

Originally, like the previous quatrain, this stanza was interpreted as a prophecy of Cromwell. The word 'divorce' had been taken figuratively to mean a 'divorce' between King and Parliament. The King was considered to be Charles II, forced to flee after the death of his father, and the one 'with no token of kingship' Oliver Cromwell. But to find a 'real' divorce in the writings of Nostradamus was a more attractive alternative, and here was an apparent prediction of Edward VIII fleeing the United Kingdom after his abdication and of his subsequent marriage to a divorced woman. But there are three adverse factors: two are flaws in the prediction, the third (and most important) is the background in which Nostradamus wrote. The 'King of the Islands' was not 'forced' to flee (or indeed to abdicate), and he did so before the 'divorce' arrangements were completed; nor can it be said that George VI (his brother) had no 'sign' or 'token' of kingship.

But it is the background that is crucial. The prophecies were published in 1555 when the divorces and subsequent marriages of Henry VIII were notorious throughout Europe. Henry had died in 1547, eight years earlier. It would not have been difficult for Nostradamus to foresee a situation in which another king divorced his wives and would be 'forced to flee' for doing so. It is no credit to Nostradamus that nearly four hundred years elapsed before the prediction applied and even then it did not involve a divorce *by* a monarch but a divorce of a 'present' husband by his intended bride.

In this historical 'build-up' to the Second World War, we have thus seen that the predictive value of Nostradamus is often minimal and faulty; that events followed interpretations, and that prominent people frequently wanted to carry

---

[34] Centuries X:22.

out Nostradamus's 'prescriptions' to the letter, while others were busy 'fitting' predictions to events and devising their strategies accordingly. Prominent in both categories were the leaders of the Third Reich, who both 'fitted' the Spanish Civil War and the abdication of Edward VIII into their scheme of things — hence the sympathetic welcome the Führer gave to the ex-monarch. He was clearly using such interptations of Nostradamus as a strategy for invading Poland and toppling Britain.

The Outbreak of War

A collection of stanzas has been used to describe the period 1939/40, some of them appropriately dealing with the German invasion of France. Many have been drained of whatever natural, contextual meaning they may have had. But some are striking examples of how Nostradamus gets most of the detail correct, yet makes a 'howler' that detracts from the value of the prophecy.

A great deal of publicity was given to an early prediction that appears to describe Hitler as a 'bird of prey':

> *The bird of prey flying for a 'semester'* [or 'to the left']
> *before conflict is made with the French*
> *Some will think this good, others sinister* [ambiguously]
> *The weaker party will think him — good augury.*[35]

The stanza can be fitted to the invasion of France by Hitler, but elsewhere in Nostradamus's writings the 'bird of prey' is supposed to signify Napoleon. Even the reference to 'to the left' (if it means 'to the West') is suspect, for the reading is 'semester' in line 1, to rhyme with 'sinister' in line 3. Of course there were pro-Hitler and anti-Hitler parties in France, represented as weak and strong in the interpretation of lines 3 and 4; but the pro-Hitler party won — the 'weaker party' of a straight interpretation of the text — in contradiction of the quatrain. Even Laver, a Nostradamus enthusiast, here admits that 'a quatrain like this is of no value or proof of the Prophet's powers'.[36]

---

[35] Centuries I:34.
[36] Laver, p. 224.

A similarly vague set of stanzas occurs in Century II. One quatrain describes a war involving Italy, Germany, France and Spain, and a 'strong one' supposed to be Hitler; the next presents an almost apocalyptic war scene.[37] A 'school-house' republic is mentioned, but this is never the subject of agreement among commentators. There is disagreement as to whether the reference is to Italy, Spain or France. What is clear is that when Hitler marched his troops into Poland in 1939 he knew of the 'seven times' prophecy of Nostradamus and its interpretation by Loog. He was certain that in doing so he would involve Britain, and imagined that, to use Loog's interpretation of Nostradamus, it would both involve Poland *and* bring about the downfall of British dynasty.

But serious Nostradamus students were finding descriptions of his actions elsewhere:

> He will change it into Great Germany
> Brabant and Flanders, Ghent, Bruges and Boulogne.
> The feigned agreement, the Great Duke of Armenia
> will assault Vienna and Cologne.[38]

This looks like a description of an enlargement of Germany. In the west Hitler would assault the Low Countries, tearing up a previous agreement as a 'scrap of paper', and move on to an invasion of France, commencing with Boulogne. Then the description turns to a 'feigned truce', and because it mentions 'Armenia' it seems like a description of the agreement that Hitler and Stalin (the 'Duke of Armenia') made over Poland — an agreement that Hitler afterwards broke when he invaded Russia. Such an interpretation is imaginative, but not consistent. Of course Stalin was later to invade Eastern Europe at Germany's expense. He did attack Vienna, and the four powers occupied Austria after the war; and overstayed their welcome; but Stalin never attacked Cologne. Characteristically, Laver retains the first two (convincing) lines in his commentary, but leaves out the difficult last two lines without explanation.[39]

It was inevitable that someone would find a reference to the swastika:

---

[37] See Centuries II:39 and 40 in combination.
[38] Centuries V:94.
[39] Laver, p. 224.

> *From the party of Mars* [Messina: Fr. *Mammer*] *a great Pontiff*
> *who will subjugate the confines of the Danube*
> *— the cross pursued by hook or crook*
> *captives, gold, jewels, more than a thousand rubies.*[40]

The verse does not describe Hitler, but a Pontiff or Pope who would, like Mussolini, try to restore the Danube as the boundary of his (Roman) Empire. It requires a stretch of the imagination to make a reference to the pursuit of a cross, *ne raffe ne riffe* ('by hook or crook'), mean a 'crooked' cross, i.e. a swastika, particularly as 'hook' and 'crook' are appropriate 'puns' for the progress of militant Catholic Christianity in Nostradamus's day — the 'hook' meaning to catch people by 'fishing' for them, sometimes brutally, the 'crook' meaning to lead them gently as a shepherd. Any suggestion of a swastika is ingenious but igores the context, and it is difficult if not impossible to apply the description 'great Pontiff' to Hitler.

Such were the preliminaries to Hitler's invasion of Poland, after a non-aggression treaty had been signed between Germany and Stalin on 23 |August 1939. The fulfilment of Nostradamus's prophecies was much in the minds of several members of the hierarchy, but it was not given official recognition for propaganda purposes. The Reich was ambivalent both towards Nostradamus and astrology: it was interested in it, but it banned public interest, lest the Reich would be brought into disrepute or its plans become more widely known. Matters took an unexpected turn with the appearance of K. E. Krafft and an attempt on Hitler's life. Krafft was no ordinary astrologer. He had developed a new astrological theory of birth patterns and was throughout 1938 preparing a treatise on astrology. Though Swiss-born, he was of German origin and became both disillusioned with Switzerland and a Hitler enthusiast. His pretensions were great. He tried to make himself available to Hitler on all occult matters, having left Switzerland for Germany before the German invasion of Poland. Shortly after the invasion and the outbreak of war in September 1939, Frau Goebbels is alleged to have 'discovered' Loog's prediction of the British

---

[40] Centuries VI:49.

involvement with Poland in 1939 while reading one night and to have drawn Goebbels' attention to it. This was a pretext for the Reich to become 'officially' interested in the Centuries, but it window-dressed its activities with respectability. A further pretext, and a precedent, were necessary.

Krafft knew little about Nostradamus and had already written to a friend, Dr Ferriere, on 26 August expressing belief that the invasion of Poland would not involve Germany in war.[41] Then, for a casual associate, Dr Fesel, he cast a horoscope of Hitler, based on his own astrological methods, predicting that Hitler's life would be in danger between 7 to 10 November 1939. Hitler had a number of important public engagements during that period and the probability of an assassination attempt was quite high.[42] An attempt on Hitler's life was indeed made during this period, and when Krafft's letter became known it caused considerable embarrassment. Either Krafft had to be silenced or he must be involved in Hitler's use of astrology and Nostradamus for propaganda purposes, particularly as the Loog interpretation of the invasion of Poland had proved so successful. Krafft was commissioned to spend a short while on a new German translation of the Centuries emphasizing pro-Nazi interpretations. He was also involved in the task of forging new Nostradamus-style stanzas that included patent Nazi-propaganda, but he was a very unwilling participant. Soon Louis de Wohl, a Hungarian Jew, was to be employed by the British to produce anti-Nazi Nostradamus-style propaganda and astrological prophecies; but Ellic Howe has shown that much of his work was quite unnecessary, for Hitler abandoned his interest in Nostradamus and astrology a short time afterwards and Krafft found himself in prison. De Wohl was accorded the honorary rank of Captain for his work. After the war he abandoned astrology, became a Catholic convert, and turned to religious novel writing.[43] By then Krafft had died in disgrace. The effect of Nostradamus on Krafft in November 1939 is often overstated,

---

[41] Ellic Howe, *Astrology and the Third Reich* (Aquarian Press, 1984).
[42] op. cit., p. 118.
[43] For example *The Restless Flame* (1952), a novel about St Augustine.

and Cheetham's speculation[44] that one stanza enabled Krafft
to foresee the attempted assassination of Hitler is certainly
unfounded:

> *The people assemble to see a new spectacle.*
> *Princes and kings among many that stand by.*
> *Pillars fall, the walls, but as by miracle.*
> *The King is saved and thirty of those present.*[45]

It requires a great deal of interpretive licence to see Hitler as
the 'king' of the passage. The 'princes and kings' at the
meeting were not conspicuous — if they were there at all.
Hitler was not saved 'as by miracles', for he left the meeting
early; and the 'thirty' cannot be, nor ever have been,
identified. So the quatrain says nothing about the attempt on
Hitler's life but refers instead to an unidentified king's
survival of an earthquake, or some similar event. Further, the
Krafft prediction letter did not even mention Nostradamus,
in whom he was not more than casually interested until
Hitler engaged him in the translation work.

We can expect to find more Nostradamus fulfilments in
1940 and 1941 after the German propaganda machine had
been to work on them. Here are a few:

> *Because of Gallic* [French] *discord and negligence*
> *there shall be an open passage to Mahomet* [the Muslims]
> *Soaked with blood shall be the land and sea of Sienna*
> *and the port of Marseilles covered with ships and sails.*[46]

This is supposed to relate to the French discord after Hitler's
invasion of 1940, which gave Mussolini the opportunity to
invade Muslim countries in North Africa. But when read
sensibly it is the prediction of a Muslim invasion, not an
invasion of Muslim countries. We should remember that the
fear of such an invasion was Nostradamus's prime concern
because of reverses in the time of Suliman prior to the battle
of Lepanto.

An apparent prediction of an air battle over fascist Italy is a
little more convincing:

---

44 See Cheetham, p. 267.
45 Centuries VI:51.
46 Centuries I:18.

Naples, Palermo, Sicily and Syracuse:
— new tyrants, lightning in the skies.[47]

The fascists *were* tyrants, and these two lines (with a subsequent mention of London) sound like a prediction of a British air raid on Italy. But let us put the quatrain into context. The first line refers to Greek colonist cities in southern Italy ruled by tyrants (*c.*7–*c.*5 BC). The lines can be distorted to mean a British aerial invasion, but the following lines contain several inaccuracies. There was no British alliance with Brussels or Ghent, or Susa (in Persia). It is difficult to know how Susa (the ancient Persian city) could have anything to do with British attacks on fascist Italy.

A subsequent stanza in the same Century looks like a prophecy of mass condemnation of an alliance between two 'monarchs' (thought to be Hitler and Stalin), after which the alliance would be broken by a misfortune.[48] When Hitler and Stalin signed their non-aggression pact in 1939 they had not previously been at war. There was subsequent condemnation by a 'great number of people', in particular the people of Poland, but this has happened repeatedly after many alliances in history. Further, the alliance was not broken by 'misfortune', but by Hitler's invasion of Russia.

There are two vague and generalized stanzas in Century III, neither of which has any serious claim as a valid prediction. One describes the 'Cimbrians' (originally a German tribe) ravaging Spain[49] and is assumed to refer to the German help given to Franco between 1936 and 1939; the other[50] describes fugitives on (French) roads being subjected to 'fire from heaven'. This, like the lightnings of the earlier stanza (II:16), are convincing pictures of modern warfare, but the symbolism is taken from John's Apocalypse. Both *may* be pictures of modern warfare; but in painting them, Nostradamus has added little to a possible pre-existent Biblical prophecy.

A later stanza in the same Century is equally vague.[51]

---

[47] Centuries II:16.
[48] Centuries II:38.
[49] Centuries III:8.
[50] Centuries III:7.
[51] Centuries III:32.

Literally, it talks of a great sepulchre for the people of
Aquitaine, coming from the direction of Tuscany and
involving Germany. Its predictive power is more of a credit
to interpreters than to Nostradamus. Aquitaine is taken to
mean France, and Tuscany to mean Italy. The prediction
states that a 'sepulchre' would be made for the French in the
direction of Italy (with German help). If anything, the
sepulchre (interpreted as the German invasion of 1940) came
to France from the direction of Germany (and with minimal
Italian help). There are other supposed descriptions of the
casualties during this period:

> *All the inhabitants of Marseilles change*
> *In flight, and pursuit to Lyons*
> *Narbonne, Toulouse angered by Bordeaux.*
> *Killed and captive about one million.*[52]

In context, it sounds like a war *between* French cities,
particularly line 2. It specifies southern cities, for Nostradamus was most concerned with them as a southern
Frenchman. It does not draw a clear line between the parts of
France that were occupied and Vichy in June 1940, and
Cheetham's contention that Nostradamus's 'one million'
must place the fulfilment in modern times must be regarded
as unsound, for the figure includes not only the recorded
fatalities but other casualties — too small an estimate for
Vichy France in 1940.

Of all the possible 'wrestings' of Nostradamus to fit the
period, the next is the most ludicrous:

> *By the Rhine and Norican mountains,*
> *will be born a 'noble' [grand de gens] come too late,*
> *who will defend Poland and Hungary.*
> *They will never know what became of him.*[53]

The first three lines were not at all difficult for Hitler
enthusiasts to make use of. 'Noricum' was Austria in the
Roman Empire. Hitler was born there, as were most of the
Holy Roman Emperors. They were 'noble' (*grand de gens*) but

---

[52] Centuries I:72.
[53] Centuries III:58.

he was not, and it is pure 'distortion' for interpreters such as Cheetham to use the phrase about his 'simple' (humble) birth. Though it was Hitler's policy to invade countries on the pretext of defending them, the use of the words 'who will defend Poland and Hungary' to mean his invasion of Poland and Hungary is indeed ludicrous.

Laver provides another 'clue' (not this time replicated by Cheetham), which is assumed to relate to the Axis division of France; he himself describes it as 'tiresome':

> *'The fighting on both sides will be so bitter —*
> *— that Mesopotamia will not be found in France'.*[54]

In this case 'both sides' is supposed to signify the north/south division of France in 1940; but, if anything, this is a reference to Nostradamus's picture of France (particularly Paris) as Babylon and hints at the destruction of pre-Bourbon or Bourbon Paris, using the model explained earlier. It adds nothing to the details of Hitler's invasion of France, but is just one of Nostradamus's many 'Babylon' references.

De Gaulle and Petain have been spotted elsewhere in the Centuries:

> *The changing will be quite difficult*
> *City and province will gain by the change*
> *A prudent one, high of heart will be chased by the 'cunning one'*
> *By sea, by land, people will change their estate.*[55]

The best that can be said of this stanza is that all the details, except one, 'fit' the 'decentralization' policy of Petain. It does tell us that De Gaulle (the 'prudent one') would be chased into exile by a 'cunning one' (Petain). But were there not other 'cunning ones' who would as easily fit the bill? One detail is clearly wrong. City and province did *not* 'gain' by the change. For most of De Gaulle's exile, Axis France was an administrative mess. Further, the quatrain draws on

---

[54] Centuries III:99.
[55] Centuries IV:21.

biblical symbols.[56] A later quatrain apparently about Petain does provide us with a little more detail that can be checked, but most of its strength comes from interpretation:

> *The old man mocked and deprived of his place*
> *By the foreigner who will subordinate him*
> *The hands of his sons are devoured before him.*
> *The brother at Chartres, Orleans and Rouen, — he will betray.*[57]

The quatrain's strength lies in the cosmetic nature of its translation. It does mention three towns that were liberated by the Allies at the same time (at about 19 August 1944), but these were not places where Petain (the assumed 'old man' of the stanza) betrayed his brother, even if this brother is interpreted to mean the Allied French. The 'hands of his sons' also have to be interpreted symbolically to mean the 'government' of which Petain had control. The only fulfilment of the prediction, if any, is the simultaneous mention of three French towns that were liberated at about the same time, but even these do not appear in the correct context.

There are two twin stanzas that provided the French Resistance with some comfort during the period of occupation. As general descriptions of an occupied country in wartime they are ideal, but otherwise they give little indication of being predictions:

> *By fraud, the kingdom — of its forces plundered*
> *— the fleet blockaded, passages for the spy*
> *Two false friends will come to rally*
> *To awaken hate, for a long time asleep*
> *With great grief will be the French nation*
> *Vain and 'light-hearted' they will believe rash things*
> *Bread, salt, nor wine, water, venom nor ale.*
> *The greater one a captive, hunger, cold and 'necessity'.*[58]

---

[56] This is an important transposition of a biblical set of symbols from the Book of Daniel. Daniel 11:21 gives a picture of a cunning contemptible traitor and of the wise (v.33-34) who would resist in persecution and exile.
[57] Centuries IV:61.
[58] Centuries VII:33 and 34.

Where was the 'rally' held, and who were the two false friends that came? It requires a strong belief in poetic or prophetic licence to assume, as Cheetham does, that they symbolize Germany and Russia, and not Germany and Italy, or Japan. And what was 'light-hearted' about the French during the years from 1940 to 1944? To a French believer in Nostradamus these lines perhaps provided some evidence that Nostradamus had foreseen the occupation and could look beyond it, and the very discouraging description was a basis of encouragement; but to a rational student of prediction they are little more than a generalized description of an occupied country. Perhaps they display Nostradamus's belief that before the end of the sixth millennium and the 'common advent' (the Second Coming of Christ), France would be occupied by an anti-Christ power.

Contemporary identifications with the Nazis (i.e. *c*.1940) appear elsewhere in interpretations of Nostradamus. Most are neither specific nor detailed and some are highly symbolic:

> *The great mastiff is chased from the city*
> *Angered* [a play on 'fascist' = *fasche*] *by the foreign alliance*
> *Afterwards, having chased the stag to the field*
> *The wolf and bear will defy each other.*[59]

Does 'wolf' mean 'Germany' or Italy, as some expositors have suggested? And how did Russia and Italy 'defy each other' when they became allies? Most people would have used a lion to symbolize Britain and her empire at the time. If Nostradamus did use the image of a mastiff to refer to Britain, he probably did so because the French call the mastiff 'the English dog'. If the interpretation of this stanza is as a prediction of Britain being chased out of Europe, angered by Hitler's alliance with Russia, and of Hitler's subsequent attack on Russia, it is based on shaky and obscure symbolism.

A similar piece of obscure symbolism occurs when Nostradamus talks of a man-woman and two eclipses:

---

[59] Centuries V:4.

> *To the north, great efforts by a man-woman*
> *to vex almost Europe and the Universe*
> *The two eclipses will be brought to rout*
> *For the Pannons [Hungarians] they will reinforce life or death.*[60]

In the hands of propagandists in the Second World War, the 'man-woman' was Hitler, though it is not clear why. The rest of the stanza is equally unclear and open to interpretation. Were the 'two eclipses' the two world wars in which Germany was involved? How did Hitler 'reinforce life or death' for the Hungarians, more than for the Czechs and the Poles? The 'man-woman' could just as easily be Russia, in which case the fulfilment becomes the invasion of Hungary in 1956. But Nostradamus wrote at a time when the Turks had not long invaded Hungary: the link with the Second World War seems slight:

> *A captain of the great Germany*
> *will come to render false help*
> *A king of kings, to support Pannonia [Hungary]*
> *His 'revolt' [war]will cause great bloodshed.*[61]

Identification of the Hungary prophecies with the Second World War rests on poor premises, though Laver uses the latter as 'proof' that Nostradamus foresaw Hitler's strategy of invading small nations on the pretext of protecting them — a strategy shared by all imperialists and dictators long before Hitler's time. The Hungary predictions are better explained by the fact that Nostradamus lived at a time when Hungary was always under the threat of Ottoman domination, and when Germany was the only real protector.

Domination and Decline

The years from 1941 onwards were momentous. They saw the attempted invasion of Britain, the attack on Pearl Harbour and the entry of America into the war, Hitler's involvement with Japan and Italy, and the liberation of

---

[60] Centuries VIII:15.
[61] Centuries IX:90.

Europe and the Far East, concluding with the bombing of Hiroshima and Nagasaki.

There is no clear picture of the attempted invasion of Britain in Nostradamus's writings. The nearest one can get is an obscure stanza, of which the first two lines read:

> Into the Isles, the infants will be transported
> Two out of seven will be in despair.[62]

It *is* a picture of flight, and the 'Isles' are probably Britain; but who are the 'two out of seven'? Is this the connection of one of the 'Medici' children (the house of the seven) with Britain via Mary Queen of Scots? The prediction is about the transportation of infants, and though children were evacuated from European countries to Britain during the Second World War, there was much more evacuation within Britain itself. The rest of the stanza is indeed obscure, though some have identified a reference to 'soil' and 'shovel' in the remaining lines with the 'digging for victory' campaign.

As for the attack on Pearl Harbour:

> Naval battle in the night will be overcome
> [By] *fire*, the ships of the West [American?] will be ruined
> By a new 'rubric' the great ship will be coloured
> Anger to the vanquished. Victory in a mist![63]

Translated literally, and without interpretational licence, it does not tell us as much about Pearl Harbour as first appears. Why should the 'West' mean America? Is the new 'rubric' (code) a new method or a new symbol (emblem)? Are not the vanquished always angered? Finally, is not the 'great ship' the papacy, as elsewhere in Nostradamus's writings? If so, is it not an unwarranted liberty of interpreters to make the 'great ship' mean one of the ships attacked at Pearl Harbour, and 'coloured' mean 'camouflaged', while the 'mist' is interpreted symbolically to mean 'hazy glimpses of victory to America'?[64]

It is this interpretational fudge that explains most of the

---

[62] Centuries VIII:64.
[63] Centuries IX:100.
[64] See Cheetham, *Nostradamus*, p. 388.

successful quatrains relating to the Second World War. The success is not Nostradamus's but that of the ingenuity of interpreters. France under occupation, for example, is cheerfully accorded one of the later stanzas:

> *Bright splendour for a joyful maiden*
> *No longer will shine. She will be without salt*
> *With mercenaries [merchants?] ruffians, an odious wolf.*
> *A universal monster, all confused.*[65]

If one interprets the 'joyful maiden' to mean France, 'salt' to mean wisdom, the 'wolf' Germany, Italy or Hitler, and the 'universal monster' Hitler, the quatrain becomes a description of the occupation period from 1940 to 1944. But the picture is that of a *general* occupation of France, or a period of discord in France — *if* the 'joyful maiden' does indeed symbolize France. Again, Nostradamus consciously or unconsciously presents us with something biblical, inverting Revelation 12 and the Sermon on the Mount.

Apocalypse	*Sermon on the Mount*
'A woman clothed with the sun'[66] 'red dragon' (universal monster)[66]	'You are the light of the world'[67] 'You are the salt of the earth'[67] 'false prophets' . . . 'ravening wolves'[68]

This is typical of the many distorted uses of the Bible in Nostradmus's writings. It illustrates that Nostradamus is referring to some latter-day persecution of the elect and depends on his understanding of the Apocalypse of John; it does not refer to the Nazi occupation of France at all. This will be explained in Chapter Seven. Also typical of this obscurity and interpretational licence is an astrological

---

[65] Centuries X:98.
[66] Revelation 12:1-3
[67] Matthew 5:14-15.
[68] Matthew 7:15.

quatrain, which is assumed to describe the politics of Italy and Japan during the same period:

> *The sea will not be safely crossed by the 'sun' ones*
> *Those of Venus [Venice] will hold all Africa*
> *Then their kingdom, Saturn will not occupy*
> *And the part of Asia will change.*[69]

This would have been good propaganda for the pro-Fascist Italians or the Japanese during the war, but one fails to see how it could still be used by Cheetham as a proof of Nostradamus's perceptiveness after the war. If the '"sun" ones' are the Japanese (the rising sun being the Japanese emblem), then the first line is correct. Their navies were insecure after they entered the war, but so were those of the Allies. However 'all Africa' never fell into the hands of the people of 'Venice' — Mussolini's Italians — unless it is understood to mean *Roman* Africa (i.e. North Africa), and even this was only a threat for a short while, for there were pockets of British resistance everywhere. But, to be consistent, if this interpretation were advanced, then 'Asia' in line 4 would also have to mean *Roman* Asia, i.e. the Roman province in what is today western Turkey. This renders line 4 meaningless and prohibits the use of it to mean the Far Eastern territories that fell under the Japanese during the war. One cannot have it both ways!

These flaws are usually glossed over by Nostradamus's enthusiasts in an attempt to put the best possible case for his perceptiveness. It may be irritating to some readers to have them exposed, but this is necessary if we are to build a useful model of human prediction and its varying quality. Such a gloss occurs in another 'Hitler-Mussolini' stanza of the same period:

> *Norneigre* ['black north' — or Norway misspelt] *and Dacia*
> *and the British Isles*
> *by the united brothers will be vexed*
> *The Roman leader came from French blood*
> *And the forces repelled into the forests.*[70]

---

[69] *Centuries* V:11.
[70] *Centuries* VI:7.

There was some resistance to Hitler in Norway and not only in Dacia but throughout the whole of the Balkan peninsula. Dacia was Roman Roumania. The resistance fighters, led by Britain, used the forests — graphically described in line 4. But who were the 'united brothers'? There need not (by the terms of the prediction) be two, and Hitler and Mussolini were not brothers. To make things worse for the Second World War interpretation there is no evidence that Mussolini (the 'Roman leader') came from French blood.

These unanswered questions again indicate that Nostradamus's prediction does not perfectly fit the picture of British, Norwegian and Balkans resistance. If so, what does the prophecy mean? It was written just before 1555 when the Holy Roman Empire was trying to resist the advances of the Turkish Empire in the east. Nostradamus used the best predictive material available in his days, taking the best of both Catholic and Protestant expositors of Biblical prophecy. To believers in a Western Antichrist, the Holy Roman Empire was a potential source of the menace, and would have to revive, some time in the remote future, before the Second Advent (of Christ). Its original founder was Charlemagne (of French blood), and so a Frenchman would probably be its reviver. Hence the quatrain also provided fuel for Napoleon's conquest of Europe. Any such emperor (like Napoleon and Hitler) would have to drive resistance either to the corners of Europe, i.e. Britain, Scandinavia and the Balkans, or into the forests. No longer is the stanza a prophecy of Hitler and Mussolini; it is another of Nostradamus's Antichrist stanzas, built on a useful biblical model, but borrowing also from Protestant expositions of Revelation.

These misinterpretations provided propaganda material for both sides during the Second World War. They seem on occasion more remarkable than they are because of the revival of a word from Nostradamus's time, so that *duc* (= duke) and *Duce* (= leader) was the term Mussolini accorded to himself:

> *The King will find that which he desires so greatly*
> *when the Prelate will be taken wrongly*
> *Reply to the 'duc' [Duce] will make him 'mal content'*
> *who in Milan will put many to death.*[71]

---

[71] Centuries VI:31.

Taking the stanza literally removes its relevance to the Second World War. The 'King' (of Italy) did *not* get what he desired when the *Duce* came to power. The 'Prelate' (Pope) was not imprisoned (as he was under Napoleon) and the Vatican was, for the most part, respected by the Fascists. The misinterpretation began in the early 1930s when it was thought that Mussolini would ultimately deport the Pope — something the King of Italy may also have desired. Unfortunately it stuck even when disproved by history, and is repeated by both Laver[72] and Cheetham[73].

★ ★ ★ ★ ★

In this chapter I have tried to show how Allied, Axis and pro-Nostradamus propaganda clothed some of his more obscure quatrains with new meaning and ignored the flaws in their interpretations. For the most part, as I have intermittently indicated, Nostradamus wrote his predictions either for his own period, or for the end of time, when by biblical criteria the people of God would suffer unspeakable persecution. As the war came to its close, the interpreters abandoned the more obscure for the more apocalyptic, which are more reliable because they depend on Nostradamus's biblical insight. I shall deal with his prediction of submarines in the next chapter; but the following is assumed to refer to a periscope:

> *From where he will think to bring famine*
> *from there will come relief*
> *The sea's eye* [periscope] *by avaricious dog*
> *From one to the other will be given oil and wheat.*[74]

The Germans used the sea to blockade Britain, but submarines were used to bring in fuel and food. Here *is* a perceptive quatrain. Fulfilment here is not the result of particpation or obscure interpretation: it is 'apocalyptic', and relies on the seer's biblical and scientific insight.

   This is true also of the conclusion of the war, the bombing of Hiroshima and Nagasaki:

[72] Laver, p. 232.
[73] Cheetham, p. 260.
[74] Centuries IV:15.

Near the harbour and in two cities
will be two scourges — of which like has not been seen
Hunger, pestilence within, people by sword evicted
Will cry for help from the great immortal God.[75]

Nostradamus was, of course, here using a biblical model and projecting it into the future. Although five cities suffered the destruction of Sodom and Gomorrah, the *two*,[76] particularly became an example for all time, and are cited repeatedly in the New Testament. The final reference in the Apocalypse is a plague on cities where *two* witnesses have testified, spiritually called 'Sodom and Egypt'. Suddenly we emerge from the morass of Nostradamus-inspired propaganda and twisted fulfilments to the remarkably perceptive use of a biblical model. Somehow Nostradamus foresaw a heaven-sent destruction of a future Sodom and Gomorrah. It needed two witnesses to testify to the destructive power of the 'atomic-bomb'. It needed two bombings to bring the Second World War to an end.

[75] Centuries II:6.
[76] Genesis 18 and 19; Isaiah 1:10; Amos 4:11; Matthew 10:15; 2 Peter 2:6; Jude 7; Revelation 11:8.

5
Prophecies of Present Times

In the previous chapters we have seen that Nostradamus's inherent ability may have given him some powers of prediction in relation to the time horizon of his own lifetime, but these do not necessarily explain the success of some of his predictions over several centuries. Some of this success can be attributed to his very close study of contemporary biblical interpretation, and to an ingenious scientific mind — a mind that, like Leonardo da Vinci's could describe and discern, for example, the functions of a submarine and a periscope long before they became a reality.

Biblical interpretation and scientific insight, however, are not enough, and we have seen that two other factors, participant fulfilment and interpretational fudge, are involved. These two factors are specifically appropriate to the long interval between Nostradamus's own times and the 'end of the world' which he awaited, for they explain many of the 'hashed' and self-fulfilling explanations of the Centuries during the intervening period. They explain why many of his most accurate and detailed prophecies are self-fulfilling in times when (as in the Second World War) there was considerable interest both in him and in them. In much the same way, a statistically larger number of his quatrains can be identified with incidents that occurred to the French monarchy and to France immediately after the first French Revolution than with other periods of comparable length between Nostradamus's time and ours. This is partly because during periods of tension and stress there is greater interest in *all* predictions (including those of Nostradamus) than at other periods, and this interest drove people with power and influence not only to interpret and reinterpret much that

Nostradamus wrote, but also (where possible) to fulfil specific predictions.

If, as we have seen, a French king, a Napoleon, or a Hitler could identify himself with some of the more complimentary of Nostradamus's predictions, he would seek to fulfil them regardless of the less complimentary aspects. In such circumstances, the very details of the prediction are themselves identified either by propaganda issues or by some topical contemporay issue. The participant then sometimes unconsciously adds his own extra matching detail by doing things that make the prophecy fit even more exactly, particularly if the prophecy is sufficiently ambiguous to have a quasi-Delphic status. The prophecy, so to speak, wins, but only on the 'heads I win, tails you lose' principle. Yet, it makes sufficient impression on contemporaries that it becomes seen as an outstanding accurate detailed fulfilment. The prediction, for example, that the British monarchy would suffer in 1939 after an invasion (?) of Poland was, as we have already seen, Loog's synthesis of two misapplications of Nostradamus in respect of a 290-year period and the identity of the Bastarniae. It *worked* because Hitler took notice of the interpretation and invaded Poland in 1939. It *did not work* in respect of determining the end of the British monarchy.

Participant fulfilment is thus inevitably bound up with the other leading factors in the period between Nostradamus's time and our own. This is what I have called interpretational fudge — the attempt on the part of interpreters to make some predictions fit events by reading misspellings and new meanings into the text on the premise and pretext that Nostradamus may have misheard or misspelt them. In this category is 'Hister',[1] by which Nostradamus invariably meant the Danube (Latin:Ister), but which Hitler (and interpreters) identified with himself because of the matching detail of some of the predictions containing this name, despite the fact that it cannot be shown why Nostradamus should have wanted to use 'Hister' to mean 'Hitler'.

With these four variables to explain the remarkable matching quality of some of Nostradamus's historical fulfilments — biblical interpretation, scientific insight,

---

[1] Centuries II:24.

participant fulfilment and interpretational fudge — we can leave out of the account for the moment his natural powers as a seer. Most of the evidence concerning this factor shows that human predictive insight does not normally extend beyond the time-horizon of the seer's own lifetime, so that it is best regarded as a 'residual' in our model. It can be offered as an explanation of the unexplained 'hardcore' of Nostradamus's fulfilments, and investigated later in Chapter Eight.

This mysterious 'X' factor may, of course, be immensely important in the Nostradamus case, but the main object of this book is to indicate how many of Nostradamus's supposed fulfilments *can* be adequately explained *without* it.

This chapter is concerned with world events after the Second World War and with Nostradamus's predictions of the end of the world, which on millenarian grounds, he dated at the end of the twentieth century. Unlike previous chapters it thus deals with events *and* likely events. I am not here arguing *for* millenarian theory — the belief in six thousand years of human history and a seventh 'millennium' to commence at the end of the present century — as a biblical model. In fact, I have argued elsewhere *against* its biblical validity.[2] What is important is that so many people, including Nostradamus, believed it, and that this very belief set in motion a trend (e.g. in scientific awareness) that produced in the twentieth century the very pre-conditions for the fulfilment of biblical (and Nostradamian) predictions of the end of the world. This chapter must thus deal with recent fulfilments of Nostradamus's predictions, *and* with his predictions of the end of the world. Further, it must progress on different lines from previous chapters. It must be thematic, considering how the four factors mentioned earlier explain Nostradamus's predictions of what has happened since the Second World War and how they determine his expectations of events at the end of the twentieth century.

'Participant fulfilment' now becomes less important. This is because, in the twentieth century, there is insufficient time (except in the case of Hitler) for such fulfilments to become fixed in the interpretational framework. We are thus left with *three* remaining variables to discuss in detail:

---

[2] D. Pitt Francis, *The Most Amazing Message Ever Written* (Castle Books, 1983). See Chapter 1 for the real preconditions of the Apocalypse.

1. The effect of early sixteenth century biblical interpretation and of Nostradamus's own biblical model;
2. scientific insight; and
3. interpretational fudge.

The State of Israel and The Coming of Antichrist

Few of Nostradamus's predictions are given in a time scale that clearly indicates twentieth-century fulfilment. There are references to 1999[3] and to astrological conjunctions that seem to relate to the end of this century;[4] but Nostradamus's preoccupation with the last decade of the twentieth century can be explained on millenarian grounds, as I shall show later. Further, as the quatrains are either jumbled or, as we have seen, arranged on a thematic basis, and not in time sequence, no prediction can be identified as a twentieth-century prophecy simply by its position in the writings. Thus most, if not all, twentieth-century identifications must be obtained by specific interpretation of details and matching them with events in the twentieth century, or those that are considered likely to happen.

Of course, there are exceptions. We shall see, for example, that Nostradamus's prophecy of the State of Israel (based on biblical prophecies) is associated with the 'century of Phoebe', which may be astrologically matched with the twentieth century. Also, if he had regarded the twentieth century as the last century in secular history, in common with the millenarian (seven thousand year) theory held by many biblical scholars of his own time, then there is some reason for thinking that he would associate the twentieth century with the revival of Israel, if only on grounds of biblical interpretation. For similar reasons, he would have associated some of the cataclysmic events described in John's Apocalypse with the present century also. There is considerable evidence, of course, that he was aware of the millenarian theory. I have mentioned this awareness of his earlier in this book, but it is now appropriate to examine some of the evidence in detail. For example:

---

[3] Centuries X:72.
[4] Centuries I:51.

Another will take up his reign for [or *'until'* — Hebraism]
   seven thousand years
when the exhausted sun takes up his cycle.[5]

The first line contains an 'elliptic' reference to the theory of 7,000 years of human history, and may mean 'until the *end* of the 7,000 years' — because, as a Jew, Nostradamus would occasionally have thought in biblical Hebraisms, the 'reign' being a reference to the Christian doctrine of the millennial 'reign' of Christ, which was assumed by millenarians to be the completing 'sabbath' between *six* and *seven* thousand years of relevant human history. The reference to the exhausted sun could be either: (i) an astrological reference to the 'century of the sun', the twentieth century; or (ii) a reference to biblical poetry often applied by Christians to the millennium — 'His name shall endure . . . as long as the sun'.[6]

Nostradamus need not, of course, have deliberately copied his Bible-interpreting commentaries; but he would have been aware of the view that associated the twentieth century both with the rejuvenation of Israel and with the 'end of the world'. He also provides us with one patent use of the word 'millennium' in X:74.

This chapter does not seek to plead for or against the long-term and large-scale prophetic qualities of the Bible in contrast with the short-term predictive material of human 'prophetic' writings, for I have already done so, to some extent in Chapter One and am only too aware of the possibility that even Israel's revival in the present century could be regarded by some as a case of mass 'participant-fulfilment' — of fulfilling the 'next year in Jerusalem' wish of every Jewish generation at a time when such fulfilment becomes politically and economically possible. This explanation would only be a partial one, for it would not explain why such Apocalyptic and biblical expositors as Joseph Mede and Isaac Newton successfully identified Israel's political regathering (on apparent biblical evidence) with the twentieth century, nor why Nostradamus seems to have accepted such an interpretation and have 'latched on' to it.

---

[5] Century I:48, and Century X:74.
[6] Psalm 72:17.

The clearest of Nostradamus's references to the rejuvenation of Israel as a political entity is:

> *A new law will occupy a new land*
> *around Syria, Judaea and Palestine.*
> *The great barbarian empire will be shattered*
> *before the century of Phoebe is finished.*[7]

The prediction may appear obscure, like all Nostradamus's predictions, but it rests on a large number of biblical passages about the regathering of the Jewish people to the area 'Syria, Judaea and Palestine'.[8] Further, the three terms are deliberately chosen to describe three political entities, mainly in the area west of Jordan:

(i) *Judaea*, the 'kernel of the *State of Israel*';
(ii) *Syria*, a 'Muslim' opponent, not itself west of Jordan, but influencing the area by infiltration; and
(iii) *Palestine*, representing the original Palestinian inhabitants, Christian and Muslim, associated with *Lebanon*.

Such perceptiveness may be partly attributable to a biblical prophetic model of a 'last-day' conflict in which Israel and Syria would be the main contestants and Lebanon (under the guise of 'Tyre' and 'Palestine') hopelessly sandwiched between.[9] Further, it uses the three main Roman and medieval names for the territory. Finally, the countries today represent the three main religious influences in the middle east: Israel (Judaea), representing Judaism; Syria, representing the Muslim influence; and Lebanon (Palestine), meaning the remains of the 'Christian' (crusader) conquests in the area. Thus the words are well chosen to describe the emergence of the state of Israel.

Similarly, the phrase 'the great barbarian empire will be shattered' is not simply a casual reference to the Ottoman Empire but a specific quotation from the prophecy of Daniel of a stone (a new Kingdom) that would shatter an image.[10] I

---

[7] Centuries III:97.
[8] Deuteronomy 28–30 inclusive; Ezekiel 37; Luke 21:24.
[9] See Obadiah 19 and Ezekiel 26.
[10] Daniel 2:44–45; but see my comments in 'The Message of Daniel' (St Brides lectures, 1969) and the application to the first century.

have shown elsewhere that this prophecy is best understood in the context of Christ's first advent, but this cannot nullify, in any way, the theory that Nostradamus used existing Christian interpretations of biblical prophecy.

Though the twentieth century is not clearly indicated, if we assume that the 'century of Phoebe' (or Apollo) can be identified (as the century of the sun) with the twentieth century on astrological grounds, then the application of the prediction to Israel becomes quite clear, even though the quatrain is sandwiched between two prophecies that are usually applied to the nineteenth[11] and seventeenth[12] centuries respectively.

For example, the 'new law' (with its double meaning of 'people of the Law', or Torah, and therefore, Israel) seems more appropriately associated with Judaism, even though a 'new' version of it — a State tolerating and officially recognizing 'orthodox' Judaism, and yet in many respects much too modern to carry out some of its demands to the letter. Further, as we have seen, the indication of the prediction is that Israel will annex parts of Syria and 'Palestine' (i.e. Lebanon, the vestige of medieval Palestine, with its masses of Palestinians) and Judaea (including a part of its own occupied territories, which is often officially described as 'Judaea and Samaria'). The terms are not only specific in so many senses, but they would have been immediately understood by Nostradamus's French contemporaries, for Syria had been used by crusaders as an all-embracing term for the land east of the Mediterranean from Turkey to Egypt.

The expression 'barbarian empire' may seem vague to us, but Nostradamus, as a French Catholic believer in a Turkish Antichrist, would have used it of the Turkish Empire. Thus, the accuracy of the prediction is somewhat blurred, for the Turkish Empire had crumbled long before the State of Israel was declared. But the expression may have a religious meaning. It could be a global term for Muslim peoples, whom Nostradamus's contemporaries would have regarded as 'barbarians'. Thus, it could accurately predict Israel's 'shattering' of the Arab (usually Muslim) peoples. If so,

[11] Century III:96.
[12] Century III:98.

'Palestine' would, as I suggested earlier, be a direct allusion to
the Palestinians (whether in Lebanon or elsewhere). But even
if this is conceded, there has to be some interpretational fudge
in modern expositions of this prediction. For Lebanon has
been the major (Muslim) victim of Israeli action in the
twentieth century — and yet Lebanon is the relic of a French
Christian (crusader) enclave in the middle east. An original
reader of Nostradamus would never have identified Lebanon, of all countries, with the 'great barbarian empire', nor
would any of his contemporaries have taken it to mean the
pounding of a part-Christian, part-French country by Israel.
Even here, then, there is predictive distortion. What other
events would Nostradamus have expected to be fulfilled in
the twentieth century?

The principle is much the same. Nostradamus makes
obscure references to the twentieth century in contexts that
match biblical expositors' ideas of this period, and there is
sufficient obscurity and/or contradiction to make some of his
predictions inevitable. Let us, in turn, explore three other
'hints' by biblical expositors of what may happen in the
twentieth century and examine how Nostradamus either
exploits or subconsciously uses them. They concern:

(i)   Antichrist
(ii)   World disasters
(iii) The Papacy

We could include a fourth category, prophecies of scientific
achievement, on the assumption that biblical prophets may
be interpreted to have foretold an increase in scientific
achievement,[13] but this will be considered when we examine
Nostradamus's scientific perceptiveness later in this chapter.

The predictions of Antichrist contain conflicting material,
but agree with each other on matters that not only seem to
have a biblical origin but were an 'understood' Catholic
picture of Antichrist in Nostradamus's own day. They are as
follows.

1. Antichrist would come from the Euphrates region
(present-day Iraq or Iran, or, at least, from the east), as the

---

[13] Daniel 12:4.

Apocalypse of John appears to indicate in some places.[14]

2. He would be a 'man of blood', for the 'blood' theme, again, spans most of John's Apocalypse[15] and in some places, in sequence, it is associated with the 'Euphrates' theme.

3. He would be a 'lawless one'[16] who would, in the ethos of the interpretations then current, also be identified with the 'lawless one' of Daniel's prophecies[17] and would, therefore, also change (or try to change) festivals and rest-days — an anathema to Catholics of that time.

The predictions that follow these three themes can thus be identified as originating from the Bible, but Nostradamus is obscure in other details. The first prediction in his writings that can be categorized as relating to Antichrist is not a direct prophecy and has no indication either of its time-scale or its fulfilment. It reads:

> *The clergy will be both exalted and ruined*
> *— by those who want to learn nothing about them.*[18]

The first line has a 'double-headed coin' ring about it, for it presages both exaltation and ruin; one or both of these events would be likely at some time or other after Nostradamus's time. However, as a prediction student who was familiar with the Bible, and with existing interpretations of its predictions, Nostradamus may have had in mind: 'In the last days perilous times shall come . . . having a form of godliness but denying its power',[19] and other predictions of a final state of irreligion in which religion would be respected only for its political and temporary advantages, hence 'exalted' (for political reasons) and 'ruined' (through the Church losing its spiritual authority). As such the quatrain ceases to be a contradiction, and simply stresses the paradox in the biblical prophecy.[19]

The prophecy has been partly fulfilled in those areas of the

---

[14] Revelation 9:14 and 16:12.
[15] See particularly Revelation 9-18.
[16] 2 Thessalonians 2:3.
[17] Daniel 11:36.
[18] Centuries I:15.
[19] 2 Timothy 3:1 and 5.

world where atheistic communism has been successful, but has no other 'origin' than the Pauline predictions. Though there is a hint of Paul's other predictions of a 'lawless one' who would set up 'irreligion' as 'god', the words 'exalted and ruined' are an intended clear interpretation of Paul's predictions of the final state of godlessness but are sufficiently obscure to fudge the central specific theme and amass a whole series of likely interpretations.

The second prediction in the Antichrist series (and the first clear reference to Antichrist) comes later in the first Century[20] where Nostradamus writes of a man born with an 'aquatic triplicate', who celebrated Thursday as his rest-day and who would bring trouble from the east. Thus he fulfils two of the conditions provided above, but not the third.

1. He comes from the east, which is specifically mentioned.

2. He is *not* stated to be a 'man of blood', but may be one.

3. He does seek to change 'times and seasons'.

Though the east is not necessarily identifiable with the Euphratean region (Iraq), the prediction does contain an obscure reference to an 'aquatic triplicate'. At first sight this looks astrological, but in fact it is a restatement of a prediction in a later quatrain to 'the *sea* and *two rivers*'[21] — that is, three elements containing water. It thus implicitly refers to a land of 'sea and two rivers', and although a number of countries would fit the description, it is in context (i.e. the 'east') a reference to the Euphratean region.

To the author of the Apocalypse, the east was a source of anti-Christian activity — at least if 'beyond Euphrates' is to be taken literally. To the Roman Empire the Euphrates would have been the boundary of the civilized world, and, although I have elsewhere suggested a better exposition of these passages in the Apocalypse,[22] medieval expositors, particularly Catholic writers, associated them with a

---

[20] Centuries I:50.
[21] Centuries VI:33.
[22] D. Pitt Francis, *The Most Amazing Message Ever Written* (Castle Books, 1983).

Turkish/Ottoman Antichrist from either the regions of Iraq or Iran.

The 'lawless one' theme is also taken up in the 'Thursday' reference. This identifies Antichrist with one who would seek to change existing festivals and rest days, such as Friday (Muslim), Saturday (Jewish) and Sunday (Christian). There is no existing fulfilment involving a religious body that uses Thursday as its rest day every week, for Communist systems often stagger holidays to discourage religious worship. But the reference is important because it illustrates that Nostradamus had a 'biblical' premise for believing (on the basis of the quotations from Daniel and Paul) that Antichrist would seek to change existing rest days and festivals with the object of destroying religious loyalties. To confuse us, and yet improve Nostradamus's predictive success, another passage[23] actually predicts that Antichrist would make Monday his rest day. Given that four days (from Monday to Thursday) are unused by the main monotheistic religions, and therefore likely choices for Antichrist, Nostradamus improves his predictive probability to 50 per cent by using Monday and Thursday in his predictions. The chance of Antichrist choosing the same days is at least as good as flipping an unbiased coin!

The next reference to Antichrist[24] describes him as a 'man of blood' who will come to prominence at a time when a 'new land' would be at the height of its power, and the 'two great leaders' are friends. The height of American ('new land' = 'new world') power is contemporaneous with the past few decades of this century, though no amount of insight based on biblical interpretation could have given Nostradamus this information. Further, if the 'friendship' between 'two great leaders' means the era of *detente* before American power started to wane, then the stanza becomes a remarkable picture of Communist inroads that took advantage of *detente*, blood and redness both being associated with communism. This, then, could be an unexplained flash of insight. Yet, the blood symbol is important, not simply as a reference to Communism, but because it satisfies the second of the conditions about Antichrist listed at the beginning of this part

---

[23] Centuries II:28.
[24] Centuries II:89.

of the chapter. Blood is identified in the Apocalypse of John with Euphrates so that at least one of the three biblical indications of Antichrist are satisfied.

Antichrist reappears in the next Century[25] in a quatrain that describes great 'proscription' (i.e., conscripted military service) in an area that can be identified as Turkey and modern Iran. Care is needed in identifying this quatrain with an Antichrist likely to appear in the twentieth century, for Nostradamus lived in the Suliman period when this area was much in mind, as previously mentioned in connection with the Araxes/Lepanto prediction in Chapter Two. But at least the stanza seems to depend on expectations of an Antichrist. The 'blood' and 'Euphrates' conditions — two of the three mentioned earlier — are both satisfied by the details given in this quatrain.

Sometimes, either subconsciously or by design, Nostradamus's mind 'hit' on the correct formula for the present time simply by synthesizing (i.e., combining) an existing Catholic interpretation of the Bible involving a Muslim Antichrist with biblical passages about the breakdown of religion before the end of the present order of things. To do so, some eastern power would have to replace Muslim domination. This insight is apparent later in a reference to a 'new order'.[26] It states that in the region of the Dneiper (i.e., in southern Russia) the 'Moorish law' (Muslim region) will be replaced by another, more pleasing, set of laws that would ultimately fail.

Though there is no timescale or time point for this prediction it is preceded by the seer's own notable '500-year' prediction, which states that his works would be understood more clearly some 500 years after his own times. This is not a twentieth-century prediction, unless Nostradamus had lunar years (i.e., those of 354 days) in mind, for 500 lunar (i.e., original Muslim) years would be about 480 calendar years, which when dated from Nostradamus's birth would terminate approximately at the end of the twentieth century. As a round figure it is one more reference that seems to depend on the millenarian theory — that the world would end at about the end of the twentieth century. This reference

---

[25] Centuries III:60.
[26] Centuries III:97.

is discussed in Chapter Eight.

Two further direct references to Antichrist occur in Century VI. The first of these reverts to the view of a Muslim Antichrist:

> *His hand finally* [or back?] *through sanguine Alus*
> *He* [Alus?] *will be unable to protect himself by sea.*
> *Between the two rivers he will be afraid of the warriors' hand*
> *The black one, angry, will make him repent!*[27]

Two of the listed conditions appear in the quatrain. They are:

(i) references to blood;

(ii) a reference to the Euphrates region, the sea and the two rivers — the 'aquatic triplicate' of an earlier reference.

The third listed condition, changing rest day (festival) dates, does not occur, but there is sufficient detail to indicate that Nostradamus was once more drawing on an existing view of Antichrist. The word 'Alus' is obscure and would be significant only if it had been Nostradamus's sole attempt at predicting the name of Antichrist, but the Centuries contain many possible 'shots' at his name, few of which sound alike. This name, Alus, could be a Latinized form of 'Allah' (the Muslim name of God) or 'Ali' or a similar cognate Muslim name. It is Muslim sounding because, at this stage, Nostradamus — probably in common with contemporary Catholics — believed that Antichrist would be Muslim, rather than irreligious or godless. Protestants would have identified Antichrist with the Papacy. If this had been the only definite name of Antichrist it would have been more convincing, but it is not. Elsewhere[28] his name is given as Mabus, which is sufficiently obscure to be either:

(i) a Latinized form of Moab, the nearest-sounding name of an Arab people to Mohammedan; or

(ii) derived from a Celtic/Welsh word 'mab' meaning 'son' and thus, possibly, meaning the 'son of perdition' of biblical prophecy.[29]

---

[27] Centuries VI:33.   [28] Centuries II:62.   [29] 2 Thessalonians 2:3.

Another passage provides an even greater opportunity for a 'free-for-all' among obscurantist interpreters in the phrase 'the last but one of the prophet's name'.[30] If this means the penultimate syllable of the name of a prophet (and it need not), then it could be that of any well-known prophet, including those of the Bible, Muhammed, or even Nostradamus himself. Consequently, a great variety of names, including Ham, Hom, Ho, Dam and Dan, have been suggested. These names, together with those of Alus and Mabus, are sufficiently different from each other for any one of them, using anagrams, to be a good guess at the name of any future Antichrist!

Most of the other Antichrist references simply follow the biblical stereotype of one of three conditions listed earlier.

Let us examine two examples and then a third, which is a little more important. First there is a Catholic-style prophecy of a Muslim assailant:

> *The great Asiatic with a great troop by land and sea*
> *So that blues [?] Pers [= Persia] he will drive out the cross to death.*[31]

This demonstrates little insight. The Antichrist comes from Persia (if my understanding of 'Pers' is correct) and he is against the cross (= Christianity), though he need not be a Muslim.

Secondly, there is a quatrain that shows a little more originality, which in one translation can read:

> *The Antichrist soon destroys three*
> *For 27 years the war will continue*
> *The heretics are dead, alive, exiled*
> *With blood, human corpses, water and red hail covering the*
> *ground.*[32]

The quatrain is an interpreter's hunting ground, particularly because the very word Antichrist occurs in it. Some have taken it to mean the 'third [Antichrist]' ('three', line 1) and

---

[30] Centuries II:28.
[31] Centuries VI:80.
[32] Centuries VIII:77.

have identified the earlier two with Cromwell, Napoleon, Hitler, or various others. Latterly, 'three' has been interpreted to many any association of three people, not of Antichrists. Cheetham even suggests the three Kennedy brothers, but this anticipates a Kennedy death that has not yet occurred. In fact, the prediction originates from borrowed and distorted biblical passages:

(i) Revelation 16, which describes the outpouring of blood in different ways and ends with the fall of 'fiery hailstones' (i.e., 'red hail') on earth: 'every one of them about the weight of a talent'.[33]

(ii) A threefold plague in the same biblical prophecy, in which 'the great city' is 'divided into *three* parts'.[34]

(iii) A Daniel reference to a beast-type ruler who would 'change times and seasons' and 'subdue *three* kings'.[35]

Interpretations may, of course, vary — as, for example, Cheetham's[36] identification of 'red hail' with radioactive fallout — but in this case the biblical origin of the detail could hardly be clearer. Even the reference to 27 years may result from a preoccupation with *three*, for 27 is 3^3. The words are changed, but the detail is essentially biblical in origin.

The third example is the most courageous on Nostradamus's part, for it provides us with a date:

> *In the year 1999 and seven months*
> *— from the sky will come the great King of Terror*
> *He will raise to life the great King of the Mongols*
> *Before and after war reign happily.*[37]

The King of Terror may of course simply mean death and be explained as a poetic allusion to judgement from heaven. Alternatively, it may be a reference to the Second Advent, when the 'king of the Mongols', the conqueror Genghis

---

[33] Revelation 16:21.
[34] Revelation 16:19.
[35] Daniel 7:24.
[36] Cheetham, *Nostradamus*, p. 337.
[37] Centuries X:72.

Khan, will be raised and judged, but at a time clearly specified.

The time period owes much to the millenarian theory, which held that the history of mankind divides into approximately 7000 years from about 4000 BC to AD 2000, with a millennium[38] of about 1000 years. Such a view is less popular now than it was in Nostradamus's time. It is neither illogical nor unimaginative that Nostradamus's date should be 1999 and seven months, for some expositors of the Apocalypse understood a period of five months' torment[39] as occurring before the advent of: '*the* hour, day, month and year'.[40] The deduction of five months from 2000 years AD gives 1999 and seven months. The choice was safe, and in a well-established tradition. Yet it was sufficiently removed from Nostradamus's own time not to disgrace its lack of accuracy if it failed.

In this section we have now dealt with predictions of the restoration of the Jewish nation and of a supposed Antichrist in the twentieth century. Before proceeding to other sources of Nostradamus's inspiration and success in predictions that appear to have present-day fulfilment, it is useful to consider two other topics that have a biblical basis of prediction:

(i) predictions of world-wide plagues; and

(ii) predictions about the Papacy.

In both these cases some inspiration came from the Bible, but the degree of applied imagination and obscurantism is greater than in the cases already considered.

Plagues and Popes

In the sacred writings of most of the main religions the end of the world is depicted and heralded by world-wide calamities. This is not only a feature of Judaism and Christianity, that is, of Old and New Testaments, but of the Qur'an and of some

---

[38] Apocalypse 20:4.
[39] Revelation 9:10.
[40] Revelation 9:15.

Buddhist writings. The Olivet prophecy of Jesus[41] has been interpreted in this way, and Nostradamus copies such interpretations in this respect. World plagues and world war are clearly depicted in the Centuries but the detail is sometimes quite original and displays some imagination. The first case is general, and may contain oblique references to the millenarians' expectations of the end of the world, and therefore of the twentieth century:

> *Plague, famine, death at the hand of warriors*
> *— the century approaching renewal.*[42]

Of course this could mean the 'turn' of any century, including the present one; but it may also mean the century 'approaching' (or 'next to') the 'renewal' of the world, and therefore, on the basis of Nostradamus's millenarian speculation, the twentieth century. The first line displays little imagination and could easily have derived from the Olivet prophecy of Jesus or the last chapter of the Apocalypse of Ezra; or it could simply be an interpretation of the four horsemen of the Apocalypse.[43]

But later in the same Century, Nostradamus becomes much more imaginative about each 'plague', and one stanza depicts world-wide famine, the cannibalism of infants and the eating of roots of trees.[44] World famine is a logical consequence of overpopulation, and could be reasonably deduced from the passage of time. Further, the reference to cannibalism of infants may derive from the Bible,[45] but the eating of tree roots seems to be original and should be noted carefully in relation to the next reference to plagues,[46] which mentions:

(i) people stripping bark from trees because of hunger; and

(ii) a man born with two teeth.

There is a further description of the hunger at the end of time in the words:

---

[41] Mark 13.
[42] Centuries I:16.
[43] Revelation 6:1-8.
[44] Centuries I:67.
[45] Deuteronomy 28:57.
[46] Centuries II:7.

The call of the unwanted bird
on the pipe of the breathing floor.
So high will the price of bushels of wheat rise,
— that man will devour fellow man.[47]

The detail of the last two lines is part-biblical. The cannibalism quotation probably derives from Deuteronomy (28:57), and the wheat price reference has its counterpart in the third of the Apocalyptic horsemen sequences (Revelation 6:1-8). But what of the first two lines of this quatrain? Imagination and obscurity are added for no apparent reason. The 'pipe of the breathing floor' is often interperted as meaning a chimney-stack: this interpretation is not the only possible one. Roots and branches of trees 'breathe' sap and provide life to them. If men eat the roots of trees (I:67) and strip the bark from each kind of tree (II:7), then the branches are bound to suffer and the 'unwanted bird' loses its nourishment. For this reason, creatures of different kinds become unwanted and extinct.

Herein lies the real clue to the quatrain's meaning. Hunger and greed not only drive mankind to the exploitation of other species, but to depriving them of their means of nourishment. Not just 'unwanted birds' but whales may be exploited. Other species, such as the African elephant, become almost extinct, not just because of greed (for ivory) but because their own means of livelihood are eroded. The drift of these quatrains is that hunger and greed drive men to rid the world of its less popular resources, including trees and the more 'unwanted' (unsavoury?) of living creatures.

The 'child born with two teeth' reappears in a later famine reference.[48] He is coupled with:

(i) 'barren rain' (an apocalyptic figure of dry hailstones falling to the ground); and

(ii) 'absence of wheat and barley'.

The 'two-tooth' reference is the only original part of this stanza, for the other lines have a biblical flavour. At one time the two 'two-tooth' references (II:7 and III:42) were thought

---

[47] *Centuries* II:75.
[48] *Centuries* III:42.

to relate to Louis XIV, who was said to have been born with teeth. But such a prediction would not be relevant to the 'hunger' theme of these stanzas. All sorts of interpretations are possible. It is a graphic picture of mankind 'consuming' by exploitation the African elephant — with two tusks'. But this fudged interpretation involves events too recent to have found their way into Nostradamus commentaries. Another, and more likely, suggestion is that Nostradamus meant that people would be born 'two-toothed' or 'doubly-greedy'. Hunger does not result only from overpopulation: it often springs from greed on the part of others. Nostradamus appears to have had sufficient foresight to see that not only would the world's population increase, but knowledge also — in particular, knowledge concerning human nutrition. This would lead to concern about nourishment and to overfeeding; generations would be born expecting never to be hungry, and thus they would suffer much more acutely when real hunger would come. This, then, is a picture of a final 'generation' expecting never to be hungry, and stripping the world's resources to satisfy itself. It is indeed an accurate picture of the twentieth century. But how much of it was dependent on a biblical vision of the troubles preceding the end of the world, and how much did scientific awareness and logical foresight play a part in constructing this picture?

Elsewhere, Nostradamus predicted other plagues associated with world war, but again his biblical-based foresight is uppermost. For example:

> *After great human 'truck'* [= misery], *greater approaches*
> *— when the great 'wheel' of centuries is renewed.*
> *It will rain blood, 'milk', famine, war and pestilence.*
> *In the sky one sees fire, dragging a long 't[r]ail' of sparks.*[49]

The flavour here is similar to that of Century I:16, but the reference to war is more specific because there seems to be a reference to aerial warfare in the fourth line, and because the reference to 'human misery' in the first line seems general, and therefore worldwide. But line 3 is unoriginal. Warfare (involving conquest), then bloodshed, then famine and then pestilence (involving death) *are* the four horsemen of the

---

[49] Centuries II:46.

Apocalypse. Though they are in logical order in Revelation, the order is slightly distorted in line 3 of this stanza. But war *does* logically produce bloodshed, famine and death, and it requires little foresight to imagine that the final 'world-ending' conflict would do the same.

Nor is line 4 original. It may also have been inspired by Apocalyptic imagery, such as the tail of a fiery dragon dragging (trailing) a third of the stars of heaven.[50] But the word 'sparks' suggests something much more human. Early expositors suggested a comet, but they do not 'trail sparks' in this sense. So the sparks are most probably of human origin, and Nostradamus, with scientific insight, gives a clear description of twentieth-century warfare. The twentieth century is also hinted by the statement that the 'great wheel of centuries is renewed'. If each millennium is regarded as a turn of the wheel of centuries, the twentieth century fits this description better than most.

What else does Nostradamus tell us about the final war at the end of the world? Modern warfare uniquely involves shelling, aerial conflict and the mass-use of chemicals. Nostradamus could have taken a good description of chemical (or of nuclear) warfare from the Bible: 'Their flesh shall rot away while they stand on their feet, their eyes rot away in their sockets . . .'.[51] But he does not do this, though, as I suggested in Chapter One, he may have used Joel's description of an atomic explosion, but in another context. Yet, possibly with biblical (or scientific) insight, he does assume that the final conflict will be aerial/chemical in nature:

> *A very great pestilence will come with the great shell.*
> *Relief is near, but remedies are far off.*[52]

The lines suggest that pestilence will come from shelling with chemicals, and the napalm bomb was a good example of this. Line 2 suggests that, although people can be relieved easily, and can continue living, they take a long time to recover, because of the permanent scars that such warfare produces.

---

[50] Revelation 12:4.
[51] Zechariah 14:12.
[52] Centuries III:75.

Two later stanzas suggest that pestilence will be caused by chemical warfare and then produce famine — a slight distortion of the order of the four horsemen of the Apocalypse.

The first associates both, but curiously with a war involving Greece (or, perhaps, the middle east generally): 'A great famine, pestilence, because of false dust [i.e., chemicals].[53] The second of the two stanzas is more general in description, and has hints of aerial (or even space) warfare, which will be considered later when Nostradamus's scientific perception is discussed:

> A grand famine by a pestilent wave
> will rain the length of the Arctic pole.[54]

There follows a description of people at war, who live without politics and law. So, again, the biblical (horsemen) connection between war, famine and pestilence is repeated, but clearly transposed to the end of the world to appear in a cosmic context.

So, our verdict about Nostradamus's prophecies of plagues is clear. Like some of his contemporaries, he used a biblical model, and in line with the 'four horsemen' expected war, bloodshed, famine and pestilence (death) on a cosmic scale at the end of the world. Further, there are at least two millenarian (and therefore twentieth-century) hints of the time horizon for fulfilment, but he introduces some unexpected and imaginative detail and strangely inverts the sequences, so that he appears to be somewhat independent of contemporary Christian expectations.

So much for his bible- and scientifically-based predictions of plagues to come shortly before the end of the world, and identified by some of his contemporaries with the twentieth century. Let us now examine his predictions regarding the Papacy in the twentieth century. Here, his use of biblical expositions is weakest, but this is understandable. Biblical expositors of the 'historical' Protestant school, such as Joseph Mede and Isaac Newton over a century later, tended to believe in a papal Antichrist. Malachy, four centuries earlier,

[53] Centuries V:90.
[54] Centuries VI:5.

had produced a list of Popes to the end of the twentieth century, and a few Catholics believed that there might ultimately be a single apostate Pope, possibly Antichrist. Somehow, though a Catholic, Nostradamus had to admit the possibility of a papal Antichrist as well as keep both themes apart, and he does! We might expect prophecies of specific Popes, and one or two about an apostate Pope; the contents of the Centuries on this subject are in just that proportion.

One detailed quatrain[55] concerns a Pope who would:

(i) minister for about four years; and

(ii) be followed by a more 'liberal' pontiff.

The details would have fitted John XXIII and Paul VI, if Paul VI had been more liberal and worldly.

Another quatrain[56] specifically mentions a 'Paul', and was thought by Cheetham[57] to be Paul VI and to contain a reference to the three Kennedy brothers. Hindsight, however, has taught us better, for:

(i) Cheetham's work did not accurately predict the manner of Paul VI's death:

(ii) she assumed that the third Kennedy brother would be assassinated; and

(iii) there were five previous Popes named Paul.

Other papal predictions are totally obscure. One[58] expects an Antichrist-Pope, but is not clearly identifiable with any Pope who has officiated this century. It states that: 'His blood' will be 'poisonous in the chalice'. Curiously, it follows Catholic scholars who believed in some future papal Antichrist, and carefully borrows a biblical reference used by contemporary Protestant biblical commentators: 'drunk of the wine of her immorality,[59] and 'the cup that she has filled, fill to her double'.[60]

No Antichrist could occupy the papal chair without a

[55] Centuries VI:26.
[56] Centuries VIII:46.
[57] Cheetham, *Nostradamus*, p. 325.
[58] Centuries III:65.
[59] Revelation 17:2.
[60] Revelation 18:6.

schism, for some Catholics would remain 'faithful'. It is reasonable to assume that, as in the case of the Rome-Avignon-Pisa schism of the Middle Ages, such a Pope would be an 'outsider'. Do such speculative data fit the stanzas? In one case,[61] Nostradamus predicts schism within the Roman Church itself (as distinct from Protestant movements), and hints at an Albanian (Sabine) north-eastern Pope, with a description that could well fit the present Polish pontiff. But if the quatrain is assumed to fit the recent tridentine schism and a non-Italian Pope, it foils the expectations of Nostradamus's original sources and readers, even though Poland is (like the Sabines) north-east of Rome.

Another quatrain makes a calculated guess at the identity of the non-Roman Pope. He is elected for a 'trembling ship' (= Church), from 'ancient France' (Gallic peoples originally came from Eastern Europe) to 'make promises to the enemy' (the communist world?).[62]

Unexpectedly, an 'eastern Pope' is here linked with promises to communist regimes.

In an obscure way the Papacy may also be identified with predictions of (i) 'a man from the east';[63] and (ii) Antichrist, by association with one about a 'long-lived Pope'.[64] There is thus a case for believing in a partly-accurate fulfilment of the detail of these quatrains, but in a way that Nostradamus would never have expected. We have seen an internal schism in the Roman Church, a Pope who is both non-Italian and a 'man from the east' (if the prediction does not relate to Iran), and promises that have been made to an 'eastern' enemy; however, in contrast to the expectations of Nostradamus and his Catholic and Protestant contemporaries, the first non-Italian Pope to occupy the chair since the first few centuries AD is far from being Antichrist!

Before examining Nostradamus's scientific insights and how they relate to the twentieth century, let us summarize the findings of the past two sections. Nostradamus's twentieth-century predictions owe a great debt to biblical

---

[61] Centuries V:46.
[62] Centuries V:49.
[63] Centuries V:54.
[64] Centuries V:56.

and other apocalyptic literature, as well as to the ideas of Catholic and Protestant biblical expositors of his day. Most of them believed the millenarian theory: that mankind would exist in its present state for only 7000 years, of which 6000 were scheduled to end in the twentieth century. Most of them believed that this would involve the regathering of the Jewish people to Israel (then Palestine) and that a lawless (Islamic, or post-Islamic) Antichrist would emerge to change existing festivals and rest-days.

I have also provided clear evidence that Nostradamus used the sequence of the apocalyptic horsemen in his descriptions of the end of the world, for example, war, bloodshed, famine and plague (with death), though the original biblical prophecy may not in fact have meant the end of the world. His prophecies of the papacy, on the other hand, are much more obscure. They are untimed, and he leaves some room for an 'Antichrist', schismatic, non-Roman Pope to satisfy, with unclear hints, the expectations of most of his Protestant, and some of his Catholic, contemporaries. That prophecies of a non-Roman Pope can now be applied to the present Pope is a matter of ingenuity of interpretation rather than original expectation.

Nostradamus, Science and Present Times

Many of Nostradamus's 'biblical insight' predictions have been fulfilled. They were unoriginal, reflected the popular beliefs of his contemporaries, and were fully in line with the biblical expositions of his own time. But his predictions of scientific inventions are often quite original, and many have been realized in the twentieth century. Before I suggest an explanation, it is appropriate to list some of them.

First of all, let us look at some related predictions from Century I: 'The fish that journeys over land and sea'[65] and 'Despite the signs of palm-branches [the palm-shaped 'pillar' — *timorah* of biblical prophecy[66]] . . . — afterward death and pillage'.[67] Elsewhere aerial travel seems to be indicated: 'People will travel safely through the sky over land and

---

[65] Centuries I:29.
[66] Joel 2:30.
[67] Centuries I:30.

seas';[68] and there are also predictions of aerial warfare: 'Weapons will be heard fighting in the skies'.[69] There is a hint of radio equipment[70] where the word 'antenne' (literally 'antenna') is used to describe a complicated mast. An earlier reference is a little more specific:

> *When the living thing* [animal] *tamed by man*
> *— with great pains and difficulty begins to speak*
> *— the lightning harmful to the rod*
> *will be taken up from the land, and suspended in the air.*[71]

This has some of the flavour of live communication by electronic means — something originally using a 'harmful' agent (electricity) but then 'taken up from the land' and employing the air itself as its agent — i.e., radio instead of the telephone and telegraph. The sequence is a precise one, for electricity is 'live' or 'animated' in the original Latin sense of the word 'animal'. Telegraph communication employed 'rod-connected' principles, but was then superseded by radio.

However, the quatrains sometimes seem to transcend the invention of radio, and to turn to something much more modern — to space stations. After describing a 'long rain' the length of the 'Arctic pole', a stanza speaks of something called Samarobrin, an object 300 miles from earth where 'they will live without law, exempt from politics'.[72] This is an amazingly accurate suggestion of a manned space station. 'A machine of flying fire' is described later in the same Century.[73]

Reference to space travel and space warfare recur later. There may be a hint of man's reaching the moon:

> *He will come to take himself to the corner of Luna* [the Moon]
> *— where he will be transported and placed on foreign soil.*[74]

These references are sufficient to show extraordinary

---

[68] Centuries I:63.
[69] Centuries IV:43.
[70] Centuries IV:92.
[71] Centuries III:44.
[72] Centuries VI:5.
[73] Centuries VI:34.
[74] Centuries IX:65.

scientific insight on the part of Nostradamus, but they do not explain how he obtained it. Scientific insight is a composite of a number of factors.

First, as suggested in Chapter One, twentieth-century discoveries use earlier inventions. Some of Nostradamus's predictions, such as the invention of the submarine, rely on earlier prototypes. Leonardo da Vinci had begun to design submarines over thirty years before Nostradamus's time. The ancient Greeks played with ideas about thermodynamics. The ancient Chinese invented gunpowder long before its use for destructive purposes.

Secondly, there is always a lag between an initial discovery and popularity during which the popularizer is accredited with the invention. Samuel Taylor provided the prototype of Pitman's shorthand nearly half a century before Pitman. Darwin simply modified explanations of existing German theories of Evolution — and did so unsuccessfully — yet was popularly accredited with their 'discovery'. Several twentieth-century inventions were thought about long before they were perfected.

A third factor is the 'hit-and-miss' nature of scientific vision — the very basis of most science fiction writing. The speculator and prophet dreams of machines that can perform impossible tasks, encourages people to want them, and thus sets the pace for a type of participative fulfilment: the prophecies become targets for human accomplishment.

Fourthly, such speculations are usually popular because most people want to see the impossible happening. The lag between prediction and fulfilment does not usually evoke the same degree of ridicule and scepticism as that to which other unfulfilled predictions are usually subjected.

These are only partial factors and do not explain why many of these predictions have been fulfilled either in or shortly before the twentieth century; thus, a fifth factor is required, which is that, even in this case, Nostradamus was partly reliant on the beliefs of contemporary biblical interpreters in assuming an increase in human knowledge during the following few hundred years, particularly in relation to the prediction 'Many shall run to and fro, and knowledge shall increase.[75]

---

[75] Daniel 12:4.

Though this passage may now be variously interpreted, it was assumed then to mean that human knowledge would increase remarkably before the Second Advent, and thus, by implication, within the next few centuries. Although Nostradamus carefully avoided assigning a specific time scale, he too worked on the premise that scientific invention would reach its climax before the world's end in the twentieth century, and his imagination focused on what people most wanted — in particular the self-fulfilling wishes and dreams of the people of his time. If a wish of this kind is strong enough, sooner or later an inventor somewhere will try to fulfil it.

All these factors in combination explain those of Nostradamus's predictions that result from scientific perceptiveness. What of participative fulfilment? Though this explains many predictions relating to the French monarchy, Napoleon and Hitler, it cannot be used sucessfully to explain late twentieth-century fulfilments with any degree of success. For a prophecy to become successfully fulfilled one requires at least ten years of continuous identification. Many of Nostradamus's 'modern' predictions have been reinterpreted over a decade: Cheetham's work, for instance,[76] is already embarrassed with predictions that encapsulate her own preoccupations with the Kennedy brothers[77,78] and with Pope Paul VI: none of these predictions involves either self-fulfilment or participatory fulfilment. Further, participatory fulfilment requires a believer in Nostradamus (such as Hitler) who is powerful enough to attempt to fulfil the relevant quatrains. Most candidates for self-fulfilment studied the Centuries thoroughly, and the more obvious quatrains have already been identified with past notorieties and are thus, in effect, 'taken out of circulation'. There are obvious exceptions. 'Hister', as we have seen, referred to a river (the Danube) until Hitler decided to identify himself with the name.

One unidentified participant does remain, however.[79] No

---

[76] E. Cheetham, *Nostradamus* (Spearman, 1973, subsequent editions unmodified by Corgi, 1975-1980; thus, less than 10 years old).
[77] Centuries II:57.
[78] Centuries II:95.
[79] Centuries III:94.

one has yet claimed *and proved* to be the interpreter who would arise after 500 years to make the whole of Nostradamus clear, though this is to be expected, since only 400 years or so have expired. But the millenarian theory, to which Nostradamus subscribed, held that all things would be revealed at the millennium — i.e., some 500 years from Nostradamus's day. Thus, in specifying 500 years for a final interpretation of his work, Nostradamus threw a two-headed coin. This quatrain will be discussed again in Chapter Eight.

Interpretational 'fudge'

We have seen in the succeeding chapters that most quatrains in the Centuries triumph by their very obscurity. In this chapter one example is useful for demonstration purposes: 'The last but one of the prophet's name'[80] can have any number of meanings, even if syllables and anagrams are the only basis of interpretations. Yet, the line's possible meanings, other than these (for example, the 'last but one' of some prophetic dynasty), boggle the imagination.

Not all Nostradamus's predictions are as obscure as this, but some present us with detail that must recur historically, and so be as applicable to the present century as to any other — such as the picture of an enslaved population chanting, with its rulers in prison.[81] This is not just a picture of the French Revolution, but of all revolutions and even counter-revolutions, and can be applied to the present-day fortunes of such organizations as Solidarity in Poland.

Some predictions, then, are historically obscure, others are verbally obscure. It was a preoccupation with astrology that gave Cheetham[82] the suggestion that the 'scythe' of an early quatrain[83] is a reference to Saturn. But there are at least two other possible meanings. The 'scythe' is a symbol of Russia, which is composed of *Scythian* peoples, among others. The French word used for 'scythe' is *'Estang'*, and is, of course, part of the name of a former French 'right-wing' leader. So the word can be contradictorily associated both with the

---

[80] Centuries II:28.
[81] Centuries I:14.
[82] See Cheetham, p. 28.
[83] Centuries I:16.

right-wing or the left-wing in politics. The net is thus cast so wide as to provide opportunity for fulfilment with any right-wing or left-wing political combination that might arise 'as the century approaches its renewal'.

Within two quatrains is another verbal/historical obscurity, for although the prediction was fulfilled in Medici times it clearly depicts a 'Troyen' (Frank = Franco) having trouble with indigenous Spanish people, and may be fitted to the Spanish Civil War, aspects of World War II or to various incidents up until the time Franco died.

Added to verbal and historical obscurity are cases of clear multiple fulfilment. In Century I is a rehash of part of Daniel 11. A man tries to change money and standards, comes from Egypt, and then attempts to 'withdraw the edict, causing Byzantium to change its laws'.[84] Anyone who reads sixteenth-century expositions of Daniel 11, particularly of the 'king of the south'[85] and the 'lawless one'[86] will notice a remarkable similarity of detail.

But interpretational fudge has produced many conflicting interpretations of this quatrain. Napoleon was suggested by early commentators. Then in the nineteenth century came Mehemet Ali, who rebelled against Ottoman rule. Modern times have produced their own interpretations. Spiritually, 'Byzantium' is the Muslim 'Arab' world, which is divided on most things but united by being Islamic and by its attitude to the State of Israel. The first attempt to 'change' and to 'withdraw' the 'edict', curiously, came from an *Egyptian,* and the stanza can be made to read as a perfect prediction of the policy of Anwar Sadat!

Finally, let me provide a case where the fertile imagination of an interpreter could work easily on both verbal and historical obscurity. I have already commented on:

> *The last but one of the prophet's name*
> *will take Diana as his 'day of rest'.*[80]

I have listed this as an Antichrist passage, and think this is correct. But slight cosmetic surgery, of the type I have shown to exist in Laver, could produce the following:

---

[84] Centuries I:40.
[85] Daniel 11:40.
[86] Daniel 11:36, 7:25.

(i) 'last but one' to mean Prince Charles, as heir to the throne meaning next to the sovereign;

(ii) 'of prophet's name' — i.e., as a name specifically mentioned by the 'prophet' (i.e., Nostradamus) elsewhere, as in the case of the beheading of Charles I;

(iii) 'will take Diana' — a marriage to Diana, and thus no longer meaning Monday (Diana) as a 'day of rest'; and

(iv) 'will deliver a great nation' — meaning Britain, but only in a promotional sense.

This seems to be a highly speculative interpretation of the quatrain and to wrest from it a meaning (the marriage of Charles to Diana) that is far from what Nostradamus intended. But it is no more fanciful than many other applications of Nostradamus's prophecies.

These, then, are obvious cases of historical and verbal fudge, where some meanings are bound to fit a given situation and where, once a few of the details fit, the interpreter is tempted to read the remainder in the same way by crediting Nostradamus with misspellings and anagrams to preserve mystery and obscurity.

Yet, despite bible-based foresight, scientific insight, participative fulfilment and interpretational fudge, there are a few post-war fulfilments that defy explanation because of their amazing detail. One of these concerns present-day Iran:

> *In a land with climate — opposite to Babylon*
> *will be great outpouring of blood.*
> *Heaven will seem unjust in land, sea and air.*
> *Sects, famine, 'kingdoms', plagues, confusion.*[87]

There is triple entendre even in line 1, for:

(i) Iran is geographically opposite Babylon, in physical contrast;

(ii) it opposes modern Iraq, which is situated in the site of ancient Babylon, both religiously and politically; and

---

[87] Centuries I:55.

(iii) its climate is also in opposition. Thus, the hanging gardens of Babylon were constructed to satisfy the whims of a princess who was accustomed to the airy climate of Persia.

The rest of the passage gives almost a complete description of the mass-killings of the Khomeini regime. It is a description of judicial executions with 'heaven' seeming unjust because the justice of Muslim courts is so rough. Given this interpretation as a possibility, the stanza is not the only possible reference to the Iran-Iraq conflict.[88] Khomeini may also appear in other references. Is he, for example, the 'man from the east' who would come to France (where incidentally Khomeini took refuge) and afterwards emerge to 'strike everyone with the rod'?[89]

Such predictions are not so easy to explain with my four factors, and there are a few others. Nostradamus's last quatrain is partly explained because it is bounded by his millenarian view:

> *A great empire will be for England*
> *— the all-powerful for over 300 years.*[90]

But it does not explain why he could predict greatness for England at a time when England was nowhere near its zenith. The best, but still unsatisfactory, explanation is that his 290-year (seven times) prophecy of judgement on England 'hedges his bets'. One or other prediction would succeed or fail as the case may be.

Nostradamus appeared to predict the rise of communism: 'a generation of intellectuals [philosophers]' who would 'despise death, gold and riches' and 'have support of masses of people'.[91] Perhaps he saw beyond communism to Hungarian/Chinese experiments to introduce revisionary restricted capitalism: 'All things common among friends . . . put far behind.'.[92] He may even have foreseen religious underground movements in communist countries:

[88] See also Centuries III:64.
[89] Centuries II:29.
[90] Centuries X:100.
[91] Centuries III:67.
[92] Centuries IV:32.

will arise against the red ones'[93] — although 'red ones' can mean cardinals and 'sects' may then, as suggested earlier, simply mean the Protestants of his day and beyond.

Finally, his predictions of inflation are graphic, unfudged and useful, though Cheetham[94] overstated the case by saying that paper money was not in use in Nostradamus's time. But he was right. Gold and silver have now been replaced by paper, and even metal coins (such as the one pound piece in the UK) are no longer sized to their value. Notoriously, France experienced the pattern of this prediction[95] more acutely than most in modern times, with the creation of a new franc to replace a debased and valueless one.

Thus, our four-part explanation of Nostradamus's success may satisfy most of his 'fulfilled' predictions. But they do not explain his genius completely. There still seems to be an X-factor, a 'residual' of astonishing detail that completely baffles us on some occasions, even when biblical interpretation, scientific insight, participative fulfilment and interpretational obscurity ('fudge') are disentangled. Sometimes the unexplained X-factor provides immense detail, but also an Achilles' heel — a flaw that shows Nostradamus to be still human. Such X-factor predictions are important, because a theory of prediction can only be constructed from unexplained data, and this is much less than most Nostradamus commentators have assumed to be the case.

We have not noticed many fulfilled astrological-based predictions. Indeed, Nostradamus's astrological references are few. Whatever may explain his predictive genius, it is *not* astrology, with which he seems to have had a love-hate relationship. He had a wealth of intelligence and perceptiveness that most people do not possess. He was a doctor, and therefore a student of human nature, and we have seen that most of his predictions can be explained by reference to our four explanatory variables.

The rest of the book will engage in statistical disentanglement in an attempt to examine the proportion of fulfilled prediction that can be explained by these four factors. What then of the X-factor? Is it something different from

---

[93] Centuries IX:51.
[94] Cheetham, *Nostradamus*, p. 317.
[95] Centuries VIII:28.

Nostradamus's 'doomsday' perspective, or do the four factors together provide us with a whole that is, so to speak, greater than the sum of the parts? X-factor predictions, as we have seen, are very detailed, and amazingly brilliant, but always (or nearly always) contain one flaw that serves to highlight their human origin. So, if Nostradamus's perceptiveness is something that we can develop simply by looking into the future in the right way, we must still not expect the 100 per cent accuracy claimed by Old Testament prophets.

6
Towards an Explanation

Nostradamus and Astrology

It is often thought, quite wrongly, that Nostradamus's knowledge of future events derived mainly from an early form of crystal-gazing[1] or from his knowledge of astrology. His attitude to astrologers and astrology was ambivalent. Professionally, he was first and foremost a medical practitioner but his academic training and earlier schooling from his grandfather had provided an insight into astronomy and astrology before these two categories of human knowledge were divorced from each other. I do not intend to argue the case for or against astrology. It is sufficient to state that in Nostradamus's time astrology was held in great respect. Though astrology was a 'second profession' for Nostradamus, particularly in his capacity as court astrologer to Catherine de'Medici, he could safely rationalize this position by reference to biblical characters, such as Daniel and Joseph, and yet have the perceptiveness to denounce astrologers as he does at the end of his sixth Century.[2]

It is not possible to check the horoscopes that Nostradamus cast of individuals, to see whether they reliably predicted the future for the people concerned. He obviously possessed natural powers of foresight that would explain his accurate prediction of events in the times with which he was familiar, though his 'Araxes' prophecy, now wrongly interpreted to be a prophecy of Lepanto, shows that he could sometimes be wrong. To a large extent such predictions, made for the seer's own times, are no longer relevant in our search for the reasons for Nostradamus's success as a

---

[1] Centuries I:1-3.
[2] Centuries VI:100.

prophet. This book is about the Centuries, in which are some stanzas that seem to have had remarkably accurate fulfilments long after Nostradamus's death, and the one question that we must now ask about them is: Does astrology in any way explain the success of the Centuries as a set of prophecies? We must answer this question from internal evidence alone. The fact that Nostradamus may or may not have been a good astrologer does not answer the question whether or not astrology was behind the apparent success of the Centuries as a series of predictions of world events. We must examine the Centuries themselves to discover how many quatrains have patent astrological references. If these are a few, we must deduce that the influence of astrology on them is small.

This may run the risk of understatement, but we can 'hedge' against the effect of this risk on our conclusions by including all patent astrological references except those where Nostradamus provides clear clues that though they seem to be astrological they are not, though most of these do not provide astrological time-references (i.e., clues about the time of fulfilment). Thus, the list of references that appears below is *inclusive* rather than *exclusive*, though my choice may *seem* arbitrary to some.

I began with all possible references to, or hints at, the names of planets and constellations. I excluded references to the sun, where they are clearly not astrological (e.g., 'City of the Sun'); then I eliminated references to eagles, lions and cocks (with a few exceptions), even though 'lion' may be Leo, a constellation.[3] References to Neptune were excluded where they are patently mythological, not astrological. One reference to Capricorn and one to Saturn have been excluded for the same reason.

Then came a few hard choices, about which some readers will disagree, but which make little difference to the statistical analysis that follows. There are only three. Century V:25 *looks* astrological (in content), and both McCann and Cheetham regard it as such; but Mars is clearly a description of 'the Arab prince', and Venus (Venice) and Lyon (Lyons) are *place names,* so I risked excluding it. Century VI:25 (line 1) is clearly (a) a duplication of the reference in VI:24, and (b)

---

[3] See, for example, Centuries I:31, with its Eagle, Cock, Moon, Lion and Sun.

symbolic, i.e., a reference to the 'young red king'. The third was simply a reference to 'revolutions' of Mars, i.e., periods of about two years.

Century	Astrological Quatrains	Frequency
I	15 16 25 28 48 49 50 51 52 54 56 62 80 83 87	15
II	5 28 35 41 43 46 48 65 78 81 88 90 98	13
III	3 16 46 57 77 92 96	7
IV	25 28 29 30 31 33 50 67 68 84 86 96 97	13
V	11 14 23 24* 53 61 62 66 70 72 87 91	12
VI	4 6 17 24* 35 50 52 98 100	9
VII	(Incomplete Century, but no astrological quatrains)	0
VIII	2 29 46 48 49 85 90	7
IX	12 19 55 72 73	5
X	8 28 50 67	4
	Total number of 'apparent' astrological quatrains	85

Note. Bunched references are underlined.
★ For exclusion of V:25 and VI:25, see the text.

None of the three references mentioned above is patently predictive of a later event. This does not seem to be of any significance at first, but let us look at the end column of the preceding table and present it in a form known to statisticians as a histogram.

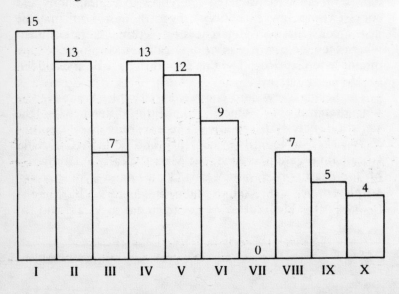

In this diagram, the number of occurrences corresponds to the size (height) of the bar, and the number of the Century concerned is printed beneath each component. Apart from two exceptions, i.e., 7 occurrences in Century III and no occurrences in Century VII (an incomplete Century), the frequency of astrological occurrences gets smaller and smaller as we progress through the book.

The second important point to notice is that 52 of the 85 stanzas with astrological references are 'bunched' or 'clustered', at intervals of less than five stanzas between one component and the next, and that a number of these items in each cluster are next to each other. Given that there are 942 extant quatrains and only 85 astrological stanzas, this set of 52 quatrains in 18 clusters is significantly large — about 61 per cent. It conforms with my theory, propounded earlier, that although the quatrains are not arranged in any known historical order, nonetheless, they have been arranged by Nostradamus, either consciously or unconsciously, in topical order, and that most of the astrological quatrains thus appear together.

A second explanation of this strange clustering of astrological stanzas may be that it is the result of Nostradamus's attitude to astrology. As we have seen, it was not his primary profession, though he was a court astrologer and 'rationalized' his position, possibly by reference to biblical precedents such as Daniel and Joseph. Yet, his biblical knowledge and scientific training led him to realize that most of the astrologers of his day were charlatans.

At first this seems improbable, but two more questions should be considered. First of all, why are so many of the astrological quatrains clustered? Was it because Nostradamus had an 'addiction' to making astrological references, and yet an addiction that he wanted to transcend? Look at the table. The first addictive streak seems to be overcome at the end of Century II, and there are relatively few astrological references in Century III. Then the whole process starts up again for a while, but by the end of Century VI the seer seems to have had enough. Indeed, the final reference in Century VI is his incantation against astrologers:

> Let the profane, unknowing crowd keep away
> — let all astrologers, simpletons and barbarians
> stay far off . . .

It is as though he feared two things: that he would be
ridiculed and ignored by the intellectuals of his day, who
were beginning to question the scientific value of astrology,
and that he would be criticized by the astrologers of the time
for not conforming with their methods, some of which were
questionable and some positively unscrupulous. Astrology
remained respectable in the very highest circles until its
divorce from astronomy over two centuries later, and even
today it has its devotees who can produce masses of statistical
evidence in its favour. But, as in the case of Nostradamus's
quatrains, the masses of apparently detailed prediction or
character-judgements in its favour may or may not prove its
total reliability or scientific value. Far less would any modern
research into astrology and its reliability prove that the
astrologers of Nostradamus's times were to be relied on. We
must remember that Nostradamus was a contemporary of
Paracelsus, who was calling much of medieval philosophy
based on astrological premises into question. Only three
more clusters of astrological quatrains occur after this point,
and these are small ones.

The second question is this. Why, after the denunciation of
astrologers at the end of Century VI, does Nostradamus
leave the seventh Century completely free of astrological
allusions? We can speculate endlessly about Century VII, and
it is even possible that Nostradamus deliberately decided to
keep us guessing. It is, after all, the incomplete Century,
having only 42 quatrains. Did he start to write astrological
quatrains at the beginning of VII:43, and then decide to tear
up that portion of the manuscript and destroy it?

This brief examination of Nostradamus's love-hate relationship with astrology may already have revealed the
answer to one mystery that has puzzled Nostradamus's
commentators for over four centuries — the real reason for
the incompleteness of Century VII. It is not the only reason.
Another is that there are proportionately less interpreted
stanzas in Century VII, compared with the other Centuries.
Nostradamus's ability was therefore at its low ebb when he
wrote it, and later stanzas may have contained immediate
predictions that subsequently proved untrue.

Finding the real reason for what may have been purely
accidental is, to some extent, a speculative process, very
much like speculating about the missing twelve verses at the

end of Mark's Gospel in some manuscripts, and giving evidence for or against the theory that Mark's Gospel was one of the earliest 'codices' (or bound books) that happened to lose its last page at an early stage. This type of explanation (i.e., an accident) may explain why material is missing in Mark's Gospel, but it does not explain why material is missing two-thirds of the way through a book. Given that it was not an accident, astrology seems the most likely reason for the incompleteness of Century VII, which comes immediately after the denunciation of astrologers, and this may also explain why the remaining stanzas contain no astrological references.

It seems, therefore, that astrology has little, if anything, to offer in explanation of the accuracy of Nostradamus's predictions, because only 85 out of 942 of them (that is about 9 per cent) have even the slightest reference to anything astrological. But not all Nostradamus's quatrains contain apparently accurate predictions or even identification with subsequent events. By examining the references to identifiable subsequent events, some of them quite inaccurate, in the quotations from the Centuries in Chapters 1 to 5 of this book, the number of 'explained' stanzas is 208. This is only an estimate of the correct number of identifiable or fulfilled predictions in the Centuries, but the detail in others is questionable, and it can be regarded as a safe figure; if it were larger, the case against my extension of proof would be even weaker.

It could be argued that, although 85 stanzas is only 9 per cent of all Nostradamus's 942 stanzas, they may represent a high proportion of the predictions that have been identified with subsequent events. For example, if all 208 'fulfilled' stanzas could be explained by astrology, the case would be unquestionable; but if all 85 references were found among the 208 stanzas alleged to have been fulfilled, there would be some reason for believing that astrology was 40 per cent responsible for their success. There would still be significant evidence to show the credibility of the popular misconception that Nostradamus obtained his information about future events from astrology.

To overcome such an objection one has to prepare what is known in statistics as a two-way table, showing how many of the 'fulfilled' stanzas are astrological, and how many of them are not. If my 208 references in Chapters 1 to 5 are counted and classified, the table looks something like this.

Astrology and Assumed Fulfilment

A Cross-Classification of Nostradamus's Quatrains

	Astrological	Non-Astrological	Totals	Percentages
Identifiable Fulfilments	17 (18.77)	191 (189.23)	208	22.08
Unidentified or of doubted Interpretation	68 (66.23)	666 (667.77)	734	77.92
Totals	85	857	942	
Percentages	9	91		100.00

These findings are almost like a statistician's dream: they are so near to being proportionate that one could rule out completely any question of astrology providing a more than proportionate number of explained (or identified, or fulfilled) stanzas. If one uses the overall percentages to calculate the expected proportions of occurrences, and compares them with actual numbers, the differences are so small that they can almost be ignored.

The difference is 1.77 in each case and has to be reduced for statistical purposes, using a correction known as Yates' correction[4] to carry out statistical testing for significance in what is known as the chi-squared test.[5] This test provides a value that is only a very small fraction of that required for proving a significant difference of any kind. In this case, the result is so near to being proportionate (and therefore to having occurred by chance) that statistical testing is hardly necessary. The table clearly shows that there can be no positive relationship between astrological quatrains and

---

[4] See D. Pitt Francis and C. A. O'Muircheartaigh, *Statistics: A Dictionary of Terms and Ideas* (Arrow, 1981), pp. 286-7 for a full explanation.

[5] Ibid., pp. 50-1 for a full explanation. I assume 942 quatrains; J. C. de Fontbrune includes a few apocryphal ones and makes 965.

supposed identifiable fulfilments.

We can carry the argument one stage further. Though astrology could only have contributed, at most, 1.8 per cent (or 0.018) to explaining Nostradamus's predictions (that is 17/942), we find, when we examine these remaining cases, that astrology has hardly any contribution to make to explaining Nostradamus's assumed predictive ability.

Let us examine these cases. The first four are more biblical in content than astrological. The first of these[6] has a doubtful reference to *Mars*, which is the only astrological content of the stanza, and is simply symbolic; but it also has a clear reference to 'seventy times' blood-shedding, which is clearly biblical.[7] The second[8] refers to a scythe, assumed by astrologers to be *Saturn*; but as pointed out in the previous chapter, this need not be the case.[9] The Archer is an obscure detail, but there is a reference to a biblical sequence,[10] the four horsemen of the Apocalypse. The third[11] simply refers to the 'reign' of the moon and is a doubtful reference to astrology, which does not help in explaining the stanza but has a relevance to the basis of the millenarian theory[12] based on the Bible's date for the Creation. Incidentally, this quatrain reveals a link between biblical interpretations and astrology in the belief of early biblical scholars that despite the Bible's denunciations of astrologers, there is a 'superior' version of astrology governing all 'Divine' times. This view was explored at length by Dr H. Grattan Guinness over a century ago.[13]

---

[6] Centuries I:15.

[7] Genesis 4:24 and Daniel chapter 9.

[8] Centuries I:16.

[9] I have already suggested that Estang could mean other things, for example, the fact that the recent French leader Giscard d'Estang, or the Scythian peoples, e.g. the Russians, who currently use a scythe in their flag.

[10] Revelation 6:1-8.

[11] Centuries I:48.

[12] The view of 7000 years' relevant human history, based on Revelation 20:2 ff. as a Sabbath. I have discussed this view earlier in this book.

[13] See H. Grattan Guinness, *The Approaching End of the Age* (Hodder and Stoughton, 1878), which specifies that biblical 'times' involve planetary cycles as well as calendar years.

The fourth passage[14] is the most doubtful of all the astrological references because it is assumed that by 'aquatic triplicate' Nostradamus meant the three water signs of the Zodiac. I have already shown that Nostradamus must have meant something entirely different (the sea and the two rivers), by comparison with a later quatrain. We can safely delete it from our list of astrological references. Again, it has a biblical reference, being based on one of Daniel's prophecies that medieval and sixteenth-century biblical expositors interpreted to mean Antichrist.[15]

The fifth[16] of our seventeen cases is quite different. It is clearly astrological and refers probably to the conjunction of Jupiter and Saturn in the constellation Aries. The prediction is vague. It says that 'great changes' will occur. The interval between conjunctions of Jupiter and Saturn in Aries is usually less than a century, but Nostradamus wrongly specifies a 'long century'. I listed it as an 'explained' predicition, because Cheetham uses it as a prediction of the War of Spanish Succession (1702) and the French Revolution (1789-1802). But there were no spectacular changes following either of the conjunctions, so that even Cheetham looks forward to a possible future fulfilment (1995). The reference, then, though clearly astrological, may not be 'predictive' in the sense of having a subsequent fulfiliment. It can therefore be safely deleted from our list.

The ground is thus sterile so far. The sixth case[17] is the reference to Diana, with which I have dealt fully earlier. I have only included it in my list of astrological references because Diana may be taken to mean the moon. But all expositors of Nostradamus assume that, because of its context, it is simply a cipher for Monday. Given some ingenuity it could be read as a proper name and as a prediction concerning the present royal family, as I have shown earlier. It is therefore not explicable as an astrological reference and must be excluded from our original list of 17 possible references in this category.

The seventh reference[18] was included simply because it

---

[14] Centuries I:50.
[15] Daniel 11:36-40 and particularly 7:25.
[16] Centuries I:51.
[17] Centuries II:28.
[18] Centuries II:46.

mentions 'the great cycle of centuries' and a comet. Astrology is only loosely implied in the phrase 'great cycle of centuries': it may be a millenarian detail (i.e., a reference to the 7000-year history of mankind). With this in mind, the comet reference may also be biblical, based on the Apocalyptic picture of the dragon;[19] it may even be a crude attempt to describe the Second Coming.

We have to move to the next Century for the eighth of our references.[20] It is the famous Bastarnian stanza, which, if my theory is correct, motivated Hitler to invade Poland. I have already shown that, though the prediction was fulfilled through Loog's misinterpretation, it relies more on the Bible's sevenfold prophecies than on any astrological calculations. The only astrological reference in the stanza is the one word 'Aries': 'Aries fears for Bastarnian support'.

Here, as earlier, Aries is merely being used as a cipher, perhaps for some nation under its sign, or perhaps because of its assumed astrological characteristics. Even Loog's interpretation of the prediction misfired for the British monarchy neither changed, nor was destroyed in 1939, though Hitler 'role-played' some of its details. But even if it had been fulfilled in detail, the word 'Aries' in context would have added little to the explanation of its fulfilment. It should, like previous components of our list, be deleted.

The ninth reference[21] is like the seventh:

> *The world approaches its last period*
> *— Saturn, again, will be late returning*

This is a reference to the end of mankind's history, and as such is possibly millenarian, displaying the characteristics of a view of biblical interpretation that I described earlier.[13] Astrology does not explain any supposed fulfilment.

At the end of this Century is the tenth reference,[22] which does specify an exact time. The events will occur when Saturn is in Leo on 13 February. An assassination will take place involving the 'leader from Fossano'. I have shown

---

[19] Revelation 12:1-4.
[20] Centuries III:57.
[21] Centuries III:92.
[22] Centuries III:96.

earlier than the picture of the assassination is not a completely accurate one, and that the probability of some assassination taking place somewhere under the conditions mentioned, is not too small for the event to have happened by chance. We are not even sure that the person behind the assassination did not know of the prediction and make use of it. Further, Ephemeris tables show that Saturn was not in Leo when the incident occurred and that the description is best understood symbolically.

The eleventh reference[23] comes nearly a Century later and simply uses the word 'Venus', thereby giving an impression of being astrological in type. It is taken by most commentators on Nostradamus in recent times as a World War II prediction, in which case 'Venus' is assumed to mean 'Venice'. It is, in any case, a cipher for a place-name, and even if the stanza were a genuine World War II prediction, astrology would not explain its predictive quality. This case has again to be deleted from our list of clear astrological references.

The twelfth of our seventeen references[24] is also a cipher. Though for Nostradamus, it may have been a hit-and-miss attempt to predict an event involving the Tudor succession, most commentators match it with the period of William and Mary over a century later. Whether it has been fulfilled or not, the astrology in the stanza is purely poetic and does not add to its predictive quality. Britain is simply described as the 'Kingdom of the Balance' (i.e., Libra), though this is not a normal cipher for Britain in astrological writings, and Nostradamus may have been alluding to some other European kingdom.

The thirteenth and fourteenth references are in Century V and are bunched close together. In the first,[25] there are two planetary allusions, but again are simply ciphers for describing places or people. They are (a) 'those of the Sun'; and (b) 'the people of Venus'. The first cannot be taken literally, and obviously Nostradamus is describing a nation. Because this stanza was used during World War II for propaganda purposes, Cheetham[26] suggests that the phrase

[23] Centuries IV:6b.
[24] Centuries IV:96.
[25] Centuries V:11.
[26] Cheetham, *Nostradamus*, p. 212.

may mean the Japanese. The second cipher is a pun, as elsewhere in Nostradamus's writings, and is only superficially astrological. Venus means Venice and therefore Italy; it is only interpretation in this century that relates the prediction to World War II. At one time, it could have been assumed to have a literal meaning, but Venus is now known to be uninhabitable.

The fourteenth reference[27] is clearly astrological and needs to be retained in our list, for it refers to astrological time intervals: 'Saturn and Mars in Leo'. There is an interpretation that assumes that Nostradamus had the Napoleonic (Peninsular) War in mind, though Saturn and Mars have been together in Leo several times in the intervening centuries, and the details of the stanza are so vague that there could have been several 'fulfilments'. But we shall retain it in our list as a case where astrological prediction could have been a reason for apparent fulfilment. So, of this pair, one is to be deleted and one remains.

We move to the fifteenth reference, which is in Century V[28] and is another use of 'Venus' as a cipher. In context, it does not this time refer to Venice but to promiscuity in a French court, based, as I have suggested earlier, on a 'daystar' reference in the Bible.[29] It can clearly be deleted from our list.

Now comes a gap of two Centuries before another possibly successful astrological prediction, for none of those in Century VI can be regarded as successful, and at the end of this Century Nostradamus denounces astrologers, so that Century VII contains no astrological references whatsoever. There are only two more, one in Century VIII and one in Century IX. In neither of these two remaining cases can astrology be given credit for the assumed predictive values of the quatrain.

The first[30] simply uses Mars as a cipher for war, as the Cock in the stanza may, perhaps, mean France and the Eagle the United States or the Austro-German nation. Although it is a papal prediction that Cheetham[31] associates with the

---

[27] Centuries V:14.
[28] Centuries V:72.
[29] Isaiah 14:12.
[30] Centuries VIII:46.
[31] Cheetham, *Nostradamus*, p. 293.

Kennedy brothers, it is now not capable of fulfilment in the way that she interprets it. Even if it were, the descriptor Mars would not indicate the context of its fulfilment or the time when it would occur.

The second, and last, of our seventeen references, in Century IX,[32] looks a little more promising, for it specifies a time of plague when Mercury, Mars and Jupiter would be in conjunction. This has happened on several occasions, as have plagues; so the fact that they once coincided at the end of World War I (1917/18) may not necessarily reflect the accuracy of Nostradamus's astrology. But let us leave it in our list, thus reducing our seventeen cases to only three.

We do not have to examine the remaining 68 astrological references, for we are only concerned with cases in which astrology could possibly have helped or supported the predictive success of Nostradamus's work. Our list has been reduced to three. To summarize the procedure: cases 10, 14 and 17 of our list remain, though even these are still a little doubtful. Cases 5, 7, 9 and 13 may be concerned with future events or be millenarian in content, and so are still potentially inaccurate; they can therefore be moved downwards in the table. Cases 1, 2, 6, 8, 11, 12, 15 and 16 have been identified with events by interpreters, but the astrological details are simply descriptive and do not support the prediction in any way. The remaining two cases, 3 and 4, are neither necessarily identifiable with specific events nor astrology-supported. So the table can now be revised.

Astrology and Assumed Fulfilment

A revised cross-classification of Nostradamus's quatrains

	Potential Astrological Fulfilment-time	Other	Totals	Percentages
Identifiable fulfilments	3 (16.08)	199 (185.88)	202	21.44
Unidentified or of unclear interpretation	72 (58.92)	668 (681.12)	740	78.56
Totals	75	867	942	
Percentages	7.96	92.04		100.00

This revised table has a kind of two-tail explanation that complements the earlier table. The earlier table showed that it was wrong to suppose that astrology could explain a disproportionately *large* number of 'fulfilled' quatrains. This table shows that astrology in fact, explains a disproportionately *small* number of 'fulfilled' quatrains, and that, in all, there are only *three* (less than 0.04 per cent) of such cases. Further, readers who are acquainted with statistics may like to try the chi-squared test (with Yates' correction) to prove that the number of fulfilled quatrains relying on astrology is disproportionately small. I am avoiding this technicality because many of the remaining 65 of the assumed astrological stanzas can be moved across into the bottom right category of the table, thus reducing the overall number of astrological stanzas even further. But as some of these have a potential future fulfilment, and are vague in their details, they cannot be examined critically and re-classified accordingly.

It is sufficient to say that a large number of the 72 quatrains in the bottom left category of the table would have to be shifted across and added to the 668 in the bottom right category, but we cannot do so until the end of the time, because those in the 'unclear/other' category may also have to be moved elsewhere. Of only *three* of Nostradamus's 942 quatrains can it be said that astrology could have enhanced their predictive qualities by prescribing the time of fulfilment. Two of these are rather vague, and the other could involve coincidence. These conclusions do not denigrate astrology as a predictive science: they mean that somehow Nostradamus transcended it, and that his predictive qualities, if any, were *in spite of, not because of* his knowledge of astrology. We can remove astrology from our list of explanatory variables.

Six Contributing Factors

We can now return to reconsider the explanatory variables largely adopted in this book. First, Nostradamus sensibly expected events to happen in his day; when they did not, they were open to reinterpretation. Secondly, Nostradamus used biblical prophecy and millenarian theories; thirdly, he possessed some scientific (science-fiction) trail-blazing quality which led, among other things, to a fourth variable, participant fulfilment. Interpreters may have made more out of his stanzas than he intended, so there is no clear distinction between the first (X_1) and fifth (X_5) factor; and there is a possible sixth — a bizarre, psychic, unexplained factor. Let us tabulate his early fulfilments, using the material from Chapter Two.

The statistical appendices at the end of the book should be read in conjunction with the tables that follow, *before* taking into account amendments and suggestions in Chapters 7 and 8. The appendices, in other words, are based on these tables and *not* on *later* refinements and explanations.

AN ANALYSIS OF EXPLANATORY VARIABLES
(1) Predictions of the French Monarchy — Part A

Stanza		Comment Details	X_1	X_2	X_3	X_4	X_5	X_6
Century	Quatrain	Details of the quatrain together with its usual interpretation/fulfilment	Reasonable contemporary expectation — reinterpreted	Biblical prophecy or reliance on a biblical model	Scientific insight	Participant fulfilment	Interpretational fudge	Unexplained fulfilment with one inaccuracy or more
		Notes This first table is about the French monarchy. Many predictions use a biblical model, though some are explained by events happening to fill details of predictions in a way that Nostradamus would not have imagined.						
VI	75	Gaspard leaves the fleet for a higher command, but seven years afterwards heads the Huguenots.	X	X		X		?(X)
VI	63	Catherine in mourning for seven years.	X	X		X		
IX	7	Nostradamus's bones, based on Joseph's bones, and Nostradamus's role-playing.	X	X		X		
III	39	Seven reduced to three, and a biblical seven-branch candlestick analogy.	X	X		X	(X)	
VI	11	Explanation of seven-branch lamp-stand similar to III:39.	X	X		X	(X)	
II	18	A tempest and battle against Henri III. Brissac was told that he was *not* a man of 'earth and sea'.				X	X	
V	67	Inaccurate because of the description of 'throat wound'; the 'head of Perousse' is assumed to be the Pope; 'naked' is based on a text in Revelation 16.		X			X	
I	10	Simple description of the burial of the Valois kings.	X	X		X	X	
X	39	Inaccurate about the two islands in discord, but reasonably expected. One line may be fully predictive.	X			X	X	

Predictions of the French Monarchy — Part B

Stanza	Comment statement, including details and assumed meaning	X_1	X_2	X_3	X_4	X_5	X_6
IV:47	Massacre of Huguenots under Charles IX.	X	X				
III:31	Wrong prophecy of a battle by the river bank of Araxes, later applied by misinterpretation to Lepanto.	X				X	
VIII:38	The King of Blois assumed to be Henri III.	X				X	
VIII:52	Another assumed prophecy of the King of Blois to be read as Henri III.	X				X	
X:44	Ambiguous prediction about the League, which could be Catholic 'holy' league or a Calvinist League.	X	X			X	
V:72	There was nothing voluptuous (i.e. associated with Venus) about the Edict of Poitiers, which granted toleration to Huguenots.	X	X			X	
X:59	Inaccurate prediction of the betrayal of Lyons to the Huguenots.	X				X	
III:41	The death of Condé. Sufficient accuracy to be unexplained.	X	X				X
IX:38	Aemathein prediction of a war involving Louis XIV and La Rochelle, but depends on the meaning of 'Aemathein'.		X			X	
I:8	Prediction of Henri IV's siege of Paris, but depends on the meaning of 'Great Hadrian' in context.	X	X			X	

The table is continued below. At this stage it is evident that no 'fulfilled' prediction can be assigned to one complete category. In explaining the predictions relating to the French monarchy I have excluded participant fulfilment where this is improbable because of the religious beliefs of the people concerned. For example, some Protestants would have had little faith in the prophecies of Nostradamus, and prophecies of scientific achievements are also absent among those that are fulfilled during this period.

Predictions of the French Monarchy — Part C

Stanza	Comment statement, including details and assumed meaning	X_1	X_2	X_3	X_4	X_5	X_6
I:9	The siege of Paris in 1589/90, followed by details of the siege of Malta in 1565, also somewhat inaccurately written.	X				X	
II:55	The conversion of Henri IV to Catholic teaching, 'seeing what is necessary' (?).	X			X	X	X
X:38	Henri as 'light of love', but with an uncharacteristic interpretation of Hadrian.					X	
IX:39	Yet another cipher for Henri IV.					X	
X:45	A reasonable expectation of Nostradamus about Henri IV and the Peace of Cambrai, later misinterpreted as the affair of Henri with the wife of a later governor of Cambrai.	X				X	
X:18	Henri IV as 'son of Hamon': unlikely participant fulfilment.					X	X
IX:45	Largely a 'failed' prophecy, but misinterpreted. Henri IV did not make great Italian conquests.	X				X	
VIII:71	A non-existent edict against astrology claimed by interpreters. Prediction failed.	X				X	
III:20	Expulsion of the Jews from Spain — inaccurate detail.	X	X			X	
III:11	Assassination of Henri IV with inaccurate details.	X				X	
IX:36	Assassination of a king, thought to be Henri IV, around Easter; Henri IV was killed on 14 May 1610.	X	X			X	

The picture is now being built up. Most of the successful predictions concerning the French monarchy could be attributed to the reasonable expectations of Nostradamus, particularly with his biblical model of a decadent 'Babylon' and the vague style in which he predicted. The data are difficult to treat, for where the predictive quality of a stanza may be attributed to more than one factor, it seems unreasonable to apportion the credit for its success between the factors. Because of lack of real evidence, it is best to give each factor equal weight. We shall, of course, be considering the 'Babylon' model in Chapter Seven.

Predictions of the French Monarchy — Part D

Stanza	Comment statement, including details and assumed meaning	X_1	X_2	X_3	X_4	X_5	X_6
IX:18	The only Louis XIII prediction. Speculates about current events; Montmorency and Flanders.	X			X	X	?(X)
VIII:68	Richelieu dispositioned by Cinq Mars. An extremely accurate and detailed prophecy.						X
X:58	Louis XIV as Aemathien makes war on Marseilles by mis-interpreting Phossens.				X	X	
X:7	Louis XIV as Aemathien again attempts conquest, while England has tax problems.				X	X	
IX:93	Louis XIV as Aemathien misread "battra" as 'bastira' and built the Languedoc Canal.				X	X	
III:87	French fleet disaster near Corsica. A likely event.	X				X	
IV:2	An invasion of Spain by French king. Louis XIV would have wanted to fulfil this prophecy.				X	X	
IX:64	As Aemathion, Louis XIV would have wanted to cross the Pyrenees into Spain.				X	X	
III:15	Though very little of Nostradamus's predictions have been applied to Louis XV, this is inexplicably accurate: 'Through death a child will rule over France'.						X

Stanza	Comment statement, including details and assumed meaning	X_1	X_2	X_3	X_4	X_5	X_6
IX:27	The prediction is applied to Dubois (de bois) by Laver and therefore the reign of Louis XV; but Cheetham applies it to the French Revolution.					X	
V:38	An inaccurate prediction, for the Sallic Law did not fail with Louis XV and Louis XVI, except in an obscure sense. Enhanced only by interpreting the stanza in one way.					X	

The reasons for assigning factors in each case will be apparent on re-reading Chapter Two. Some X's are doubtful, but they are better included than excluded. This table of the first two centuries or so from Nostradamus's times onwards (with a few exceptions relating to England) shows that, initially, contemporary expectations by Nostradamus (with a possible biblical/historical model) played a major part in fulfilment, though the Valois kings and Catherine were sympathetic to him and may have attempted to fulfil some of his prophecies themselves. Later, however, reasonable contemporary expectations cannot explain certain details, but Louis XIV was powerful enough to have used the predictions (or his advisors) to his own ends. The following table gives an approximate picture over some two hundred years.

Predictions of French Monarchy and its times	Assumed 16th-century fulfilments	Assumed 17th-century fulfilments	Assumed 18th-century fulfilments
X_1 Reasonable expectations during Nostradamus's time	20	6	—
X_2 Use of a biblical model — history repeating itself	12	3	—
X_3 Scientific insight	—	—	—
X_4 Participant fulfilment	9	4	2
X_5 Interpretational fudge	20	10	4
X_6 Unexplained hardcore	4	2	1
Totals	65	25	7

Side-totals for each variable are not shown because they will
have to be adjusted later. Some of the material assumed to
have been fulfilled by Henri IV and Louis XIV spans two
centuries, so that the effects of participant fulfilment appear
less clear by being placed in two categories. It is safe to say,
however, that the bulk of Nostradamus's assumed fulfilments result from quatrains written so obscurely that they
could either be flexed ('fudged') by interpreters to fit
particular events after Nostradamus's time, or actually
role-played by someone like Louis XIV. The rest derive from
Nostradamus's expectations based on a biblical model of a
decadent dynasty.

Let us now move to his 'revolutionary' predictions,
remembering that they reflect Jesus's Olivet prophecy; that
wars and revolutions will continue intermittently throughout
human history.[33]

AN ANALYSIS OF EXPLANATORY VARIABLES
(2) Predictions of the Revolutions — Part A

Stanza		Comment, including details and assumed meaning	X_1	X_2	X_3	X_4	X_5	X_6
Century	Quatrain	*Details of the quatrain together with its usual interpretation/fulfilment* Notes Many of the quatrains in this section have a biblical-style 'woe' (= disaster) flavour. There is a reasonably high proportion of 'fulfilments' due to 'fudged' interpretation and some participant fulfilment in the case of Napoleon and his successors.	Reasonable contemporary expectation — reinterpreted	Biblical prophecy or reliance on a biblical model	Scientific insight	Participant fulfilment	Interpretational fudge	Unexplained fulfilment with one inaccuracy or more
X:7		'Wine and Salt' and Charles I. This has been included in the previous table.						
IX:49		Another 'wine and salt' stanza with much better insight.					X	X
X:40		Interpreted twice of Charles I but later of the abdication of Edward VIII (Lonole).	X				X	
X:22		This stanza has also been applied to Charles I and Edward VIII. The chance of fulfilment increases with time.	X				X	

[33] Matthew 24:6–8.

Stanza	Comment, including details and assumed meaning	X_1	X_2	X_3	X_4	X_5	X_6
III: 80	Could be applied to Cromwell, Charles II, or later old and young pretenders.	X				X	
VIII:76	Prediction of Cromwell with three incorrect details, 'strained' to match events.	X				X	X
III:81	Obscure reference to Pontefract may be disregarded. It was one of many similar cities.					X	
VIII:56	The reference to D.nebro is difficult to explain.					X	X
II:68	This could refer to almost any threatened invasion of England.	X				X	
II:67	Description of William of Orange as the 'blonde one'.					X	
VIII:58	James II and William of Orange.					X	
VIII:40	Misinterpretation of a contemporary warning about Toulouse, to fit the events of James II's time (Taur).	X				X	
II:51	The fire of London 1666. Some perceptiveness, but not as much as commonly held, because of mistakes of detail.					X	X

Predictions of Revolutions — Part B

Stanza	Comment statement, including details and assumed meaning	X_1	X_2	X_3	X_4	X_5	X_6
II:53	Good with one inaccurate statement. The Great Plague.	X				X	X
IV:89	Some perception, but inaccurate middle lines — London 1689/90.					X	?(X)
IV:96	Probably about Elizabeth I but hopelessly inaccurate about William III and Mary.	X				X	
III:57	Very vague about British change. Later used by Hitler.	X	X		X	X	
X:100	Very vague but depends on apocalyptic expections (300 years).	X	X			X	
I:53	Probably an expectation of Antichrist, misapplied to the French Revolution.	X	X			X	
I:3	The only French Revolution context elsewhere applies to cardinals (reds) and Church.		X			X	
I:14	No more applicable to French Revolution than present Polish Solidarity struggles.	X	X			X	
II:12	An Antichrist prediction applied to French Revolution.	X	X			X	
VI:23	Taken from John's Apocalypse but 'fits' French Revolution.	X	X			X	
IX:20	The most remarkable of the quatrains. Difficult to fulfil willingly in detail. The 'Varennes' stanza.		X			X	X
IX:23	Clear expectations ('roof falls on childs head') were not fulfilled.					X	
IX:22	Louis XVI's imprisonment but with inaccurate detail.	X	X			X	?(X)

Stanza	Comment statement, including details and assumed meaning	X_1	X_2	X_3	X_4	X_5	X_6
IX:34	Only two amazing details. Contemporary expectations and some clear inaccuracies.	X				X	?(X)
IX:77	Some perceptiveness of collapse of monarchy, but events did not occur as foretold.	X				X	?(X)
IX:51	Could be French Revolution, or communism in Poland. Depends on meanings of 'red ones'.	X	X			X	
I:57	Only applied to French Revolution, by ingeniously interpreting 'milk and honey'.	X	X			X	

Predictions of Revolutions — Part C

Stanza	Comment statement, including details and assumed meaning	X_1	X_2	X_3	X_4	X_5	X_6
III:59	France would hardly be a 'barbarian empire'.		?(X)			X	
V:33	Amazingly accurate description of atrocities in the period.						X
VI:92	Little real reference to the execution of Louis XVI.					X	
VIII:19	Variously interpreted. 'Cappe' can mean different things.	X				X	
VIII:80	Great red one. Betrayal of Louis XVI. Vague predictions.	X	X			X	
X:17	Marie Antoinette in prison.						X
X:43	The necklace affair.					X	
III:35	Antichrist prediction applied later to Napoleon.	X	X			X	
X:86	Biblical prediction of Cyrus's conquest of Babylon reapplied to Paris, misapplied to Napoleon.	X	X			X	
I:98	Another use of the biblical model of history repeating itself. Alexander=Napoleon	X	X			X	

Stanza	Comment statement, including details and assumed meaning	X_1	X_2	X_3	X_4	X_5	X_6
II:29	Prediction of an eastern Antichrist reapplied to 'Babylon' then to Napoleon.	X	X			X	
I:60	Nostradamus taking pot-luck with probabilities (see above). Napoleon did come from south.	X				X	
I:76	A twist (barbaric name) by interpreters. Napoleon does *not* mean 'Yes, destroyer'.	X				X	
IV:54	This may even be a case of participant fulfilment. Other French kings had foreign ladies.	X			X	X	
I:88	'Shaven head' variously applied to Cromwell and Napoleon.					X	
V:30	A vague reference to Pontiff.					X	
VIII:46	Vaguely applied to Napoleon's Pope and to modern times.					X	
V:57	Montgolfier and the hot air balloon, and Sext (= Sixtus?).	X		X			X
II:97	The biblical, Babylonian model later misapplied to Lyons.	X	X			X	

Predictions of Revolutions — Part D

Stanza	Comment statement, including details and assumed meaning	X_1	X_2	X_3	X_4	X_5	X_6
II:99	A good pretext for Napoleon's invasion of Papal States.				X	X	
V:15	Another papal prediction which Napoleon fulfilled.	X	X		X	X	
I:4	Originally a prediction of an Antichrist-Pope, which Napoleon fulfilled. Short life participant. He was murdered.	X	X		X	X	

Stanza	Comment statement, including details and assumed meaning	X_1	X_2	X_3	X_4	X_5	X_6
III:37	Conscious fulfilment of the capture of Milan by Napoleon on two occasions.				X	X	
II:94	Distortion of biblical phrase re. Antichrist conquests. 'Shall not escape' (Napoleon).	X	X		X	X	
I:24	'Bird of prey' vague prediction.		?(X)			X	
V:14	Libyan prediction. Violent distortion of text and context.					X	
VIII:53	Vague reference to Boulogne wrested by interpreters.					X	
II:68 VIII:37	This pair of quatrains may refer either to Napoleon or time of Charles I (see Laver).					X X	
I:77	Greek mythology reference with some perceptiveness about Nelson's mortal wound.					X	X
IV:82	Unconvincing interpretation about retreat from Moscow.					X	
II:44	References to eagles are common in Nostradamus and can mean almost any nation.					X	
I:89	Haute-velle = Wellington is no more than a play on words.					X	
III:45	It needs ingenuity to apply the 'five strangers in temple' stanza to occupation of France.					X	
X:87	Nisse may mean Nice, where Louis XVIII was proclaimed. Antipolles *may be* antipodes.					X	
X:23	Antibe could mean Nice also, but quite indefinite.					X	
I:23	Why does a leopard represent Britain, not a lion?					X	
III:83	Most Bourbon kings were 'long-haired', thus prediction is vague.					X	

Predictions of Revolutions — Part E

Stanza	Comment statement, including details and assumed meaning	X_1	X_2	X_3	X_4	X_5	X_6
II:87	Vague reference to German prince, capable of several meanings.				X	X	
X:10	Another stanza capable of several interpretations.				X	X	
X:90	Reference capable of application to Louis XVIII or Napoleon.				X	X	
I:100	Vague reference to Italy applied to Louis XVIII.				(X)	X	
V:39	A similar case to above. An Italian reference applied to Louis XVIII by Laver.				(X)	X	
III:96	The famous Fossano reference involving the use of astrology Perceptive but with several flaws of detail.						X
VIII:42	Pun on Orleans; possible participant fulfilment by Louis-Philippe.					X	
VI:84 VIII:38 V:7 V:6	Possible interpretational 'fudge' but much could be explained by Louis-Philippe's possible self-identification with the Philip of the quatrains.		?(X)		X X X X	X X X X	
IX:89	The most obvious case of 'multiple' fulfilment because interpreters disagree over 'Ognion' — a French coin, Mehemet Ali, the new Republic or Napoleon.		X		X	X	
V:69	An inaccurate description of the French tricolour, but otherwise perceptive.					X	X
V:92	Nostradamus may have obtained his 17 years from a biblical model, but there is some perceptiveness.		X			X	?(X)

This is the longest series of tables in the book, because it
spans the whole period of revolutions, including a few earlier
ones in England, and contains the largest number of
identified predictions in Nostradamus's writings. Some
readers may have doubts, in individual cases, about the
categories of explanation. I have used brackets or question
marks or both where there are doubts about the factor
explaining the fulfilment of a given quatrain, and there is, in
any case, bound to be some subjectiveness about the 'weight'
of some of the factors. But the distribution of variables is,
despite everything, reasonably similar to that in the first
series of tables. If we adopt the method used earlier and
examine the differences between variables in fulfilments
ascribed to different centuries, we get the following results.

Predictions of Revolutions	*Assumed times of fulfilments*			*Totals*
	17th-century	*18th-century*	*19th-century*	
X_1 Reasonable expectations during Nostradamus's time later re-interpreted	8	22	3	33
X_2 Use of a biblical model — history repeating itself	—	18	7	25
X_3 Scientific insight	—	1	—	1
X_4 Participant fulfilment	—	3	14	17
X_5 Interpretational fudge	15	31	31	77
X_6 Unexplained hardcore	6	7	4	17
Totals	29	82	59	170

This table shows a similar distribution to the table based on
Chapter Two, but some of the reasons are different. The
most common variables are still X_1 and X_5, but the character
of X_1 is now different. Many of those in the previous table
were events that Nostradamus could reasonably have
expected to occur in the immediate future. We are now well
beyond the time of Nostradamus, and the explanation
combines X_1 with X_5 in many cases. In other words,
Nostradamus expected an event to have happened in a given

way, but it did not occur. The event was obscurely described, and an interpreter later 'fudged' or 'flexed' the prediction to match a completely different event in another time period. These, together with other occurrences of X_5, such as those where Nostradamus is deliberately obscure and meets with an equally obscure interpretation to match a future set of events, account for 77/80, or over 96 per cent of fulfilments.

Nostradamus's use of the Bible is different in this set. Predictions based on his Babylonian model do not recur until the time of Napoleon, and there are no 'biblical model' predictions that can be assumed to apply to seventeenth-century England. Most are ascribed to the eighteenth century, based on Jesus's predictions of revolutions, 'wars and rumours of wars', but assumed by interpreters to apply to the French Revolution. Only one indicates scientific insight, and that may be a 'fluke' of interpretation. The most outstanding cases of participant fulfilment in this section relate to Napoleon Bonaparte, but some refer to his enemies and successors. There are a larger number of 'unexplained' predictions, but few of these are beyond question, and it must be remembered that with the passage of time, the probability of a fluke set of coincidences for an undated prophecy becomes greater. One of these outstanding fulfilments is astrological, but it is the only clear indication anywhere in the 942 quatrains that Nostradamus actually used astrology to predict an event that was fulfilled, though with some inaccuracy. The odds are very much in favour of contemporary expectations or Bible-based expectations that were fudged and distorted by interpreters to relate to events that happened very much later. But let us reserve judgement for a while, and analyze Chapter Four.

AN ANALYSIS OF EXPLANATORY VARIABLES
(3) Predictions leading to World War II — Part A

Stanza		Comment statement, including details and assumed meaning	X_1	X_2	X_3	X_4	X_5	X_6
Century	Quatrain	Details of the quatrain together with its usual interpretation/fulfilment	Reasonable contemporary expectation — reinterpreted	Biblical prophecy or reliance on a biblical model	Scientific insight	Participant fulfilment	Interpretational fudge	Unexplained fulfilment with one inaccuracy or more
		Notes This table summarizes Chapter Four of the present book, and includes the late nineteenth century, the yawning 'chasm' of apathy about Nostradamus, his revival after World War I *and* the use made by several interpreters of Nostradamus during World War II.						
VII:11		The 'unheeding child' stanza, interpreted differently by Laver and Cheetham.					X	
VI:6		A plague associated with a cluster in Cancer, wrongly interpreted to mean death of Pius XI.		?(X)			X	
II:1		The only quatrain applied to World War I, but not without considerable text distortion.					X	
VIII:80		A Bible-based revolution prediction of Antichrist, variously applied to French and Russian (1917) crises.		X			X	

Predictions leading to World War II — Part B

Stanza	Comment statement, including details and assumed meaning	X_1	X_2	X_3	X_4	X_5	X_6
IX:55	A prediction of post-war plague associated by interpreters with the end of World War I.		X			X	
III:57	The Bastarnian prediction again. Not included, because it appeared in the previous table.						
I:47	Not as ingenious a prediction of the League of Nations as is often thought.	X				X	
V:85	Another Nostradamus prediction aginst Swiss Calvinists later interpreted to mean the League of Nations (and its failure?).	X				X	
II:24	A prediction about Germany with Rhine and Hister (i.e., Danube) as its known boundaries, later 'adopted' by Hitler (Hister).	X			X	X	
IV:68	Another 'Hister' (i.e., Danube) prediction of Germany's assumed boundaries long before Nostradamus, 'borrowed' and enacted by Hitler.	X			X	X	
III:63	A Nostradamus prediction of Roman (Catholic) suffering under a 'Protestant' Antichrist, distorted to refer to Mussolini and Hitler.	X	X		X	X	
V:29	Clearly originally a prophecy about a bridge over the Danube, *not* about the Concordat, Mussolini, Hitler or the Papacy.	X	X			X	
VIII:31	The Selin prophecy, clearly originally Muslim, but wrongly taken to be Mussolini; Cheetham admits this weakness.	X	X			X	

Stanza	Comment statement, including details and assumed meaning	X_1	X_2	X_3	X_4	X_5	X_6
VIII:33	A curious attempt to make the 'un-worthy name' mean Mussolini.					X	
III:54	Exceptionally accurate quatrain about Franco's rise to power.						X
III:68	Not an accurate picture of the end of Mussolini, and Spain was never leaderless.					X	
IX:16	A remarkable prediction of Franco's rise to power in Spain, but with one flaw.						X
X:48	A flaw that led many wrongly to expect a Spanish Fascist invasion of Europe.					X	

Predictions leading to World War II — Part C

Stanza	Comment statement, including details and assumed meaning	X_1	X_2	X_3	X_4	X_5	X_6
X:40	The Lonole prediction. This was included in a previous table.						
X:22	This also was included in the previous table. Both it and X:40 may refer to Edward VIII.						
I:34	A weak prediction of Hitler as bird of prey. Laver admits this.		?(X)		X	X	
II:39/40	The 'school' house prediction and an apocalyptic stanza.		X X		X X	X X	
V:94	Assumed to relate to Hitler's con-quests, but Armenia was important in Nostradamus's time.	X			X	X	
VI:49	In context, a Bible-based verse of a crusade against Antichrist distorted to mean the swastika.	X	X		X	X	

Stanza	*Comment statement, including details and assumed meaning*	X_1	X_2	X_3	X_4	X_5	X_6
VI:51	Based on the story of Samson and about the monarchy, *not* Hitler, who was *not* 'saved by miracle'.	X	X			X	
I:18	Prediction of a Muslim invasion, not of an Italian invasion of Africa. A contemporary fear.	X				X	
II:16	Looks like an air-raid on Italy but 'Susa' and 'lightning in the skies' quotes the Bible?	X	X	?(X)	?(X)	X	
II:38	Simple reference to alliance between monarchs (Daniel 11:27) taken to mean Hitler and Mussolini without evidence.	X	X			X	
III:8	Cimbrian invasion of Spain, but the Germans never invaded Spain though they gave Franco considerable military support.	?(X)				X	
III:7	'fire from heaven' (= modern bombing of French fugitives in World War II), but the reference is clearly biblical, and no more than one of many meanings.	X	X	?(X)		X	
III:32	A distorted reference to a sepulchre, wrongly interpreted to mean the German (World War II) invasion of France.	X	X			X	
I:72	Originally a prediction of civil war between French cities, wrongly applied to the State of Vichy France.	X				X	
III:58	A real 'stretch' of genius by interpreters. Hitler never protected Poland and Hungary, though he would have argued to the contrary.	X	?(X)		X	X	

Predictions leading to World War II — Part D

Stanza	Comment statement, including details and assumed meaning	X_1	X_2	X_3	X_4	X_5	X_6
III:99	A prediction of pre-Bourbon Paris as Babylon, based on biblical model, reinterpreted to mean World War II France.	X	X			X	
IV:21	A Daniel prediction (11:21-23) distorted to refer to Petain and De Gaulle by interpreters.	X	X			X	
IV:61	French liberated towns, but mentioned out of context of allied liberation (? betrayal).	X				X	
VII:33 VII:34	A two-stanza prediction of an occupied France, based on Nostradamus's fear that it would be occupied by an Antichrist power, distorted to refer to World War II.	X X	X X		?(X) ?(X)	X X	
V:4	Symbolic prediction involving animals, and hence a very obscure reference, assumed to be to World War II.					X	
VIII:15	An Austro-Hungarian prediction wrongly applied to World War II.	X	?(X)			X	
IX:90	Another quatrain revealing Nostradamus's imperial (i.e., Austro-Hungarian) obsession, applied again to Hitler.	X	?(X)			X	
VIII:64	Something to do with the royal 'house of seven' children going to Britain, 'fudged' to mean wartime evacuation.	X	?(X)			X	
IX:100	May originally have been about the British (American) slave triangle of trade. Fudged to refer to Pearl Harbour.	X	X	X		X	
X:98	Prediction of a latter-day Antichrist (based on the Bible), applied to Nazi occupation.	X	X			X	

Stanza	Comment statement, including details and assumed meaning	X_1	X_2	X_3	X_4	X_5	X_6
V:11	A restricted prediction of the decline of Venice, distorted to mean the modern Japanese.	X	?(X)			X	
VI:7	Built on confused ideas of Antichrist associated with the Holy Roman and Turkish empires, *not* of the Norwegian resistance.	X	?(X)			X	
VI:31	A prediction disproved by history, when applied to Mussolini and the monarchy.	?(X)				X	
IV:15	A 'periscope' prediction about submarines and blockade, but obscure (World War II?).		?(X)	X	X	X	
II:6	Sodom and Gomorrah, taken by Nostradamus, and applied by interpreters to the bombing of Hiroshima and Nagasaki.		X	X	X	X	

We are now almost there. Apart from predictions that are assumed to have been fulfilled since World War II, and a few that speculate about events to happen at the end of this century, most of Nostradamus's well-known 'fulfilled' predictions can be seen to have resulted from one or other of our five factors, or a combination of them. Few are astoundingly detailed, and most of these contain an Achilles' heel, some inaccuracy that prevents them from being regarded as entirely reliable predictions. Most of the predictions in the previous table are assumed to have been 'fulfilled' during the present century; but two fulfilments occurred before that chasm of comparative lack of interest in Nostradamus's writings, so that, when tabulating the 'weights' of each factor on the apparent success of the prediction, we still require two columns, for the nineteenth and twentieth centuries respectively. The following table summarizes the position.

Predictions leading to World War II	Assumed times of fulfilments		Totals
	19th century	20th century	
X_1 Reasonable expectations during Nostradamus's time later re-interpreted	—	31	31
X_2 Use of a biblical model — history repeating itself	1	28	29
X_3 Scientific insight	—	5	5
X_4 Participant fulfilment	—	14	14
X_5 Interpretational fudge	2	43	45
X_6 Unexplained hardcore	—	2	2
Totals	3	123	126

Again, the two most popular variables are X_1 and X_5. A mainstream source of explanation of the stanzas is that many of them obscurely reflect events that were likely to happen in Nostradamus's own time. Some of these did not happen as expected, and so were 'fudged' (= 'flexed') by interpreters to apply to events in later times, in this case World War II, when interest in his writings had been revived, initially after World War I, then by the Nazis, Hitler and his opponents. Thus $31/50$ (62 per cent) of 'fulfilled' stanzas are explained by X_1, and $45/50$ (90 per cent) by X_5, and most of them by both. There is a correspondingly high ($29/50$) number of stanzas with a 'biblical' element, many of which reveal Nostradamus's expectations of Antichrist, later applied to Hitler. The number of stanzas reflecting scientific insight is still small ($5/50$) or 10 per cent. With this in mind, let us now analyze the quatrains quoted in Chapter Five.

AN ANALYSIS OF EXPLANATORY VARIABLES
(4) Predictions assumed to relate to Present Times — Part A

Century	Quatrain	Details of the quatrain together with its usual interpretation/fulfilment	X_1 Reasonable contemporary expectation — reinterpreted	X_2 Biblical prophecy or reliance on a biblical model	X_3 Scientific insight	X_4 Participant fulfilment	X_5 Interpretational fudge	X_6 Unexplained fulfilment with one inaccuracy or more
		Notes This final table classifies the quatrains assumed to relate to the late 20th century in the order given in Chapter Five. They may neither be (a) assumed fulfilled, or (b) expected to be fulfilled before the end of the present century.						
	II:24	A 'Hister' passage, already included in a previous table.						
	X:72	A reference to 1999, probably based on biblical ideas of 6000 years of human history.		X				
	I:51	Though astrological, this reference to 1995 can also be explained on millenarian grounds, like the previous one.		X				
	I:48	A clear reference to the 7000-year view of world history, with 1000 years as millennium.		X				
	III:97	Prediction of the modern State of Israel, but with considerable 'help' from biblical prophecy.		X				
	III:96 III:98	These two stanzas were only mentioned to indicate the lack of context in III:97.						
	I:15	Undated prediction of an 'Antichrist' clergy, clearly dependent on biblical passages for its predictive value.		X				
	I:50	A middle-east Antichrist, who fulfils Catholic expectations (*could* be applied to modern Iran). Changes times and laws.		X			?(X)	
	VI:33	The 'Alus' prediction, with Muslim expectations (the sea and two rivers) as above.		X			?(X)	

The *Stanza* column groups: Century | Quatrain.

Stanza	Comment statement, including details and assumed meaning	X_1	X_2	X_3	X_4	X_5	X_6
II:28	Antichrist's 'rest-day', a use of Daniel 7:25.		X			X	
II:89	Again Daniel 11:27 with modern applications to 'detente'.		X			?(X)	

Predictions assumed to relate to Present Times — Part B

Stanza	Comment statement, including details and assumed meaning	X_1	X_2	X_3	X_4	X_5	X_6
III:60	Probably a match between current expectations of Suliman, and the contemporary view of Antichrist. May relate to present mid-east.	X	X			X	
III:97	'New order' already considered earlier in this table.						
VI:33	Alus prediction already analyzed in this table.						
II:62	Speculative 'Mabus' prophecy of Antichrist (Muslim).		X				
II:28	'Rest-day' prediction already considered in this table.						
VI:80	Another typical 'Catholic' expectation of a Turkish (great Asiatic) Antichrist.	X	X				
VIII:77	A clear Antichrist prediction using several biblical texts.	X	X				
X:72	A known millenarian reference mentioned earlier in the table.						
I:16	Another millenarian reference, which also uses the horsemen of the Apocalypse.		X			X	
I:67	Possible reference to world famine, using biblical texts.	X	X				
II:75 III:42	Two reasonable expectations of final times of hunger at the end of the world, with some biblical references.	X X	X X				

Stanza	Comment statement, including details and assumed meaning	X_1	X_2	X_3	X_4	X_5	X_6
II:7	The child with two teeth. Another 'hunger' reference.	X	?(X)				
II:46	Renewal of centuries may be a millenarian reference. Almost certain usage of Apocalypse chapters 6 and 12.		X				
III:75	Pestilence from chemical warfare. Almost certainly a 'napalm'-type prediction.		X	X			
V:90	Chemical warfare implied by the reference to 'false dust'.		?(X)	X			
VI:5	The pestilent wave and the Apocalyptic horsemen.		X	X		X	
VI:26	A misinterpreted, unfulfilled expectation of the Papacy.		?(X)			X	
VIII:46	Another of Cheetham's papal predictions that is wrong viewed from hindsight.		?(X)			X	
III:65	A prediction of an Antichrist Pope, to match both papal and Protestant expectations.	X	X				

Predictions assumed to relate to Present Times — Part C

Stanza	Comment statement, including details and assumed meaning	X_1	X_2	X_3	X_4	X_5	X_6
V:46	Schism and a non-Italian Pope	X	X			?(X)	
V:49	A Pope who may make overtures to the Communist world.	X	X			?(X)	
V:54	A power from the east, follows the papal view of Antichrist and perhaps Rev 9:14, etc.	X	X			?(X)	
V:56	A long-lived Pope, not perhaps Antichrist, but a statistical probablity in any case.	X					

Stanza	Comment statement, including details and assumed meaning	X_1	X_2	X_3	X_4	X_5	X_6
I:29	'Fish' journeying over land and sea. The myth of leviathan with some scientific insight.		X	X		X	
I:30	'Palm branches' and a possible insight into nuclear bombing, but based on biblical 'Joel'.		X	X		?(X)	
I:63	Aerial travel.			X			
IV:43	Aerial warfare, with perhaps some usage of Revelation 12:7.		X	X			
IV:92	Radio equipment (antennae).			X		?(X)	
III:44	Telegraph communication then super-seded by radio.			X		?(X)	
VI:5	Could be fulfilled in space satellites. Already appears in this table.						
VI:34	'Flying fire' machine; as, for example, a Spitfire.			X			
IX:65	Walking on the moon, if it means that. 'Luna' could be a simple cipher for some other country, as elsewhere.			X		?(X)	
II:57	Already fudged because of Cheetham's preoccupation with Kennedy brothers, and partly unfulfilled.					X	
III:94	Not yet fulfilled. The future exponent of Nostradamus, who used a precedent in the biblical Daniel (12:9) about a 'sealed book' in reference to his own writings.		X		X	X	
II:28	An obscure name for Antichrist. Appears earlier in this table.						
I:14	The French Revolution or present-day Poland(?).		X			X	
I:16	Scythian reference. Appears earlier in this table.						

Predictions assumed to relate to Present Times — Part D

Stanza	Comment statement, including details and assumed meaning	X_1	X_2	X_3	X_4	X_5	X_6
I:40	The biblical 'lawless one', Antichrist predictions.	X	X			X	
I:55	Amazing insight about the Khomeini regime, but with some help from biblical sources.	X	X				X
III:64	Another reference to the Iraq-Iran conflict.		?(X)			?(X)	X
X:100	A 300-year prediction of England's greatness, partly explained by Millenarianism.	X	X			X	
III:67	A prophecy of the rise of Communism, but anticipated from the Bible and from the rise of intellectual Protestants in his own time.	X	X			X	
IV:32	The restoration of capitalism in Communist countries.					?(X)	X
IX:51	Could just as well have meant divisions in the Catholic Church ('red ones' = cardinals) as underground movements in Communist countries.	?(X)	X			X	
VIII:28	A prediction of inflation, but this was a phenomenon in times of crisis even in the ancient world.	X	?(X)				X
I:40	This has already been analyzed earlier in this table.						

So ends our analysis of the 'modern' chapter. This, as can be seen contains several points of difference from previous ones. Some of the quatrains have been mentioned more than once, consistent with their place in the chapter, but have only been counted once. Also, this chapter contained two elements: (a) those predictions thought to have already been fulfilled this century, and (b) those predictions that are likely to be fulfilled before the end of this century. Some partial fulfilments have had to be treated either as (a) unfulfilled or (b) fulfilled, dependent on the degree of fulfilment, and one, the interpreter stanza has simply been categorized as 'future'.

Some cases are difficult. The famine predictions can be regarded as likely future events (as a world-wide phenomenon) or as 'fulfilled' (as far as the 'third world' is already concerned). The position may be tabulated thus:

Predictions of Modern Times	Likely 20th century fulfilments, or unfulfilled		Totals
	Fulfilled	Unfulfilled	
X_1 Reasonable expectations of Nostradamus, subject to re-interpretation	7	11	18
X_2 Use of a biblical model — history repeating itself	18	22	40
X_3 Scientific insight	11	—	11
X_4 Participant fulfilment	—	1 (?)	1
X_5 Interpretational fudge	16	10	26
X_6 Unexplained hardcore	4	—	4
Totals	56	44	100

The pattern of variables has now changed. Of the predictions already fulfilled this century, the largest number may be attributed to Nostradamus's use of Bible prophecy, with obscurantism on his part (interpretational fudge) accounting for almost as many. But a number of predictions demonstrate his scientific insight; that is, his ability, in science-fiction fashion, to dream up ideas that were regarded as 'impossible' by his contemporaries but that later came to fruition. In some cases, he was helped by the apocalyptic language of some biblical prophecies; in others he relied on his own genius and imagination. Let us end this chapter with a table that combines each of the four summary tables, and so gives the effects of explanatory factors in different centuries.

	X_1	X_2	X_3	X_4	X_5	X_6	Totals
16th century	20	12	—	9	20	4	65
17th century	14	3	—	4	25	8	54
18th century	22	18	1	5	35	8	89
19th century	3	8	—	14	33	4	62
20th century fulfilled	38	46	16	14	59	6	179
20th century likely future	11	22	—	1	10	—	44
Total	108	109	17	47	182	30	493

For the sake of simplicity, the total values in this summary do not take into account a very small amount of double counting (or reverse) where quatrains are assigned to historical periods covered by two different sets of tables. The totals are adjusted in the appendices (with lists that justify the adjustments) to:

107, 109, 18, 48, 181 and 30.

7
Precognition, Coincidence, and the Doomsday Message

Patterns in Obscurity

The table at the end of the previous chapter is not ideal in statistical terms and results from the search for the best explanations in doubtful cases. The first limitation of the table is that, though I have included at least one 'X' for each quatrain that has been either explained or supposedly fulfilled, I have not divided the factors where there is evidence of two, three, or more in combination (for example, using a half-X, where two explanations are probable, or a third-X where three are possible for the same quatrain). There are several reasons for not doing so: for instance, (a) there is no evidence that each factor should carry equal weight; (b) they often interact with each other, particularly X_1 and X_5; and (c) though such a rigorous analysis (if it were possible) would produce greater accuracy, it would be far more difficult for the non-statistician to follow.

Secondly, I have exercised my own judgement in deciding which factors explain a supposed fulfilment in each case. Some readers may suggest different ones in some cases, so that, though they would probably agree with the importance of each of the factors, their assessments would impede any attempt to construct a rigorously accurate model. So the numbers in each of the categories (or boxes) in the table are not definite but approximate.

A third limitation is that the table cannot be used for easy statistical analysis (such as the chi-squared test mentioned earlier) to see if there is significant difference in the explanation of quatrains supposedly fulfilled from one century to another. This is because some of the boxes (or 'cells') in the table have values of less than 6. The results would therefore be limited in value. A set of chi-squared tests on the data at this stage appears in the appendices.

Fourthly, the use of century-divisions (of time) for classification is an arbitrary one. It *does* show that there is little difference in importance of our explanatory variables up to the twentieth century, when X_3 (scientific insight) becomes important. But such an arbitrary division ignores the fact that people have tended to find suitable prophecies in Nostradamus to 'fit' events at times when they are interested in his writings, and that most of Nostradamus's 'fulfilled' predictions have been identified with predictions of Valois and Bourbon Kings, various revolutions, including the French Revolution, Napoleon, World War II and in relation to the last few decades, leaving long periods about which Nostradamus appears to be silent, at times when there is very little interest in his writings. In Chapter Four I showed that the largest of these lasted for nearly fifty years over the end of the nineteenth century and the beginning of the twentieth, with only one or two references that may have applied to World War I and the Russian Revolution. These gaps are important, for they show us that much of Nostradamus's strength lies in his *interpreters* rather than in his *writings*, for those interpreters have often provided prescriptive guidance for a powerful statesman who is able to exploit popular belief in Nostradamus; he is in a position literally to make an interpretation of Nostradamus come true, simply by political design. This is my X_4, *participant fulfilment*.

Though the table at the end of Chapter Six shows that most of the forty-seven cases occurred in the nineteenth and twentieth centuries, they are not evenly spread, and are usually associated with individuals who were devoted either to Nostradamus or to his interpreters. Of the nine cases of participant fulfilment in the sixteenth century, most are associated with Catherine de'Médici or other Valois rulers who would superstitiously have carried out their interpretations of Nostradamus's prescriptions (e.g., Catherine mourning for seven years). The seventeenth century is rather low in possible participant fulfilment, because (i) Henri IV was a Huguenot who, as far as we know, took little interest in Nostradamus, and (ii) Louis XIII was a weak king and similarly uninterested in the seer. Only in Louis XIV do we find a king who relied on his political ability to fulfil Nostradamus, and so enhance his status among those with whom Nostradamus was popular. But he did so at the expense of interpretation. For example, he misread '*battra*' as '*bastira*', and thus used Nostradamus as a pretext for building the Languedoc Canal (for which there were other sound reasons at the time).

The nineteenth century abounds with cases of possible participant fulfilment, but some of the most outstanding of the fourteen cases that I have suggested can be ascribed to the genius and power of one man, Napoleon, who was clearly familar with the writings of the sage. But again, the renowned interpretations of M. Belland, who in 1806 flattered Napoleon with a dedicated commentary, rather than Nostradamus's writings themselves, motivated the Emperor. Nor need he (as I have already said) have actually *tried* to fulfil Nostradamus's alleged prediction of his flight from Moscow, for the prediction is couched in obscure language that could have described a Russian invasion of Europe, which Napoleon (like Cyrus consulting the Delphic oracle) would do his best to avert, and yet he fulfilled the very words of Nostradamus by a trick of circumstance.

The twentieth century also contains cases that have been identified as participant fulfilment, but these are mainly confined to Hitler and his opponents, and it is again noteworthy that most of the occurrences (like Loog's prediction of the invasion of Poland in 1939) are based again on *interpretations* of Nostradamus rather than on the words of Nostradamus himself. Thus, apart from a few early instances of people, such as Catherine de Médici, who knew Nostradamus so well that they were able to fulfil his exact words (for example, her own period of mourning), we are able to exclude participant fulfilment as an isolated variable. Most of the cases that we have identified are of prominent people (Louis XIV, Napoleon, Hitler and a few others) who successfully (and mostly consciously) fulfilled an *expectation based on a Nostradamus prophecy, rather than the exact words of the original prophecy itself.*

So much for the most obvious cases of participant fulfilment. I have shown earlier in the book that 'scientific insight' presumes later fulfilment by conscious consent. The man with a scientific (or a science-fiction) brain isolates things that people may ultimately desire to have (aerial transport, submarines, telegraphic communication, computers, etc.), and in so doing is either interpreting and expounding a known human wish, or prescribing goals for people. If no time-horizon is specified, the whole human race has an unlimited amount of time to 'participate' in fulfilling the prophecy by discovering how to produce the inventions 'dreamed' of earlier. But all this will be considered when we examine Nostradamus's scientific predictions. It is sufficient to say that most cases of apparent 'consenting' participation in fulfilment by some prominent person have been based on a later interpretation of an earlier obscure prophecy of Nostradamus rather than on the words of the prophecy itself.

So, we can leave X_4, participant fulfilment, because it requires no further explanation than to say that, in general, some prominent person is fired by a sense of destiny to perform an act that he is advised (or led to think) that Nostradamus may have written of him. Such acts are rarely anything more than a credit to the obscurity of Nostradamus's writing and to the ingenuity of some later interpreter. With this in mind we can now consider the two most popular explanatory variables to which the apparent success of Nostradamus's prophecies may be ascribed: X_1, reasonable expectations of Nostradamus during his own times, and X_5, what I have called interpretational fudge, the ability of a later interpreter to 'fudge' or 'flex' a text of Nostradamus to suit the events of his times.

It is clear that these two variables are the most popular explanations of fulfilled prophecy, though X_2 (use of biblical prophecy) catches up with, and slightly overtakes X_1 (109 in comparison with 108) if partially fulfilled (or likely future) twentieth-century events are also included. This is evidenced by the table, and it does not require complicated statistical tests to demonstrate. It is perhaps just as well that the table is not be subjected to the less simple statistical tests. Many of the later fulfilments are X_1 and X_5 in combination; they are cases in which Nostradamus 'saw' an event that he imagined would happen in the near future. It did not happen as expected, though long afterwards an interpreter found a combination of events in more recent history that seemed to match the details of the prediction.

To demonstrate this, we must make a rough classification of the quatrains. Though nearly all of them are obscure, some appear to come from the non-rational part of Nostradamus's mind, 'seen' in a presumably clairvoyant way (or dreamed), though they are possibly nothing more than a subconscious jumble of ideas — for instance, fragmented biblical quotations. At the other end of the spectrum are predictions of *reasonable expectations,* deliberately written in an obscure language to avoid immediate identification and detection. They would reflect rational predictions mostly involving the immediate future, some of which would be mistaken. Nostradamus's mind would be preoccupied with (i) the decadence of the House of Valois; (ii) the problems of Protestant and intellectual attacks on the Roman Church; (iii) rivalry between France, England and Germany; (iv) the German and 'Roman' Empires with the traditional Rhine and Hister (Danube) demarcations; (v) the Suliman (Turkish) threat from the east and (vi) contemporary places of tension, such as the Netherlands and a disunited Italy. If predictions about any of these six topics were undated, they would be accepted as possible future occurrences by people of the time. Nostradamus would have retrospective credit if they were fulfilled; if they were not immediately fulfilled, most of them could later be reclothed with meaning to match other events. This, of course, is precisely what happened. Let us remind ourselves of just a few cases.

It is unnecessary to discuss these cases in detail. I list these examples below as interesting illustrations of the ingenuity of Nostrdamus's commentators; for it is clear that Nostradamus must have meant *one thing* in the context of his own times, but interpreters 'flexed' (or 'fudged') his words, sometimes centuries later, to make him *mean something quite different.* Nor are these quatrains necessarily examples of 'fudge' or obscurity on the part of Nostradamus himself. His meaning may have been relatively clear to his contemporaries. Most of my examples will be self-evident, and, to avoid discussing each of them in detail, a comparison table is given so that each change of meaning will be easily grasped. The quatrains are in Nostradamus's order, rather than in order of assumed fulfilment, and are obvious cases of X_1 and X_5 operating together, which must be distinguished from examples of X_5

alone — where Nostradamus is being deliberately obscure, allowing a later interpreter to produce an improbable (but apparently plausible) fulfilment.

EXAMPLES OF NOSTRADAMUS EXPECTATIONS 'FUDGED' BY LATER INTERPRETERS

Quatrain	Probable meaning in the time of Nostradamus	Fulfilment assumed by later interpreters
I:3	Ideas of 'Republic' were common in Nostradamus's own times. 'Reds' and 'whites' would have meant types of Catholic clergy. Nostradamus may have expected an immediate reaction to the corrupt Valois family. The 'seize' and the 'leaguers' were examples during his time.	The description 'fits' the French Revolution (1789) on three or four points of detail, but also the Russian Revolution of 1917 (Red and White Russia). For reasons such as Luke 21:25-28 in symbol, he would have expected several. There was a French Revolution in 1589/90.
I:9	Clearly about an Asian/African (therefore Turkish) invasion of the Mediterranean (Malta and Rome). Hadrian signifies Rome or its heirs (e.g., the Papacy). A clear expectation in the days of Suliman, shortly before the battle of Lepanto.	Taken out of context to refer to two completely different events (the siege of Malta, 1565, and the raising of the siege of Paris, 1590), in the wrong order and 25 years apart. The 'eastern menace' becomes the Spanish in the Netherlands.
I:47	The 'angry speeches' of Lake Leman (Geneva) are a clear reference to the Calvinist attacks on the Roman Church.	Geneva became an important city because of the establishment of the League of Nations there in 1920.
II:18	'Fire from heaven' in this context has continued to mean a thunderstorm in 1588.	Though the meaning of this particular reference has not been changed, 'fire from heaven' is elsewhere taken to mean a bombing raid.

Quatrain	Probable meaning in the time of Nostradamus	Fulfilment assumed by later interpreters
II:24	In context, a prediction of an eastern invasion of Germany (barbarian, Mongol, Turkish or Russian), with Germany being a poor defender of 'Holy Roman Empire' rights. Hister is the Danube (Latin = Ister) and *'rien'* is a 'pun' on the Rhine.	Though there were intermittent part-fulfilments of this prediction when the Turks later marched up the Danube to within miles of Vienna, it was none other than Hitler himself who believed that 'Hister' could possibly be an anagram for 'Hitler' (which it is not).
II:29	Another clear prediction of an eastern threat, similar to the previous one, dated by the context of Suliman's reign, during which Nostradamus lived.	Taken to mean a number of different things during different centuries of exposition, including Napoleon and the rulers of the Kremlin, the North Vietnamese, and de Gaulle, from *'sa gaule'* (his rod) — a pun on a name of France.
II:68	London 'fearful of the fleet when sighted'. The Spanish armada 1588 was the culmination of vast preparation and naval rivalry between Spain and England that were in preparation during the lifetime of Nostradamus, 1555.	Though he clearly anticipated a Spanish naval invasion of England, Nostradamus 'had it wrong'. The main impact was Plymouth not London, and London was not 'fearful'. Interpreters found a later incident involving William III and the Dutch fleet in 1667, which clearly fitted the details of the quatrain better.
II:90	A clear and reasonable anticipation of Turkish invasion of Hungary, the sensitive side of the Austro-Hungarian Empire.	Again, taken out of its sixteenth-century setting to mean a number of events, including Hitler's supposed defence of Hungary against the Soviets and the Hungarian rising of 1956.

Quatrain	*Probable meaning in the time of Nostradamus*	*Fulfilment assumed by later interpreters*
III:31	A prediction of internal troubles during Suliman's reign on the river bank of Araxes (Armenia and Media) involving 'Arabs' (= Muslims), and therefore, loosely, the Turkish Empire.	There was no conflict during Suliman's reign, though there had been a battle of Araxes in 1514, on which Nostradamus's expectations were based. Instead, Araxes was distorted to mean Araxum, and therefore Cape Papa (or Lepanto) and the reign of Selim II (1571).
III:58	Another 'Rhine and Noricum' (Danube) prediction of a saviour of Hungary and Poland against eastern invasions (Russian and Turkish, 'Mongol', etc.).	This is similar to II:90. Poland and Hungary were on the eastern flank of Germany. They needed protection against repeated invasions from the east. Hitler did not protect them but 'politically used' their fears.
IV:68	A 'Rhine and Hister' (or Rhine and Danube) passage. The Turks advanced up the Danube (the greatest ones of Asia and Africa) and were supreme in the Mediterranean reducing the importance of Venice (Venus) and Malta.	There is clear distortion of the quatrain to make it apply to the incidents of World War II. Venus (Venice) is taken to mean all Italy. 'Asia' is taken to mean the Japanese. 'Hister', of course, becomes Hitler and the whole applied to a Treaty signed at the Brenner Pass.
IV:82	The fear of a 'mass of men' under a Destroyer (Rev. 9) from Slavonia (Russia) invading 'Romania', the Eastern edge of what was the Roman empire.	Napoleon tried to avert this threat and thus, in a most curious way, what was evidently a prediction of an invasion from Russia became one of Napoleon's retreat from Moscow, 1812/13.

Quatrain	Probable meaning in the time of Nostradamus	Fulfilment assumed by later interpreters
V:14	This is yet another one of many of Nostradamus's pictures of a sea battle in the Mediterranean in which the Turks gain supremacy. I:9 and IV:68 are other examples of fears for the Mediterranean in Suliman's reign, involving Malta, Libya (African Muslims) and Venice.	The use by Nostradamus of a likely repeat of history and exploitation of a popular fear (Moors invading Spain) became distorted to make the 'Libyan leader' mean Napoleon (and his invasion of Malta held by the Knights of Rhodes).
V:72	The French (Valois) court was so immoral that Nostradamus clearly expected an edict tolerating voluptuousness (Venus), 'the pleasure of an edict of vice'.	There was no edict of this kind. In a desperate attempt to find one, interpreters decided on the Edict of Poitiers 1577, tolerating the Huguenots.
V:94	Attempted German unification because of a threat from the 'duke of Armenia' — the great Suliman and Turkish threat.	Some of the places mentioned were assimilated by Hitler who broke his 'truce' with Stalin (supposedly the 'duke of Armenia').
VIII:40	In context, a clear reference to two churches in Toulouse with which Nostradamus was preoccupied, St Saturnin du Taur, and Ste Marie de la Daurade, and a possible attack on Alba in Italy.	Ingeniously used by Laver and others to refer to seventeenth-century England. '*Taur*' is taken to mean 'Torah' and 'Tory', and the attack on Alba a Stuart or Orange invasion of England.

Quatrain	*Probable meaning in the time of Nostradamus*	*Fulfilment assumed by later interpreters*
IX:77	A useful reflection of royal plots such as those of Henry VIII at the time of Mary Queen of Scots, '*the King* will plot'.	Identified very much later by interpreters as a prediction of the fate of royal mistresses before the French Revolution.
X:22	Born of a deep-seated dislike of Henry VIII and his divorces, and 'loyalty' to papal disapproval. Nostradamus speculates about a future 'Henry VIII-type' British king who would have to flee because of his divorces. Henry died earlier.	Until Edward VIII's time this had various interpretations, notoriously the flight of Charles II, who was not involved in divorce. The prediction was 'fulfilled' by Edward VIII in a rather unexpected way.
X:40	The 'young one' is clearly Edward VI, who died in 1553 at sixteen years of age. It did not need speculation for Nostradamus to state that there would be dispute in London about the succession via Lady Jane Grey. Lonole is probably 'Londe' (Londres) with a 'd' looking like 'ol'.	The word 'Lonole' introduced a whole range of fantastic speculations, including those relating to Cromwell at the death of Charles I (1649) and even a prediction of Edward VIII and Mrs Simpson. The original meaning would have been clear.
X:45	In context, the reference to Cambrai refers to the Peace of Cambrai in 1529 when the French gave up claims in the Netherlands.	The words were wrested not long afterwards to refer to an affair between Henri IV and the wife of Balagny, at the time a governor of Cambrai.
X:58	A reference to a treaty for the protection of France. Aemathien, Phossens and the 'barque' may all be terms for 'light' (or Catholic Christianity) in Nostradamus's mind.	'Aemathien' is distorted to mean the Sun King. Phossens is misread Phocens (Phoceans = Phoenicians, who built Marseilles), so Louis attacked Marseilles.

These are all examples of reasonable expectations on the part of Nostradamus during his own time, or of current popular fears, expressed concisely by him. They illustrate the rational side of Nostradamus's predictions. There is an element of model-building, but it is not based on the expectations of biblical expositors, or on Nostradamus's own use of the Bible. The twenty-one examples that I have cited are only the 'tip of an iceberg'. They are examples that spring most clearly to mind. I have illustrated that subsequent expositors could take these comparatively clear quatrains about contemporary happenings and distort them to mean something quite different. If this could occur to relatively clear predictions, what would happen when, for whatever reason, the prophecies were obscure. Clearly, this would provide far wider scope for multiple interpretation and multiple fulfilment.

Thus, there are two distinct kinds of interpretational fudge:

(i)   when Nostradamus reasonably expects an event to occur, probably within the *sixteenth century* (or perhaps as a result of one of the other factors, such as 'Bible-based' or 'scientific' foresight, at a *later time*), but an interpreter alters its meaning to 'fit' a *later* (*which then becomes past*) event, or some expectation (*future* to the interpreter's) time:

(ii) when Nostradamus was himself obscure, and an interpreter matches the details of his prediction with a later, or possible future, event.

These are the two main divisions, though there are many combinations of factors. Though the prediction is often 'fudged' to suit the event, sometimes the details of the event can be 'fudged' to suit the prediction. Further, in *all* cases, there may, or may not, be an element of participant fulfilment. I showed earlier in this chapter that most examples of participant fulfilment involve a prominent person attempting to fulfil an *interpretation* of Nostradamus (for example, Hitler and 'Hister'), rather than *what Nostradamus actually said*.

The combination X_1 and X_5 (later 'fudging' of reasonable and relatively clear expectations) explains a large number of fulfilments. What then of the second category of interpreters' 'fudge'? Many of the prophecies in this category appear to use the Bible, or biblical expressions, with little regard to their contextual meaning. We must distinguish this use of biblical passages from the three biblical models, with which we have dealt earlier:

(i)   passages relating to Paris as Babylon;

(ii) passages predicting periods of revolutions (wars and rumours of wars) and attacks on social order and the Church;

(iii) passages predicting the time of doomsday — preceded by famines and other troubles, the rise of Antichrist, the political restoration of Israel, at the end of the second millennium AD.

The first of these was a reasonable attempt to apply a decadent Babylonian model to Paris, but may have been a peculiar concern of Nostradamus's. The others are common to many biblical expositors. We shall deal with these three strands of rational biblical usage later. We must first deal with the *obscure* use of the Bible, a patterned, sequential stringing-together of biblical references and quotations, without any clear expectation of a future event, to provide something that appears prophetic and excites the imaginations of later interpretators. It is impossible to say whether, in these cases, Nostradamus is being deliberately obscure or not; whether he seriously believed that using the Bible in this way would provide a prophetic calculus for later investigators; or whether we are face to face with the inspired regurgitation of biblical quotations by Nostradamus's subconscious mind. It is not wise to speculate. Let us instead provide clear examples.

Obscurity and Biblical Quotations

In Chapter One I provided two parallel sequences of eight examples of biblical references (mainly from Revelation 6:1-12) in Nostradamus's Centuries (I:15-20). The chances of their occurring randomly are 1/(8!), a mathematical expression meaning $1/(8 \times 7 \times 6 \times 5 \times 4 \times 3 \times 2 \times 1)$, or $\frac{1}{40320}$. Though they appear to be predictions of the end of time, most of them do not signal a single rational expectation on his part, and, of course, interpreters have subsequently applied them to several different events in the intervening period. Here are some examples of the obscure sequential use of biblical passages:

Century/ Quatrain	Details	Biblical source
II:27, line 3	'Hidden secrets and revelations'	Isaiah 45:3
II:27, line 4	People 'walk over'	Isaiah 45:13/14
II:29	'man', 'bird of prey' — 'from the east'	Isaiah 46:11
II:30	reference to 'Babel' or 'Babylon'	Isaiah 47
II:35	Sagittarius (arrows) associated with two rivers (Babylon)	Isaiah 49:2

Interspersed with these five sequential references are other, jumbled allusions to the prophecies of Isaiah. For example: 'he will strike everyone with his rod' (II:29) looks like: 'he will strike the earth with the rod of his mouth' (Isaiah 11:3).

Thus, though there is less evidence of sequential, systematic usage of Isaiah, the fact that Isaiah is drawn on heavily cannot be questioned. The probability that it could have arisen purely randomly (coincidence) is less than the probability that any of Nostradamus's 'unexplained' prophecies could have been fulfilled purely because of coincidence, for such fulfilments usually have *less* than five coincidental elements of detail in any one quatrain.

Even if one cannot appreciate the nature of clusters such as this, and looks instead for random, confused, scattered, non-sequential references to the Bible, the case for biblical usage would not be lessened, except that it would be more difficult to prove that Nostradamus was using the Bible on each isolated occurrence. Only a few examples of this are necessary.

1. *I:21* talks of the foundation of earth being clay, and releases a whole number of references (Isaiah 41:25; 45:9

and 64:8), including also Daniel's picture (2:33) of mankind as an 'image' founded on clay. Ingenuity could, of course, make this into a Nostradamus prophecy of bauxite–aluminium derived from clay, as a foundation of the modern age, though no one seems to have done so as yet.

2. *I:23,* which pictures a battle between boar, leopard, and an eagle around the sun, has clear affinity to Daniel's pictures (Chapter 7) of a leopard and a 'wild beast' and a picture of an eagle flying in midheaven (Revelation 9).

3. *I:69* talks of a 'flood' involving a 'great mountain — seven stadia round'. The association of the number 'seven' with the mountain looks like a confusion of the Apocalyptic figure of a woman enthroned on seven mountains (Revelation 17), particularly as she is also associated with a flood (many waters), and the 'stadia' measurement appears in the Apocalypse a little earlier (Revelation 14:20).

4. *I:87* (line 4) involves the reddening of a river. Both in the Apocalypse of John and in the Old Testament, rivers are turned into blood. Similarly, the picture of the moon being turned into blood *(I:84)* looks like another borrowing from both Old and New Testaments (Joel 2:31, Revelation 6:12).

5. *II:41* mentions the burning of a great star in heaven, a cloud and a double sun. Revelation 8:10 mentions a great star burning as a torch in heaven, which subsequently falls and produces a cloud of smoke (9:1, 2).

6. *II:46,* uses the symbol of a fire in the sky and a trail of sparks. The Apocalyptic dragon has a 'trail' drawn by its tail, which includes a third of the stars of the heaven. It is described as fiery.

7. *II:57* includes a 'river of blood', reminiscent of the plagues of Egypt. The symbol is repeated in *II:60.* Also in *II:85,* the Ligurian sea is 'red'.

8. *II:89* uses a prophecy of renewed friendship between two leaders taken from Daniel 11:27. As this precedes a

passage in Daniel (11:36), used by many Christian expositors of Antichrist, we would expect Nostradamus to use it in the same way. Hence, there is a reference to a 'man of blood' and a 'number' (the number of the beast) immediately afterwards.

9. *II:96* repeats the figure of a 'burning torch' in the sky. These are the exact words used in Revelation 8:10.

10. *III:57* uses a 'seven times' prophecy, as does *III:10*. The Bible uses it for both Israel (Lev. 26) and Nebuchadnezzar (Daniel 4). Apocalyptic time periods are based on half of seven times (Daniel 7, Rev. 11, 12 and 13). These are associated with the subjugation of a 'third' of something, as Daniel 7:24, 25 and Revelation 12:2. It is thus curious that the conquest of a 'third' occurs in Nostradamus only two stanzas later in *III:59*, and the 'seven kings' (seven heads) in *IV:50*.

11. *III:82* specifies a plague of locusts 'by land and sea'. The biblical plagues of locusts were known to have come from the *sea* by an east wind (Exodus 10:13), and from the *land* (Joel 2). See also IV:48).

12. The phrase 'gifts and tongues' occurs in *III:95*. Curiously, it specifies an area of the world, Southern Russia, from which Jews were reputed to have come (Acts 2:9) when the biblical 'gift of tongues' was first displayed by Christians during the Jewish feast of Pentecost.

13. *IV:92* mentions the head of a captain being thrown in front of an adversary, and the body being hanged. There are several biblical examples of similar events happening (e.g., I Samuel 31:8-10).

14. *IV:94* provides yet another picture of a sea being turned into blood. See Revelation 16:3.

15. *V:32* only slightly disguises the Apocalyptic picture of a seven-hilled city (Rev. 17), 'seventh rock'. Rock in Aramaic often means 'mountain'.

16. *V:35* is one of several references to a 'branch'. The term is frequently used in Old Testament symbolism (see Isaiah 11:1; Zechariah 3:8). The figure is repeated shortly afterwards in *V:39*.

17. *V:53* curiously mixes many of the symbols of Revelation 12 — including the birth of a Messiah from a 'woman clothed with the Sun', which Nostradamus has curiously confused with Venus.

18. Another reference to a 'morning star' obscuring the sun in *V:72* is based probably on Isaiah 14. The corrupt Valois dynasty obscured the glory of a greater France, as did the rulership of Isaiah's Babylon.

19. *V:83* includes the subversion of a kingdom, a three-night warning and a reading of the Bible. One can think easily of a Daniel parallel, including the fall of a kingdom after a threefold warning, 'Mene, Tekel, Peres' (Daniel 5:26).

20. *VI:11* is based on an apocalyptic ratio (4:3) used in John's Revelation of the seal and trumpet sequences. The ratio has to be adapted to make it fit the actual fortunes of the Valois family.

21. There is a millenarian prediction in *VI:24*, based on the belief in a Second Advent at the end of twentieth century when Jupiter and Mars are in Cancer. The three terms *'roi oingt'*, 'Messiah' and 'Christ' all mean anointed. Nostradamus has clearly combined his Messianic expectations (as a Jew) with his belief in astrology.

22. In *VI:28* *'grand pasteur'* means Great Shepherd and is probably a quotation of the Petrine references to Christ (1 Peter 5:4) and some 'judgement' that Nostradamus would have expected. It is curious that most expositors have taken this passage as an incorrect reference to Pius VII (a failed prophecy), while earlier a Pasteur allusion is regarded gratuitously as a prediction of Louis Pasteur (see *I:25*).

23. *VI:51* may have been used by Krafft as a prophecy for Hitler's escape from assassination in November 1939; but apart from the last line, it and the next stanza are curious reminiscences of the exhibition of Samson's strength in Gaza, when the pillars were broken and the walls fell, particularly as the theme is continued. *VI:52* mentions 'a great one . . . in prison', and *VI:56* 'the blind one' (= Samson).

24. *VI:89* contains one of several references to 'milk and honey'. The phrase is, of course, biblical, and was used at the Exodus of Israel from Egypt (Exodus 3:8).

25. *VIII:2* contains one of the many references to 'fire from heaven'. This was used primarily of Elijah in the Bible, but the phrase occurs in other biblical contexts.

26. *VIII:70* indicates that a King of Mesopotamia will have a wicked and adulterous wife. Mesopotamia is Babylon. Hence, there is another indirect reference to the 'Mystery Babylon' woman of Revelation 17.

27. *VIII:96* distorts the symbolism of Daniel 7:4, which depicts Babylon as a lion with its wings clipped. The Jews are called 'daughter of the persecuted of Babylon', because of Isaiah's phrase 'daughter of Babylon' to describe exiled Jews fleeing from captivity. In this case, they flee from Christian persecution to Muslim countries.

28. Three temporal kings are said to restore the papal seat in *VIII:99*. Though this is based on a Protestant interpretation of Daniel 7:24, of a papal 'king' who puts down three kings, some Catholics believed that there would be (ultimately) an apostate Pope.

29. *IX:17* looks like a conflation of the story of Nero supposedly burning Rome and the biblical narrative of the 'fiery furnace' and the golden image (golden century) in Daniel 3. See also *IX:53*.

30. The white stone of *IX:20* comes from an apocalyptic promise (Revelation 2:17).

31. *IX:41* contains the phrase 'honeyed letters full of bitterness'. This is clearly a reference to Revelation 10:9, to a scroll that would taste as sweet as honey, but be bitter afterwards.

32. *IX:60* may contain a reference to the biblical plague of frogs or to an apocalyptic reference (Revelation 16:13). It is clear that Nostradamus is preoccupied at this stage with the plagues of Egypt, for he mentions both the plagues of hail and locusts in *IX:69* and the escape from Egypt (with the institution of 'new leaven' [= the

Passover]) in *IX:72*. It would be illogical to attribute such a large number of references clustered together purely to coincidence.

33. Though there are many references to plagues and earthquakes in the quatrains, the 'great earthquake' of *IX:83* looks suspiciously like a borrowing from Revelation 6:12-17 (for example, because of the darkness that accompanies it).

34. Alexander, the Macedonian 'Hercules', used the crumbled walls of old Tyre to provide a 'bastion' of a land bridge to conquer island Tyre in fulfilment of Ezekiel's prediction (26:12-14). Nostradamus has this event in mind when writing *IX:93*.

35. *X:18* curiously borrows a phrase from Isaiah 40, 'The low one exalted and the high one put low'. In the Isaiah original 'every valley is exalted and every mountain and hill made low'.

36. *X:31* contains an obscure reference to Carmania. This appears to be a misspelt version of Carmonia, a nation mentioned in the Apocalypse of Ezra (II Esdras XV).

37. *X:67* states that hailstones will fall like an egg, i.e., 'each hailstone the size of an egg'. The Apocalypse of John speaks of hailstones each the 'weight of a talent' (Revelation 16:21).

38. *X:74* contains an obvious millenarian reference, in a confused setting:

> *not long before the age of the great millennium,*
> *— when the dead will rise up out of their graves.*

This is clearly Revelation 20:6, 11-15.

39. In *X:80* the 'great gates of brass' are opened. This is a reference to a biblical prediction about Cyrus. See Isaiah 45:2.

40. *X:99* contains a triple reference to the Bible. Animals such as 'ox', 'wolf', 'lion' are evidently taken from Isaiah 11:6-9, in combination with references to 'ox and ass' such as Deuteronomy 5:14 and 21; while 'sweet

manna' is an obvious reference to Israel's early wilderness history, or to the 'hidden manna' (Revelation 2:17).

These forty cases, some containing as many as three Nostradamus references, have been chosen because they are mostly illustrations of a non-systematic 'confused' use of biblical passages by Nostradamus. They are evidence that the Bible provided the source material for some of his non-rational expectations, which were expressed in obscure, confusing quatrains. Most of my examples are provided because they avoid the more obvious references to famine, plagues, death, earthquakes and other woes, which are obviously taken from apocalyptic prophecies in the Bible and formed part of Nostradamus's expectations. But the influence of the Bible on Nostradamus extended much further than this: biblical fragments, symbolism and allusions appear almost everywhere, mixed up with references to Greek mythology and medieval magic — and scattered astrological references. Very rarely, if ever, are these quotations derived from simple biblical statements, from the Gospels or the Pauline epistles, for example. Instead, they reflect matters with which Nostradamus's mind was most preoccupied and draw mainly on Exodus, Isaiah, Ezekiel, Daniel and John's Apocalypse. This may suggest that after Nostradamus's mind had done its best to think logically about the future, it simply regurgitated in a confused way those references in biblical, pagan and magical literature that it was not able to digest and perceive correctly, in the hope that a later expositor would be able to make sense of them, or at the least believe that Nostradamus was somehow aware of their meaning. This need not mean that Nostradamus was being deliberately obscure; subconsciously, he may have believed that there was virtue in drawing on references that were, even to him, confusing.

Further, as I have already stated, although much of his material, whether derived from the Bible or from other sources, is confusing and we are rarely able to identify a quatrain that is entirely based on rational expectations, this confusion *is* a systematic one. He does not arrange his stanzas chronologically, but he *does* arrange them topically — for example, the astrological clusters of stanzas to which I drew attention in Chapter Six. Some of these systematic sequences only appear to be unsystematic because later expositors have wrenched one or two quatrains out of their context and applied them to later events. For example, I:44-52 is a sequence about Protestants and persecution, including the beliefs of contemporary millenarians. It only seems confusing to us because I:47 has been wrenched out of context to apply to the League of Nations. Similarly, stanzas II:1-8 are about fish and the sea, maritime topics, islands, etc. Nostradamus was here following an apocalyptic precedent (Revelations 8 and 16) to announce the second series of woes (i.e., beginning his second Century) with woes on the sea. Unless one is aware of the systematic arrangement of what appear to be confusedly arranged stanzas, this fact is completely lost. Later, in II:27-35, is a cluster of references to Isaiah, with which we have dealt earlier in this chapter. When one adds four clusters of astrological references (I:25-28, I:48-56 and I:80-87) and one later (II:41-48), the confused contents of Centuries I and II suddenly become somewhat clearer, even though I:44-52 and I:48-56 overlap.

So much for Centuries I and II, apart from a set of clustered British (Celtic) stanzas from II:67-72. Century III:3 and 4 are preoccupied with drought, reminiscent of the 'third' apocalyptic woe, which was directed at 'rivers and fountains of water'. III:20-31 are preoccupied with Muslims in one way or another, and then follow in III:37-44 a series of stanzas mainly concerned with Italy. Similarly, stanzas III:70-81 mention England and Scotland; the references to these place names elsewhere (e.g., Marseilles) are scarce or non-existent. The Century ends with a small bunch of astrological references (III:92-96). Century III also contains, in its first half, a large cluster of contemporary expectations about the reign of Henri III, reasonable expectations that were fulfilled, possibly because Nostradamus wanted to make his mark as a prophet of contemporary events and so avoided obscurity.

Century IV contains several sequences of astrological references, including the largest, IV:29-33, and three others, IV:67-68; IV:84-86 and IV:96-97. The early part of Century V blossoms with references to ancient Rome — augurs, triumvirs and barbarian warriors, together with Sabines (see V:1-16). Again, though the stanzas seem to be jumbled, they are arranged in systematic sets with a common theme, for there are scattered references to Roman augury later in this Century. It also contains its four clusters of astrological references, V:11-14 V:23-25; V:61-66 and V:70-72.

Century VI is an exception, for apart from a few references of the apocalyptic type and two small astrological clusters, there is no systematic organization. Century VII is incomplete, but seems to have a large number of Italian references from VII:5-20. Though there is deliberate confusion later, references to Italian cities recur and are prominent in this Century.

Century VIII contains another two astrological clusters (VIII:46-49 and VIII:85-90), together with a whole series of references to England and Scotland or the British Isles (VIII:54-66). Century IX has the final astrological cluster (IX:72-73) and a high incidence of revolutionary stanzas.

All this illustrates that there are systematic arrangements of quatrains throughout the Centuries. Yet, despite this they still appear haphazard and confused: perhaps this was also done deliberately, to make them appear more enigmatic than they really are. This obscurity was capable of firing the imaginations of generation after generation of experts in the occult sciences, politics and linguistics. It was Nostradamus's later interpreters, not the seer himself, who would have to make sense of these quatrains, which were interspersed with accurate predictions based on rational expectations. What better way of ensuring that his work would endure than to stretch the imaginations of future experts and challenge them to find new significance in the jumble of Graeco-Roman, biblical and occult references?

Yet it was at times of widespread belief in Nostradamus's powers that he particularly captured the imaginations of interpreters. There are, as I have shown, more fulfilments of Nostradamus's predictions at such times than when interest in him waned. This cannot be coincidence. It is evidence that there are more meanings, more fulfilments, because the search for meaning is strongest at those times. Some have been so implausible that I have not even mentioned them, and Laver, whose own work does not lack implausible fulfilments, himself criticizes the Abbé du Vignois for doing exactly the same thing. If an interpreter identifies in his own time three coincident elements of a prophecy he will seek good reasons for explaining away (or disregarding) the rest. We are now left with a small number of genuine fulfilments for which to account:

(i)   those involving rational interpretations of biblical prophecy, or expectations based on them:

(ii)   a series of 'science-fiction' statements indicating an optimism about scientific achievement, and acting as a pace-setter for 'participant fulfilment' on the part of inventors; and

(iii)   a very small series of quatrains, so detailed in their accuracy that they are difficult to explain by either of these means.

The Bible and the Doomsday Message

We turn now from the rational expectations of Nostradamus about the *immediate future* and the jungle of non-rational, obscure statements about the intervening centuries to his Bible-based conception of the end of time.

The New Testament, in passages such as Jesus' Olivet Prophecy[1] and in the Apocalypse[2] makes clear statements about the end of humanity as we know it, and about a new age to commence with the Second Advent of Christ. However, in contrast with Jewish apocalyptic literature of its time, such as the Book of Enoch, the New Testament does not provide a date for the Second Advent, but says that the exact time cannot be known[3] and that the event will occur when the ground has been sufficiently prepared by a process of educating nations.[4] I have discussed this view of the Second Advent extensively elsewhere.[5] In spite of this, calculations were made and the idea that human history would last for 7000 years, with the seventh millennium as a 'new age' (as foretold in Revelation) became widely accepted. It was believed (based on the chronologies of the Greek

---

[1] Matthew 24; Mark 13 and Luke 21.

[2] Particularly Revelation chapters 20 to 22.

[3] Mark 13:32.

[4] Matthew 24:14 and 28:18-20.

[5] D. Pitt Francis, *The Most Amazing Message Ever Written* (Castle Books, 1983). I am not convinced with J. C. de Fontbrune's non-mathematical use of Nostradamus's letter to Henri II, but believe that Nostradamus produced these calculations to convince him that the Second Advent could have occurred at an earlier time than he himself had envisioned.

translation of Genesis) that humanity was about 6000 years old in the first century AD and it was thought that AD 1000 would be the time when John's millennium would be inaugurated.[6]

There was wild expectation when the year 1000 came round, but the millennium was not forthcoming. Because people continued to think in round numbers, Creation was redated, using the present Masoretic age-spans of the Genesis patriarchs, from 5000 to 4000 BC approximately, and speculators in biblical prophecy simply 'found' another thousand years (AD 1000–2000). It had already become a Church tradition to think of the Second Advent taking place at the end of the second millennium AD before Nostradamus was born, and certainly before Archbishop Ussher calculated that the Creation took place in October 4004 BC. Thus, there is a preponderance of references in Nostradamus's writings to events that must take place at the end of this century (1988, 1995 and 1999), and though some of these may be couched in astrological language, the expectations are certainly not primarily astrological, but conform to orthodox Christian views about the end of time.

The clearest reference to John's millennium, as we have seen, is:

> *At the return of the great seventh number*
> *It will appear at the time of the games of Hecatombe*
> *Not far from the age of the great millennium*
> *When the dead will come forth from their graves.*[7]

This is clearly a reference to the final chapters of the Apocalypse of John, where there is an allusion to vast carnage[8] and then to two resurrections of the dead with an intervening reign of Christ for a thousand years or possibly to one continuous resurrection spanning a thousand years. From this definite reference to the Bible, it is not difficult to prove that Nostradamus expected the millennium to begin with the end of the twentieth century from the cluster of quatrains that

---

[6] Revelation 20 and Genesis chapters 5 and 11 (Septuagint Version). See A. Wolben, *After Nostradamus* (Spearman, 1973) for details of expectation at about 1000 AD (see pp. 38–41).

[7] Centuries X:74.

[8] Revelation chapters 18 and 19, followed by chapter 20 on the millennium.

point to the 1990s. The clearest of these is a reference to 1999[9] and this is supported by reference to an astrological conjunction planned to occur in 1995,[10] and to the millenarian 'seven-thousand' year theory.[11] Such references indicate a conformity with 'orthodox' Christian belief in a new age, to begin with a resurrection of the dead and a Second Advent of Christ at the end of the twentieth century. To construct this model from Nostradamus does not imply that the 'end of the age' will necessarily occur at the end of the twentieth century. The Bible indicates other conditions for the Second Advent of Christ — conditions related to human knowledge, rather than to the termination of a given time-period. This model, however, *does* show the way in which Nostradamus's mind was working. It provides evidence that Nostradamus was simply using a 'traditional' Judaeo-Christian picture of the end of the world and the 'seventh millennium' as a model for his prophecies. If this is so, then there is every probability that he would have accepted without question the chain of events usually identified by most Christian apocalyptists as 'preliminaries' to the Second Advent, such as:

1. the decline of authority, particularly that of the Church

2. the rise of atheism

3. the political revival of the Jewish State (Israel)

4. periods of wars, pestilences, earthquakes, famines and revolutions

5. the rise of Antichrist (from either a Muslim or papal source, or both)

6. considerable increase in human knowledge

7. Armageddon, probably in the Middle East

It is unnecessary to discuss each of these seven preliminaries. Adventist and evangelical Christian bodies during the

---

[9] Centuries X:72.
[10] Centuries I:51.
[11] Centuries I:48.

twentieth century have produced a large body of literature on the preliminaries to the Second Advent of Christ, some of it at variance with the Bible itself. It is important, instead, to be aware that Nostradamus's mind would have built a flexible model of the 'end of time' that included *each* of these seven elements, without putting them in a given sequence and thus risk being proved wrong by the passage of time. If this is so, then many of the prophecies that have been applied to Louis XIV, Napoleon, Hitler and Mussolini and others *could and should* be read as Nostradamus's opinions of events that would happen *at the end of time;* if they do, then they could not also have been fulfilled earlier.

This view is not mine alone, but has been partly derived from the study of a futurist Italian school of Nostradamus commentators, such as P. I. Rissaut and A. Woldben. [12] However, as futurist commentators of the Apocalypse of John (in contrast with expositors of the 'historical school'), they also tried to predict the point during the twentieth century when the Third World War would break out and speculated about events that would occur between 1973 and 1983. Most of these did not occur. Nostradamus's 27-year Armageddon was pictured as beginning in 1973, and some of these interpreters produced clear pictures of an army of Crucifiers in Middle Europe, a great north-German ruler and a Muslim invasion. Clearly, this futurist school of Nostradamus has speculated about detailed fulfilments in exactly the same way as doomsday-style interpreters of the Book of Revelation. But John's Revelation provides a logical spiritual message about the development of Christianity until the Second Advent, without any deliberate obscurantism, and is a *Christian answer to* doomsday speculation rather than an example of it. Nostradamus's predictions are neither wholly derived from doomsday speculations about the Apocalypse of John, nor sequentially arranged. Instead, we are given to understand that they were deliberately jumbled to avoid interpretation by the unenlightened. Thus, though both John's Revelation and Nostradamus's writings have each had historical expositors (who look for fulfilments in the past)

---

[12] P. I. Rissaut, *La fine dei tempi. Profezie e predizioni di Nostradamus* (Padua, 1948); A. Woldben, *After Nostradamus* (Spearman, 1973), pp. 54–80. J. C. de Fontbrune (1983) moves a little in this direction.

and futuristic expositors (who believe the documents in each case to relate almost exclusively to the end of time), this is where comparison between the two must largely end, for Nostradamus's predictions are, for the most part, a confusingly shadowy copy of the apocalyptic model.

If a 'futurist' view of Nostradamus is accepted, then it is clear that a quatrain whose fulfilment is supposedly in the future cannot already have been fulfilled. A study of Woldben's interpretation illustrates this clearly. The Nazis used Century X:31 as a prediction of the Third Reich. Woldben[13] turns it into a prophecy of a northern German Emperor in the late eighties of this century. A Hadrian prediction, assumed to have been fulfilled by Henri IV by the historical school,[14] is, together with another prediction of murder in a Church,[15] used as a prediction of an anti-pope appointee made by the northern German emperor in the late eighties of the present century. Then, according to this fanciful futurist explanation, he is replaced by an angelic pastor and ten kings allied to a 'Great Monarch', followed by Crucifier Crusaders.

The final twenty-seven years of the twentieth century are assumed to be a period of intermittent world war. The 'Slavonia' prediction,[16] interpreted by the historical school to mean Napoleon's retreat from Moscow in 1812/3, is at least given its more 'natural' meaning and is assumed to mean an invasion of Arabs (and/or Slavs) during this final conflict. Predictions assumed to have been fulfilled during the Second World War are similarly assigned to the final conflict,[17] as is another prediction assumed to have been fulfilled by Henri IV at the time of the siege of Malta.[18] Other well-established traditional meanings are similarly set aside for more exciting

---

[13] Woldben, (ibid., p. 60).
[14] Centuries II:55; cf. Woldben (op. cit.) p. 60.
[15] Centuries VI:76; cf. Woldben (op. cit.) p. 60.
[16] Centuries IV:82; cf. Woldben (op. cit.) p. 67.
[17] Centuries V:34; cf. Woldben (op. cit.) p. 67-68.
[18] Centuries I:9; cf. Woldben (op. cit.) pp. 68-69. Similar use of associated Centuries is made by E. M. Ruir, *Nostradamus, les proches et derniers evenements* (Medicis, Paris 1953), where there is speculation about a seventh Antichrist who would arise during the 1970s, i.e., in 1973, or thereabouts. These years are now past history.

future possibilities. A statement about a Romano-Belgian King, assumed to have been fulfilled during the Thirty Years' War in the seventeenth century,[19] is applied to the defeat of Arab invaders, and the Selim predictions, which in context are about either Henri II or Selin, the son of Suliman the Great,[20] are made to mean a Christian King who will reign in the late 1980s before the emergence of the Final Antichrist.

The Woldben model of the future has long been disproved. It provides us with pictures of Kings and Crusaders, almost as though the French Revolution and the fall of European monarchies had never occurred. Its picture of an Arab invasion is perhaps feasible in the twentieth century, but for the fact that Muslims are never in any true sense united and that only a few Muslim countries, such as Iran and Libya, and perhaps the Palestine Liberation Organization, engage in fanatical ventures. Woldben and his school were not content to take Bible-based Armageddon-style prophecies and find their counterparts in the Centuries; they also projected Nostradamus's expectations about his own times into the twentieth century.

After speculating on the immediate future, using a scientific assessment of contemporary politics and on the twentieth century, using the seven preliminaries to the Second Advent, Nostradamus was left with a handful of events with which to fill the intervening period of about 400 years. Of course he drew on the Bible-based picture of revolutions, wars, famines, pestilences and earthquakes, scheduled by the words of Jesus[21] to happen in practically every age from his day to our own. And there was one thing besides — Nostradamus's interpretation of Apocalyptic Babylon.

To early Christians and Roman Catholics alike, Babylon[22] represented pagan Rome; but to Protestants of Nostradamus's time, it came to represent papal Rome. To a scholar like Nostradamus, the first interpretation would have been anachronistic. Though pagan Rome fell (after its conversion) to the Visigoths in 410, Nostradamus did not expect the end of the present age until the twentieth century, leaving a

---

[19] Centuries V:13; cf. Woldben (op. cit.), p. 71.

[20] Centuries IV:77; cf. Woldben (op. cit.), p. 73.

[21] See Jesus' Olivet prophecy, Matthew 24; Mark 13 and Luke 21.

[22] Revelation 17 and 18.

'gap' of about 1500 years — assuming the Babylon of John's Apocalypse to mean pagan Rome. Conversely, as a Roman Catholic he could hardly accept that the 'mystical Babylon' of the Apocalypse of John represented papal Rome. At the truest possible level, the Apocalypse of John is a spiritual drama, and 'mystical Babylon' need not represent any specific city but refers to the whole world, to the extent that it opposes God. However, the Apocalypse is written in such a way that it can also provide symbolic models, drawn from history, for application to similar circumstances in the future.

At this lower level of interpretation only, Nostradamus may have been correct in seeking a European city whose morality and decadent politics matched that of the Babylon of the sixth century BC. But why did he choose Paris? Clearly, Rome would not have been identified with Babylon by Nostradamus because, apart from its papal connection, it had little political status, for Italy was then divided. Paris, on the other hand, was ruled by the corrupt Medici family, who had supplied the Papacy with three Popes. The French had territories in Poland and elsewhere and had helped to avert the Turkish threat to the Mediterranean. Paris (and France generally) was, above all, both a hub of civilization and a corrupt custodian of Western Christendom. It was situated on two rivers, the Seine and Marne, as the original Babylon was situated on the Tigris and the Euphrates. Further, such an interpretation would have done much to enhance Nostradamus's own image of himself as a kind of Daniel to the corrupt royal family of his time. If he believed that the Second Advent of Christ would take place at about AD 2000 then there would have been almost the same time-span betweeen his time and the Second Advent as there was between Daniel's (540 BC) and the First Advent.

To those who believe that Apocalyptic Babylon is not a specific place but a spiritual figure of the whole world, Nostradamus's identification of it with Paris is inadequate. It is, however, plausible, and although John's Apocalypse was primarily written to be understood as a spiritual message of a battle between the City of God (mystical Jerusalem) and the City of Man (Babylon), it *does* contain insights that were intended to be specific as well as general, and to be repeatedly applicable to varying situations and contexts from John's time to the Second Advent. This is what is probably what is meant by the words: 'the testimony of Jesus is the spirit of prophecy'.[23]

Nostradamus may have thought in the same way, disregarding the overall message of John's Revelation and considering how its specific symbols could be made to 'fit' his own generation. Inductive logic would have led him to Paris. If (in common with some commentators on John's Apocalypse) he had regarded Europe as one of the apocalyptic beasts, he would have sufficient evidence from John's Apocalypse to believe that Paris, with its primary position in Europe, would suffer — as Apocalyptic Babylon suffered at the hands of 'ten kings' associated with the beast. Though this may not be the interpretation of the Apocalypse at its highest spiritual level, it provided Nostradamus with a partial insight that, because of the various levels of understanding for which John's Apocalypse provides, happened to be accurate.

He may also have looked back at the original Babylon, which fell twice (to Cyrus in 538 BC, and to Alexander the Great two hundred years afterwards), and speculated about possible periods of anarchy and subsequent dynasty replacement (in 1589 and 1789/93) with a similar period of approximately 200 years between, and paralleled the rise of Alexander the Great with that of Napoleon I. On the other hand, he may simply have identified similarities between historical Babylon (sixth century BC) and the Paris of his times: I have already sketched some of these at the beginning of Chapter Two. It was introduced at that stage as a conjecture, partly to explain how Nostradamus, with reference to the biblical Daniel, 'rationalized' or 'excused' his position as a court astrologer, and at the same time was able to condemn astrologers. We can now see how obvious it was for Nostradamus to have identified Paris with Apocalyptic Babylon, and it is not surprisng that he should have sought parallels with historical Babylon. He was simply using, as so many other biblical commentators have done, a 'lower', 'secondary' or 'local' application of John's Apocalypse as a predictive model, and thus was proved right to the extent

---

[23] Revelation 19:10.

that his model fitted the circumstances.

What then of the specific, or near-specific, references to Babylon in Nostradamus's work? Does he identify Babylon as Paris in any way, or does he simply play with obscurity? The references in Century II are not specific. The first [24] is to 'Babel' and the context does not suggest that Paris is definitely intended. The other principal reference in this Century does not mention Babylon but is more specific:

> Roman Pontiff do not approach
> — a city watered by two rivers.
> You will come to spit blood in that place.
> You and yours when the rose flowers. [25]

Though some historical commentators on Nostradamus[26] have associated this quatrain with the death of Pius VI at Lyons, there is little doubt that the quatrain is born from the tension in Nostradamus's mind between those (i.e., Protestants) who wanted 'Babylon' (the city on *two* rivers) to represent the Papacy, and his own view that Babylon represented Paris. In this context, 'spitting blood' is clearly associated with drinking blood. The Babylon of John's Apocalypse was said to have been 'drunk with the blood of the saints, and the blood of the martyrs of Jesus'. [27]

With this clear allusion to the Apocalypse in mind, we can re-read a better-defined reference:

> The King of Europe will come like a griffin
> accompanied by those from the north.
> He will lead a great army of reds and whites,
> and they will go against the King of Babylon. [28]

This quatrain has been misapplied both to Napoleon's flight from Moscow and to his reverses in the spring of 1814, when the allies advanced on Paris, with 'reds and whites' being taken to mean English and Austrian armies because of the colour of their tunics. Laver is inconsistent[29] in assuming

---

[24] Centuries II:30.
[25] Centuries II:97.
[26] Cheetham, p. 114.
[27] Revelation 17:6.
[28] Centuries X:86.
[29] See Laver, *Nostradamus: The Future Foretold*, pp. 184 and 185.

'King of Europe' to mean Napoleon (or his legitimate alternative) and then, in the same paragraph, making 'King of Babylon' also refer to Napoleon. The stanza explicitly states that the King of Europe comes against the King of Babylon. However, he does provide evidence that Babylon means Paris:

1. In the Epistle to Henri II, Nostradamus actually called Paris *'Neufve Babylon'*, making a pun on Mesopotamia which means 'between the rivers'.

2. Elsewhere[30] Nostradamus describes an 'inhuman Nero' who would be 'between two rivers'.

In conjunction with the Mesopotamia reference, the phrase 'between two rivers' is useful evidence that Nostradamus thought of Babylon as Paris. But the word 'new' in the first reference is also useful, for it means that Nostradamus had not dismissed earlier interpretations of the Apocalypse (i.e., identifying Babylon with first-century pagan Rome) out of hand, and his reference to 'inhuman Nero' seems to indicate this. Yet, John's Apocalyptic Babylon had been pagan Rome in an earlier era, in Nero's time, but the lapse of time between the first century and the Second Advent was so large that it was necessary to find a 'modern' (i.e., sixteenth-century) counterpart. To Nostradamus, Paris (i.e., 'new Babylon', clearly described as such in his Epistle to Henri II) would play that role, and be the political 'city of corruption' to fall at the hand of ten kings between his time and the Second Advent.

This is where Laver's case ends, for Laver has not succeeded in proving that the 'King of Babylon' was Napoleon or that 'inhuman Nero' was the revolutionary government or the government of Napoleon. The first of the two quatrains is a clear borrowing from the Revelation of John, which describes a 'beast from the abyss' that would dethrone its Babylonian mistress. This beast has elements of an earlier dragon,[31] so the description 'griffin' is also slavishly copied from John's Revelation. There was some tension between North Germany and France. The word *'aquilon'*

---

[30] Centuries IX:76.
[31] Revelation 12.

('north') is associated in French with 'eagle'. The eagle symbol was also associated in the Apocalypse of John with the fall of Babylon. In common with many Protestant expositors of the historical school, Nostradamus thought that John's Revelation would have a future 'European' fulfilment, and having already identified Babylon with Paris he looked for some European confederacy, headed by Germany, to dethrone Paris — the 'scarlet woman, Babylon' of the Apocalypse — and produce a period of anarchy that would terminate with the Second Advent. It was Nostradamus's Catholicism that prevented him identifying Babylon with papal Rome. It was part coincidence, and part participant-fulfilment that produced the conditions that seemed to be fulfilments during the Napoleonic wars. The fact that Woldben, as we have seen, applies the predictions to a 'future' twentieth-century war indicates the real gist of Nostradamus's expectations, and demonstrates that he was simply describing, in somewhat different terms, a set of events predicted nearly fifteen hundred years earlier by the Apostle John.

The Doomsday Framework

We have not yet commented fully on Nostradamus's 'scientific' expectations, nor upon those thirty or so predictions that have been fulfilled in such a remarkable way that they seem to be beyond explanation. Any study of his long-term psychic gifts has to be based on this final 'unexplained hardcore' variable, and I shall comment on his scientific perceptiveness to show that Nostradamus used all his resources, rational and obscurantist, in the production of his predictions.

However, I believe I have unclouded *most* of the mystery of Nostradamus's quatrains without any reference to these, and have produced from the jig-saw puzzle of the Centuries an incomplete picture of his expectations of the future history of the world. Nostradamus did not simply rely on his personal powers of clairvoyance: he drew on all the resources at his disposal, including his rational, 'personal' expectations and his knowledge of the way in which biblical (particularly Apocalyptic) commentators of his time viewed the few centuries to the end of the present millennium, and the dawn of a future age. This partly complete 'doomsday' framework includes the following elements:

1. Nostradamus moved in political circles. He had a brilliant mind, and was able to voice his rational expectations about the future of most European countries. He was aware of the main threats to Europe during his time, from Russia, the Turks and, to some extent, from Britain. Austria was vulnerable, but Germany (i.e., the northern German states) could champion Europe if France became weak. Some of his predictions in this category were clearly wrong (such as the Araxes prediction in context) but most of them were fulfilled (a) because of his powers of political perception, (b) because he may have had some intuitive powers, and (c) because some predictions are so vaguely written that they can be 'fudged' to fit events in his immediate future.

2. He was a student of biblical prophecy — traditionally as a Jew, religiously as a Catholic and perhaps secretly, with some Protestant leanings — and tried to form a 'biblical' picture of future events that would combine the best of all traditions, be 'safe' from opposition, and be made even safer by the obscure language in which this synthesized view of the future was couched. This picture was largely based on John's Apocalypse.

3. If traditional interpretations of the Bible, and particularly of John's Apocalypse, were subsequently proved to be wrong, Nostradamus had nothing to lose, for most of his work *copies* rather than *interprets*. The culmination of the Christian era may take place around the year 2000: if the prophecy fails, no one will be able to confront Nostradamus personally!

4. The Apocalypse envisaged that the chaos at the end of the Christian era would occur with the destruction of a 'Great Babylon'. At its highest level of interpretation this city is the unredeemed world. However, unlike Nostradamus's Centuries, which, because of the detailed way in which they are written, presume one fulfilment each, the Apocalypse, in complete contrast, is written to provide

models from the past (e.g. Babylon, Tyre, Sodom and Egypt) as moral lessons for every age. It is thus capable, at lower level, of multiple fulfilment, in the sense that its 'models' apply to every age — for the 'testimony of Jesus in the spirit of prophecy'.[32]

5. Though he accepted most Protestant/Catholic, Bible-based speculations about the chaos at the end of the Chrisian era, presumed to be a few hundred years ahead of his own time, Nostradamus could not, as a Catholic, regard 'Great Babylon' of John's Apocalypse as being papal Rome, but would seek another European city to fit the description — failing to realize the real meaning of Babylon, depicted in 4 above.[33] His Epistle to Henri II clearly indicates that he identified Apocalyptic Babylon with the Paris of his day.

6. Then something 'clicked' in his own mind, for the model on which Apocalyptic Babylon was based was the centre of an empire in the sixth century BC, with about the same time-period to the First Advent as there was between his own times (AD 1555) and the end of the twentieth century, when it was thought the Second Advent would occur. Though astrology was a respectable science even among the most religious of his day, Nostradamus could use Daniel in Babylon (sixth century BC) to rationalize his own position. He, like the biblical Daniel, could occupy the position of court magician (even, in his case, court astrologer) and yet generally condemn the practice of astrology,[34] not because he was a hypocrite but because he assumed he had powers beyond those of contemporary astrologers.

7. The fact that there is an historical comparison/model between Babylon of the sixth century BC and Paris of the sixteenth century AD of the type that I have displayed in Chapter Two in a table-comparison does *not necessarily*

---

[32] Revelation 19:10.
[33] See D. Pitt Francis, *The Most Amazing Message Ever Written* (Castle Books, 1983).
[34] Centuries VI:100.

presuppose that Nostradamus knew *all* or *any* of it. It is primarily evidence of the remarkable way in which history repeats itself. However, if he *did* work out some of the historical parallels he would have guessed that the Valois dynasty was about to fall, that another Cyrus would conquer Paris after a siege in 1588/9 in the person of the Bourbon Henri IV, and that 200 years afterwards there would be yet one more change of dynasty, for another Alexander the Great would conquer Babylon (= Paris) in the person of Napoleon. These details would, at least, sketchily fill the gap of several hundred years between his time and his presumed date for the end of the world.

8. With the fall of the Parisian aristocracy, and of other aristocracies, there would be a decline in the influence of the Church, and the chaotic conditions of Armageddon would be produced — the rise of atheism, the revival of Israel, a period of wars, pestilences, earthquakes, famines and revolutions, the increase in human knowledge and a literal battle of Armageddon, involving the whole world, probably fought in the Middle East, before the end of the world and the Second Advent. Most of these elements were to be found in the Bible.

9. Thus, apart from his ingenuity in identifying Babylon with Paris, Nostradamus used a popular framework for his doomsday expectations. However, he resorted to obscure language, jumbling of stanzas, and double meanings: (i) to 'play safe' with history, so that his predictions could be 'fudged' to fit future happenings, and (ii) so that the very interest in his predictions could be increased, and people motivated to see how his predictions could be re-read to fit the events of their own time.

This framework does not include the probability that some prominent people would actively try to fulfil his prophecies, and it leaves a small mystery for us to tackle in the next chapter.

8
The Last Mystery

Scientist before his Time?

The propositions with which the previous chapter ended not only explain why so many of Nostradamus's quatrains have identifiable fulfilments, but also suggest why they were couched in such an obscure style. His immediate expectations were rational ones. His distant expectations generally followed those of contemporary biblical interpreters. It made good political sense to concur with these, whether they proved to be right or wrong, and to the extent that the Bible tends to predict events that are characteristics of human history. Some of his predictions, such as the political revival of the State of Israel, are a credit to biblical prophecy, irrespective of interpreters, because the Bible is quite clear on such matters;[1] in other cases, such as Babylon, though he may have used an inadequate interpretation he was vindicated because of the way in which history tends to repeat itself.

Using an Ockham's razor approach[2] to the problem we could halt further enquiry at this stage, for at least we have a framework to explain *most* of the fulfilled prophecies of Nostradamus, and because we have identified the 'glosses' that have been made to the picture in that framework — by *rulers*, who believed him and were sufficiently powerful to fulfil some of his predictions or interpretations of them; and by *interpreters*, who used some of his worst howlers, such as

---

[1] See Deuteronomy 30:3-4; Ezekiel 37; Luke 21:24.
[2] Attributed to William of Ockham (1285-1349): 'Entities must not be multiplied beyond necessity'.

his rational expectations of historical repetitions (e.g., the repeat of an Araxes battle or of the infidelities of a Henry VIII, distorted to mean the Battle of Lepanto, the affairs of the English Commonwealth, or of Edward VIII). But to go thus far, and only thus far, is to fail in my task. No science is satisfactory if it is only reasoned from what can be explained. There are still some predictions in Nostradamus's writings that defy such explanations, predictions providing such detail that they indicate the probability of foreknowledge, yet that do not seem to have been borrowed from the Bible or from biblical commentators. How great is this problem, and how else could Nostradamus have acquired detailed knowledge about the distant future?

Before attempting to answer these questions, we have a remaining task: to look at an area where Nostradamus's rational expectations and his knowledge of the Bible converge — the variable that I have conveniently called X_3 and simply defined as *scientific insight*. This has seemed like a distinct variable and has been classified as such, to measure how important it is, in the full explanation of Nostradamus's predictive powers. In Chapter One, I sketched the way in which this variable may work, and, in summary, suggested the following:

1. Design often anticipates complete discovery and invention. People often make imperfect plans for accomplishing seemingly impossible things, long before such plans are perfected. In this context, I cited Leonardo da Vinci's submarine plans.

2. Many inventions are not necessarily accredited to their first inventors. Often, the real inventor dies in obscurity without any credit being given for his work. A subsequent inventor may either arrive at the discovery independently or use some or all of the original inventor's work (with or without giving him credit).

3. Before either design or discovery occur, such possibilities are often conceived, if even only for science-fiction purposes.

4. The very conception (even in science-fiction) acts as a motivator, and provides a goal for some subsequent

inventor. Hence, the *'prediction' itself* directs people's energies towards the methods of achievement.

5. In Nostradamus's work no time-scale ever accompanies such predictions. Given that human knowledge continually increases, and that the minds of specialists are subsequently being directed to make a specific invention possible, the probability of fulfilment increases with time.

These five factors provided a partial and temporary explanation of how the variable 'scientific perceptiveness' may have worked in practice. It was partly ingenuity, partly reasonable perceptiveness with respect to available knowledge in Nostradamus's own times, and partly a trail-blazing, goal-setting exercise for participant fulfilment on the part of specialists in later generations.

These five factors provide a complete explanation of the predictive value of Nostradamus's scientific perceptiveness and show that it is really a composite of some of the other variables; but they do not entirely explain his motivation for including such prophecies in the first place. In the previous chapter, X_1 (reasonable foresight) and X_2 (Bible-based expectations) were studied in some depth. Scientific perceptiveness provides a kind of bridgehead between both these variables, for it was derived from both sources: it was the point where contemporary trends and explanations of Bible prophecy both concurred and converged.

The sixteenth century was a century of inventions. For nearly a millennium, Western Europe had stagnated in learning, from the Gothic invasions of the fifth and sixth centuries to the Fall of Constantinople to the Turks in the fifteenth century, when scholars fled westward, bringing with them many forgotten ancient Greek works, Arab scholarship, and Chinese inventions. In science, the mechanistic doctrines of Copernicus, Harvey, Galileo, and later of Newton, were to replace a view of the world that had been based on the physics of Aristotle, Christian mysticism and an astronomy that was inferior to Ptolemaic thought.

Western Europe was suddenly flooded with both originals and translations of ancient Greek works on astronomy, botany, medicine and physics. Zabarella formulated rules of inductive and deductive logic, and shortly before Nostradamus's *Centuries* were written translations of unknown mathematical works of Archimedes had appeared, together with the mathematical works of Tartaglia. Such works were disseminated widely because of the replacement of woodblock printing by metal type. Gunpowder had already been invented by the Chinese and had been used by the Turks a century earlier at the Fall of Constantinople. The Americas had been discovered just before Nostradamus was born, and some 'modern' inventions, such as the submarine, had already been contemplated by men like Leonardo da Vinci.

Such developments emphasize the fact that Nostradamus lived in an atmosphere of intense expectation. So much had been discovered or revived in such a short time that, not only did he himself conclude that the future would realize nearly every invention about which mankind had previously dreamed, but his contemporaries also shared this belief. But there were contemporary Bible-based expectations as well. The conservative wing of the Church attacked such discoveries as the work of the Devil. True miracles came only from God: 'miracles' produced by human invention were not necessarily of divine origin. So, biblical passages that predicted a beast that produced 'fire from heaven'[3] or false 'signs and wonders'[4] could be regarded as prophecies of a 'science falsely so called'.[5] The liberal-minded biblical scholar could understand the words spoken to Daniel, 'Many shall run to and fro, and knowledge shall be increased',[6] to be a prediction of phenomenal increase in knowledge and discovery, even though the words themselves refer to an understanding of spiritual things. Such a scholar had already seen knowledge increase with the Renaissance, and would use the Bible as a justification for expecting an even greater increase.

Let us now look once more at some of the examples of scientific insight, and judge how strong the predictive element in them really is.

First of all, it is clear that nearly all such predictions are

---

[3] Revelation 13:13.
[4] Matthew 24:24.
[5] 1 Timothy 6:20.
[6] Daniel 12:4.

assumed to have been fulfilled in the twentieth century. The exceptions are those of Pasteur and the discovery of the hot-air balloon by the Mongolfier brothers. I have already shown that references to Pasteur may have been entirely misinterpreted, for the word is simply the French for 'shepherd'. Some commentators have assumed that, in other contexts, the word refers to the Papacy, although I have shown that Nostradamus probably meant none other than the Great Shepherd, Christ Himself. The apparent reference to Montgolfier may have been similarly misunderstood. The reference[7] says nothing about a hot-air balloon or about air travel. The only reference to a hole is not about one through which air passes, but through which an army is warned. Mont Gaulfier is mentioned as a place-name, not as the name Montgolfier; together with Aventine mountain it is a cryptic reference to an incident involving the Aventine Hill at Rome, when the attacking Gaulish army had been spotted through a hole in the wall. It seems probable that Nostradamus thought history would repeat itself, though this has never happened.

Leaving aside those references to scientific foresight that are clearly spurious, let us turn to the remainder, which are assumed to have been fulfilled in the twentieth century and all of which have biblical parallels. Let us take these in order of assumed historical fulfilment. There is an early reference to air-raids in Italy,[8] but the words are simply: 'thunder and lightning in the skies'. The phrase is apocalyptic, deriving perhaps from John's Apocalypse,[9] and are no more a prediction of aerial warfare than the similar words of the Apocalypse. A similar, but later, reference is assumed to describe the bombing of French fugitives in World War II:[10] 'The fugitives, *fire from heaven on* (reading *'sur'* for *'sus'*) their weapons'; but again, this phrase is often used in the Bible, both of biblical prophets[11] and of their false counterparts.

There is a reference assumed by some to be about the bombing of Pearl Harbour: 'Fire in the ruined ships of the West'.[12] This line could literally have been fulfilled in the

---

[7] Centuries V:57.
[8] Centuries II:16.
[9] Revelation 8:5.
[10] Centuries III:7.
[11] 2 Kings 1:10.
[12] Centuries IX:100.

sixteenth century, as in the case of the destruction of the Spanish Armada. The only scientific foresight that some interpretations assume is the use of the word 'rubric' to mean a particular bombing formation used by the Japanese.

Nostradamus could have reasonably expected the advent of the submarine but could he have reasonably foreseen the invention of the periscope, used in German U-boats in World War II? The answer is probably 'Yes'. Whether he actually did so is a different question. The prediction is couched in the words: 'The eye of the sea, like a covetous dog'.[13] Clearly it makes no sense as a prediction of German U-boats tracking down British relief supplies, for it is said *of* the 'eye of the sea': 'the one shall relieve the other'. Anatomically, one eye 'relieves' or compensates for the other. As a physician, Nostradamus was simply using a human analogy to tell us that when the land failed[14] the covetous sea would watch over the people concerned and supply them. The periscope prediction does not either patently or latently occur in the reference, which makes perfectly good sense without it.

There is only one other reference to inventions up to and including the end of World War II. This describes the atomic bombing of Japan, with which the war concluded. I have already shown earlier that Nostradamus has simply borrowed a reference from the biblical account of the destruction of two cities, Sodom and Gomorrah. The reference[15] mentions two catastrophes on two cities, but they may simply be 'hunger and plague' as the text states. Even if the calamities were 'fire from heaven' there would have been enough material in the biblical account for such a prediction,[16] and precedent enough in the Apocalypse[17] to expect a repeat of history.

With the end of World War II we reach a few more apparent prophecies of scientific inventions before their time. In Chapter Five I cited 11 references in all. The first three are references to chemical warfare: 'A pestilence will come with a great shell';[18] 'A great famine, pestilence, because of false

---

[13] Centuries IV:15.
[14] This 'land and sea' reference is clear from Centuries IV:14.
[15] Centuries II:6.
[16] Genesis 19:24.
[17] Revelation 11:8.
[18] Centuries III:75.

dust';[19] 'A grand famine by a pestilent wave . . . the length of the Arctic'.[20]

Taken together, these references assume the ultimate use of chemical warfare, or perhaps the pestilence resulting from warfare. The Bible describes a pestilence in the future when people's flesh would rot away while they stood on their feet.[21] As a doctor, Nostradamus would have believed that plagues could be carried by dust. The science of shelling had undergone improvements since the use of gunpowder in the conquest of Istanbul. But it required Nostradamus's foresight and ingenuity to put all three factors together and anticipate that chemical warfare would one day be a fact of life. This has taken four centuries.

With regard to the submarine prediction, I have mentioned Leonardo da Vinci as a possible source of Nostradamus's interest in the subject. During the late Renaissance, ideas about submarine transport were available in the writings of Aristotle, Herodotus and Pliny, and while Nostradamus was writing the Centuries an Englishman, William Bourne, was working on a set of inventions that included the submarine. But again, we must ask what Nostradamus's intentions were in making the prediction. Was he simply giving us 'inside information' about the science of his time, or was he making an obscure prediction to get the best of both worlds? The prediction reads:

> *When the fish terrestrial and aquatic*
> *— is cast on the shore by a great wave.*[22]

This vague statement now becomes less definite. Ancient nations had their myths about sea-monsters that could travel on land and sea. The Bible also used such myths (e.g., Leviathan) in its symbolism. Of course, Nostradamus may have intended to prophesy about submarines, and the prediction ingeniously anticipates Polaris-type warfare; but his forecast is draped in mysterious language that could just as well describe an apocalyptic sea-monster.

---

[19] Centuries V:90.
[20] Centuries VI:5.
[21] Zechariah 14:12.
[22] Centuries I:29.

There is a prediction concerning palms, which, as we have seen, is closely associated with death and pillage and which may be a prediction of nuclear war;[23] but again, there is a close similarity to a biblical prophecy of 'palm trees of smoke' (nuclear clouds).[24]

There are two passages about aerial warfare or of aerial travel,[25] but Nostradamus lived in an age that expected that aerial travel would ultimately be possible. Further, the Apocalypse speaks of a 'war in heaven', and aerial warfare presupposes aerial transport. Thus, Nostradamus could write speculatively about the conquest of the air, *and* draw support from the Bible. The statement 'weapons will be heard battling in the skies' could read 'armies will be heard battling in the skies' as in the Apocalyptic picture of 'war in heaven'. The other 'aerial battle' quatrain describes a 'machine of flying fire', which could refer to several weapons already in use in Nostradamus's time for raising sieges, or to the rockets invented by the Chinese long before. It is a credit to the ingenuity of interpreters that it is now usually understood to mean modern bombing raids.

The remaining three quatrains apparently incorporate two references to communications and one about space travel. The first simply uses the word 'antennae',[26] which was then understood to mean the masts of a ship. The nautical context is reinforced by a reference to a captain, and it thus seems clear that Nostradamus is not here referring to a telecommunications mast.

The next passage is more difficult:

> *When the 'animal' tamed by man*
> *— with great pains and difficulty begins to speak*
> *— the lightning harmful to the rod, will be taken from the earth*
> *— and suspended in the air.*[27]

The word translated here as 'rod' is *vierge* (virgin) in the original, not *verge* (rod or wand). The virgin is surrounded by

---

[23] Centuries I:30.
[24] Joel 2:30.
[25] Revelation 12:7.
[26] Centuries IV:92.
[27] Centuries III:44.

'lightning' (clothed with the sun), suspended in air, and an 'animal' (tamed by man) tries to speak. It now seems like a conflation of two apocalyptic scenes: the woman confronted with a dragon, and the giving of breath and speech to an image of the beast.[28,29] Using apocalyptic references, the quatrain seems less like a prediction of electricity or telecommunications. On the other hand it was perhaps not beyond the ingenuity of Nostradamus to foresee a time when energy and communication would be transmited via 'rods'.

The remaining science stanza supposedly concerns space-travel, on the basis of a reference to Luna and an assumed reference to a walk on the moon, though Luna may just as easily be the name of a country. It seems therefore, that most of the quatrains in this category are either biblical references, speculations in biblical guise, or misinterpretations by later commentators.

The Unexplained Hardcore

The previous discussion has shown that what was labelled 'scientific insight' earlier is basically a combination of the factors explained in Chapter Seven. Nostradamus had seen a considerable increase in human knowledge within his lifetime. Like a modern production expert he could plot a 'trend-line' to predict an even greater increase during the next few centuries, such as would bring the Church and science in opposition and usher in the reign of Antichrist. Further, he could 'play safe' with these ideas, by writing in an obscure symbolic style common to classical soothsayers, of the sort that characterized his contemporary Shakespeare's Cymbe-line: if he made his 'mark', interpreters would always overlook or explain away his errors.

Not only would interpreters rectify some of his predic-tions, they would also distort others to match scientific inventions of which he could know nothing. The 'Pasteur' and 'hot-air balloon' predictions, as we have seen, probably related to the Papacy (or, alternatively, to the Great Shepherd, Christ) and to the incident involving a hole in the wall on the Aventine hill. He may well have expected the

---

[28] Centuries I:64.
[29] Revelation 12:1-6; 13:13-15.

'palm-tree' passage in Joel to relate to a kind of explosion, but his references to it in the 'palm-branch' passage[8] were sufficiently veiled. Conversely, there were biblical passages that he originally quoted with no 'scientific' meaning, but which, because of their obscurity, it was easy for later commentators to interpret in this way.

We can thus conclude that Nostradamus's 'scientific perception' existed, that his intelligence, ingenuity and the times in which he lived helped him to foresee *probable* scientific and innovative achievements. But let us not overstate this ability, for (i) he played safe with some of his guesses, couching them in biblical or quasi-biblical imagery, and (ii) some of his 'scientific' stanzas are not about scientific inventions at all, but have been fudged by later interpreters.

We are left with about thirty quatrains, which we have designated X_6 and called the 'unexplained hardcore'. This treatment of Nostradamus's 'psychic' residuum as a separate variable may disturb some statistical purists, who would prefer to treat these cases as a 'residual' to the model and given them the usual letter, U (= unexplained) or ε (epsilon), used in regression models. I have deliberately used X_6 because I have made the assumption that there could still be a 'psychic' factor at work, which explains what cannot be explained by the other factors. A further reason is that none of these reasons is 'separate' or 'independent', for they all seem to interact with each other. The fact that the 'psychic factor' (if provable) *could* explain everything explained by all other factors ought not to detract from our treating it differently from those predictions of Nostradamus that can be explained either by his use of biblical prophecy or by rational explanation (i.e., X_1 to X_5).

We now have to examine these thirty 'unexplained' predictions and ask whether they can only be explained by a psychic factor (X_6) or by normal means. Even if 'psychic' phenomena were to be conceded in these cases, i.e., that Nostradamus had (on rare occasions) a prophetic gift that spanned the centuries, this would not prove his reliability as a prophet (in comparison with the Bible's prophecies of the downfall of Tyre and Babylon and the fate of the Jewish people), for many mistakes in his work have already been discovered. But how much must the 'unexplained' predictions be regarded? Are all of them evidence of Nostradamus's psychic ability, or only some of them, or none? As a proportion of the 942 quatrains, the thirty or so unexplained stanzas are only 3.2 per cent and have to be contrasted with over 50 per cent of his quatrains that have not even been successfully interpreted. Further, most, if not all, of the thirty contain minor inaccuracies when matched with the events in subsequent history of which they are supposed to be such powerful predictions, and many of them can be partly, though not completely explained by some of the other factors (X_1 to X_5).

It is worthwhile considering whether these thirty predictions vary in frequency across the Centuries. A frequency diagram, using the thirty cases, appears below.

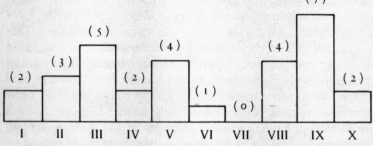

Unexplained Predictions of Actual Occurrences — A Frequency Distribution.

Compare this diagram first with that at the beginning of Chapter Six (p. 178). If we leave out occurrences in Century VII, which is, in any case, incomplete, we have an interesting picture. Those Centuries that contain the largest number of astrological quatrains contain relatively few 'predictive quatrains'; and those, such as Century IX, in which Nostradamus's apparent predictiveness is unexplained, have few astrological quatrains. The inverse correlation is not perfect; but at least it shows that astrology does not explain Nostradamus's 'psychic' gift.

Most of the stanzas are partly explained by the study of the other factors. However, we shall find that some stanzas that did not seem to involve Nostradamus's obscure usage of Bible prophecy now do so, as with the 'scientific' stanzas. Let us travel through the Centuries quickly.

Century I contains two 'hardcore' predictions:[30] about

---

[30] *Centuries* I:55, 77.

Khomeini and about Nelson's mortal wound. The interpretation of first case assumes that by the 'land with climate opposite to Babylon' Nostradamus meant Persia (or Iran), and the reference to the 'air' gives it a twentieth-century application. But earlier in this chapter I showed that Nostradamus may have drawn on Revelation 12 for the aerial battle image, and from references to Euphrates in Revelation it was commonly thought that Antichrist would come from the Persian region. Further, earlier administrators of Muslim Law have been harsh, so the reference to 'heaven seeming unjust' is not uniquely applicable to Khomeini. The prediction looks remarkable, but can be explained by a combination of factors X_1 to X_5.

The later stanza was assumed to have been fulfilled when Nelson was mortally wounded at the Battle of Trafalgar in 1805. Earlier, I suggested that its assumed predictive value was partly due to the ingenuity of interpreters and explained some of the flaws in the common interpretation (see p. 102). Nostradamus derived the prediction from a Greek legend involving a rocky cape. The fact that Gibraltar *is* a rocky cape (one of many) is, to some extent, irrelevant. Some predictive genius may have been at work in providing a picture of black sail being hoisted by a mortally-wounded victor (Nelson) but there was a flaw in the prophecy, for there is no evidence that Villeneuve died of the 'bit' of a horse; he is usually said to have been strangled.

Century II provides only three 'unexplained' fulfilments[31] but they occur within a few stanzas of each other. Their proximity may be evidence of their 'psychic' nature. The flash of genius, so to speak, came and went within five stanzas.

The first is often thought to refer to Charles I, but Charles was not 'the just'; on the contrary, he 'bled' the country by his expenditure. The expression 'three times twenty plus six' does not necessarily mean '66', for, as I showed earlier, Nostradamus was probably using a Babylonian measure; and would Nostradamus really have meant the destruction of St Paul's Cathedral by fire when he spoke of the 'ancient lady'? Would he not have had Elizabeth I in mind? It is reasonable to suppose that he was inveighing against the treatment of

---

[31] Century II:51, 53 and 55.

Catholics under Elizabeth, and that he took an apocalyptic figure about fiery judgement being wreaked on merchant peoples as the basis of the stanza.[32] Application to the Fire of London (1666) is inconsistent, for if Nostradamus really meant that the 'just man' was Charles I (as II:53 is also assumed to indicate), then why did judgement come on London in the reign of Charles II, and not that of Cromwell? The lady and the just man also appear in the latter stanza, and a plague is also mentioned. That London suffered from both fire and plague at about the same time seems to indicate incredible perception on Nostradamus's part, but the same apocalyptic judgements couple fire with plague, which reduces the originality of the predictions.

The third of the stanzas in Century II is supposed to concern Henri IV (assumed to be the Hadrian of the passage). He invites the 'Seize' to a banquet and then has them all killed ('stabs the proud'), afterwards doing 'what is necessary' (assumed to mean adopting the Catholic faith). This scenario would be plausible if 'Hadrie' in Nostradamus referred only to Henri IV, but I have already shown that it does not. Thus, the two salient features of these quatrains in Century II are (a) that they come close together, so may indicate a sudden outburst of 'inspiration', and (b) that two of them use apocalyptic symbolism. Could it be that the former was prompted by the latter?

By contrast, the five occurrences of apparently outstanding perception in Century III are scattered and diverse. Century III:15 is a prediction of a regency. Most dynasties have a regency at some time or other, and Nostradamus plays safe by not specifying dates. The words 'through death a child will rule over France' look like an accurate prediction of the spate of poisoning that preceded the regency of Philippe, Duke of Orleans, in the early years of Louis XV (1710-74), though the text does not specify this. Its apparent predictive quality is largely the result of hindsight.

Century III:41 specifies the death of Louis de Bourbone, Prince de Condé (1530-69). At the time of writing it, Nostradamus would probably have known that Condé had ambitions of becoming a Huguenot leader, and this occurred in 1560, just over four years afterwards. The term

---

[32] Revelation 17 and 18.

'hunchback' is used so that the prediction could be reinterpreted later in the event of failure. The description of Condé as a 'hideous monster' simply betrays Nostradamus's Catholic prejudices. Condé was indeed killed by a gunshot in apparent fulfilment of the prophecy, but was shot in the head, not in the eye. As he was captive at the time, it would have been easy (and ironic) for a contemporary to have used a well-known Nostradamus prophecy as an excuse for killing him in cold blood. Here, as in the previous case, nothing defies explanation.

Next is a Franco prediction, III:54. The distinguishing features are a flight *to* Spain, a battle in Spain and a 'reign' of peace. Only *two* of these elements are accurate: the description of the Spanish Civil War, and of Spain's neutrality afterwards. Franco did not flee *to* Spain: he was exiled *from* it, though he *flew* back to it to commence his rebellion. This distinction is important, for it means that a third of the distinguishing detail of the prediction rests on an unlikely and inaccurate meaning of a French word. As no time of fulfilment is specified, this prediction can also be written off our list.

Century III:64 is also obscure in places, and like I:55 it rests heavily on Nostradamus's (Catholic) expectation of an Antichrist who would come from beyond the Euphrates. Given the Antichrist explanation, it can also be written off because it is unclear.

Finally in Century III is the Fossano prediction, with its amazing detail. This[33] must be retained as evidence of outstanding perception on Nostradamus's part, though it does contain one potential flaw, which is that death is predicted by cutting the throat, whereas the assumed fulfilment involved stabbing. The accurate use of 13 February and other details, however, must place the prediction in the 'psychic' category. So, out of five cases in Century III, one must be retained in our list.

There are only two cases in Century IV. The first[34] looks like an extraordinary prediction of Communism, but it is open to a number of different interpretations. For example, when Nostradamus says: 'In places and time, when meat is replaced

---

[33] Centuries III:96.
[34] Centuries IV:32.

by fish' is he really describing some future time when the
world's meat resources will be used up, or is it simply a
reference to the existing Catholic practice of not eating meat
at specified times (e.g., Fridays and Lent)? If it is, the words
'all things common among friends' do not look like a
description of Communism at all, but of the 'old' (i.e.,
monastic) order of which Nostradamus has been writing.

The other Century III reference[35] also relies heavily on the
ingenuity of interpreters. But it has a redeeming feature
which merits its retention in our list. There were no Dutch
(Frize = Friesland) candidates for the English throne in
Nostrdamus's time.

There are four possibly unexplainable cases in Century V.
The first[36] is an outstanding accurate description of France in
a state of revolution, and fits the French Revolution (1789)
like a glove. But Nostradamus could easily have based his
prediction on biblical expectations of Antichrist and the
anarchy that would accompany his reign. The second,[37] the
'Mont Gaulfier' passage, has already been discussed.

The third[38] of the stanzas is supposed to describe the
French tricolour: 'The "phalange" of gold, blue and
vermillion'. To interpreters, the importance of the text is that
Louis Philippe was the first monarch to adopt the tricolour
(red, *white* and blue) after the 1830 Revolution. But if that is
so, why was Nostradamus wrong in one of the three colours
drawn from a possible eight? Laver's comment that the
prophet can be 'pardoned' for being 'colour-blind' is quite
unsatisfactory. In fact, the stanza was never intended to be a
prediction of the tricolour. It was derived from John's
Apocalypse, where after 'an arousal of a great one'
(Nostradamus) and 'innumerable multitude' (the 'phalange'
or host of Nostradamus) emerge whose colours are described
as: 'fire [red], hyacinth [blue] and sulphur [yellow]', and 'fire
[red], smoke [blue?] and sulphur [yellow].'[39]

The fourth stanza is the seventeen-year passage.[40]
Cheetham has rebutted the suggestion of a nineteenth-

[35] Centuries IV:89.
[36] Centuries V:33.
[37] Centuries V:57.
[38] Century V:69.
[39] Revelation 9:17.
[40] Century V:92.

century fulfilment and maintains that it relates to Pius XII in this century, who reigned for nineteen, not seventeen years. The five remaining Popes (who will officiate until the end of the twentieth century) have thus not been identified (except by reference to an obscure unfulfilled prediction of Malachy of Armagh). These unfulfilled elements in the stanza are sufficient to merit its exclusion from our list of extraordinary quatrains.

Century VI only produces one stanza of possibly unusual foresight,[41] and concerns Gaspard de Coligny (1519-72). For reasons detailed earlier (see p. 38), this case must also leave our list.

As with astrological stanzas, the incomplete nature of Century VII means that its chance of containing unexplainably perceptive stanzas is reduced: in fact, it does not contain any. Century VIII includes four unexplained stanzas: one has been interpeted as a prediction of contemporary inflation; one apparently concerns Richelieu, and the others are said to refer to the time of Cromwell. They are well-spaced, and so do not seem to indicate a sudden flash of inspiration. Cheetham seems convincing about the inflation stanza,[42] since it uses the word *enflez* (inflated) and talks of 'scrips and bonds' being wiped out. However, some of her information is wrong. Paper money existed long before the time of Nostradamus, and inflation occurred in the ancient world. Further, the stanza does not purport to be a general prophecy of inflation, for it mentions theft and stolen material being thrown into a lake. This incident has never been identified. The predictive value of the stanza is therefore reduced.

The next 'unexplained' stanza[43] is a muddle. It does not explicitly refer to the landing of Charles II in Scotland in 1650, and few of its details can really be fitted to that event. Its only claim to credibility is the phrase 'D-nebro', which looks like a compressed anagram for Edinburgh, though it is not tied to any specific event in relation to the city. But even this anagram is suspect. Those who take the trouble to count 'national' references in each of the Centuries will find that Century VIII contains several Spanish references, as in 54 ('Spanish'), 51 ('Cordoba'), and 67 ('Ferera'). Throughout

---

[41] Century VI:75.
[42] Centuries VIII:28.
[43] Centuries VIII:56.

these stanzas Nostradamus's mind was evidently on Spanish things, but there is no other mention of Scotland, assuming the anagram to be one. Context therefore dictates that 'D'nebro' is not an anagram for either Edinburgh or Dunbar, but an abbreviation of 'dans Ebro', the Ebro being one of Spain's great rivers. It had topical significance in the seer's times because of the irrigation works that were being carried out.

Another unexplained stanza in this Century[44] is its weakest. It includes many inaccuracies, which are excused by interpreters who apply it to Cromwell, because of Nostradamus's Catholic bias.

Though we may dispense with this and the other two stanzas, the fourth[45] is still convincing. It is Nostradamus's picture of the deaths of the Louis XIII and Cardinal Richelieu. It contains so many accurate details — travelling by barge (Liqueduct = 'drawn along water'), the word 'Cardinal', the death and the embalming of both men — that it must be regarded as a genuine flash of predictive inspiration.

Most of the predictions of Century IX fall into the same category. The hypothesis that whatever genuine 'predictive insight' Nostradamus received came in sudden flashes over very small sequences of stanzas is confirmed by the fact that four of Century IX's seven 'unexplained' quatrains come between IX:16 and IX23. They are:

IX: 16: an assumed prediction of Franco's rise to power

IX: 18: the 'Montmorency' passage

IX: 20: the description of the flight to Varennes

IX: 23: a picture of Louis XVI in prison.

The first of these is remarkable in that it does contain the names of Franco and De Riviera, his predecessor, but its validity depends on reading 'Castel' as 'Castille' (in Spain), and by interpeting 'Goulphre' as the Mediterranean. I have already explained that the association of Montmorency with

---

[44] Centuries VIII:76.
[45] Centuries VIII:68.

Lyons, and the problem of Flanders, reflects an historical problem dating back to 1529, of which Nostradamus would have known something.

The third of these, the famous 'Varennes' prediction, has an apparently astounding 'psychic' quality. Interpreters have enhanced its quality by specific atypical reading of some of its words. The most notorious example of this is that the quatrain mentions a 'forest of Reines'. To combat this inaccuracy, for there is no 'forest' in Reines, the word 'forest' has to be read as *fores* — meaning 'door'. Nor was there 'fire' or 'tempest' associated with the actual incident. Yet, the very mention of a royal flight by a roundabout route through a forest to Varennes is sufficiently accurate to merit the retention of this quatrain in our shortlist.

The last of the four quatrains in Century IX has been previously discussed. Literally read, it describes the top of a roof falling on the head of the imprisoned son of Louis XVI. This, of course, never happened.

Taken together, these four stanzas display an undoubted degree of insight. The combination of details is convincing, but in each case at least one element is inaccurate.

These four closely positioned stanzas virtually exhaust the cases of unexplained perceptiveness in Century IX. There are three more that were mentioned earlier, simply as problem cases. The first[46] assumes that Sauce (= Saulce) would betray Louis XVI to the revolutionaries and play a part in his execution. Nostradamus's prophecy is often coloured by interpreters who have a tendency to misread history. Circumstances were such that Saulce could not avoid preventing the King's flight. Though he was rewarded afterwards by the revolutionaries, there is no evidence that he played an active role in the King's execution.

The second stanza is a 'wine and salt' passage,[47] which describes the execution of Charles I but is allied with a seemingly unrelated incident involving the Low Countries (line 1). As Nostradamus elsewhere talks of an heir to the throne from the 'Frize' (i.e., Friesland), which historically did not occur until much later, it is just possible that his mind was muddled about how the execution would occur, for

---

[46] Centuries IX:34.
[47] Centuries IX:49.

when read in conjunction with Century IV:89, this seems to associate the rise of a Dutch king in England with the execution of Charles I. It was not an outstanding feat for Nostradamus to predict the execution of a British king at *some* unspecified future time, and the predictive value of the quatrain is only enhanced by the assuming that 'wine and salt' mean 'taxable things', and that the king was condemned because of his 'taxation excesses'. If so, Nostradamus contradicts his earlier description of Charles I as the 'just one'.

The third remaining quatrain[48] looks like a perceptive stanza but contains the most strikingly accurate detail of all. It fairly describes the arraignment of Louis XVII and his condemnation (with Marie Antoinette), but 'Life to the King's son' was not 'refused' until some time afterwards. In the circumstances depicted, he was not denied his life, but his kingdom.

Century X contains only two cases suggesting inexplicable perceptiveness,[49] and these are positioned together, implying another flash of inspiration. The first is a description of Marie Antoinette in prison, though it wrongly describes her as being *ergaste* (sterile). Next to it is the vague description of Henri IV as son of Hamon. Its credibility as a 'fulfilled prophecy' owes much to the enthusiasm of interpreters in assuming Henri IV to be the fulfilment.

A Theory of Prophecy

The number of stanzas whose perception of future events are unexplained has now been reduced to about ten, and most of these contain errors of detail. There are other fulfilled prophecies throughout the Centuries, but most of these, as we have now established, can be explained by the following: (i) Nostradamus's use of the Bible, which has proven predictive value; (ii) his reliance on his knowledge of how things would develop (either politically or scientifically) in the future; (iii) his use of popular theories, some based on the Bible, concerning the future of the world; the construction of his own 'Bible-based' models of the future, and his use of the Bible's style and symbolism, sometimes for obscurantist

---

[48] Centuries IX:77.
[49] Centuries X:17 and 18.

reasons; (iv) the designing of some of his 'prophecies' so that future interpreters could 'bend' or 'fudge' them to suit the facts of subsequent history; and (v) the conscious attempt by persons in positions of power (for example, Napoleon and Hitler) to 'fulfil' some of Nostradamus's quatrains.

What of the ten or so cases in which, despite some errors, details clearly match later events? Should they still remain a mystery? They are not explained fully by any of our variables X_1 to X_5, or by the factors listed in the above paragraph, which are a refined listing of those factors. Are they then simply coincidence? This is equivalent to saying that they are random outcomes, comprising only 1 per cent (i.e., ten) of a series of nearly 1000 quatrains. Is this probable? If we take a cold 'scientific' view of Nostradamus, it most certainly is.

Let us assume that each of these contains as many as seven conditions, all to be fulfilled in some combination, and that there would be a 0.5 probability of each condition occurring at some time or other. The probability of all seven events occurring in combination would be $(0.5)^7$ or $1/(2^7)$. This is $1/128$, and just under 1 per cent (in fact, 0.78125 per cent). This would amount, among 943 quatrains, to between 7 and 8 — just about the number we have. Most of our quatrains do not contain seven necessary conditions to be fulfilled, and some, as we have seen, contain predictive errors (equivalent, statistically, to getting six heads and one tail, when flipping a coin, instead of seven heads). The probability of general fulfilment, but with only one error, is considerably greater in these circumstances than 1 per cent — it would be approximately 6 per cent, or about 57 stanzas. Some of Nostradamus's events did not have a 0.5 probability of occurrence: the figure is much smaller, but to compensate most quatrains do not specify a necessary combination of as many as seven events. We can therefore say, with some degree of confidence, that the ten or so 'unexplained' fulfilments in Nostradamus could be reasonably expected to have occurred by chance, and that, even in these cases, he is not a completely reliable prophet; that is to say, the accuracy of detail in each prediction is something like 80 per cent on average, rather than 100 per cent.

Yet there is one remaining problem: the fact that most of the 'unexplained fulfilment' quatrains occur together. We have written off most of the 'unexplained fulfilment' stanzas in Centuries I, III, IV, V, VI, and VIII (there being none in VII). In fact, only the Fosano reference and one in VIII are left in this 'unexplained' category. But those in the remaining Centuries are in outbursts, apparently indicating sudden flashes of inspiration (3 in combination in Century II, 4 in combination in Century IX, and 2 in X). It is this subtle positioning that creates just one more mystery — a mystery that chance may not explain. For these three sudden outbursts in a wilderness of stanzas that are generally sterile, obscure or explainable, betray the existence of a factor that manifested itself very rarely in his writings, providing oases in a mass of peculiar and unintelligible allusions.

If it is admitted that these are rare prophetic gems, closely positioned together, then we must ask how they got there. Time travel is still a matter of science fiction. Indeed, a series of recent works by Dewey B. Larson[50] has indicated that, although time has often been regarded as a single 'dimension', it may in fact be a composition of three dimensions, forming a counter-universe. But, if this is so, Larson shows clearly that one can never travel along a time-dimension and return to the same point in both time and space. Although his views have not been universally accepted, they show that something superior to the universe is necessary for 'time travel'. Logically, this must either be either divine inspiration, or a divine concession.

Divine inspiration, by definition, presupposes lack of error. This does not mean that any prophecy of the future is (or ought to be) perfect. The future has to be lived. Absolute knowledge of the future may save us from some of the cares of life, but it would also rob us of many of its enjoyments and pleasures. Thus, every prophecy must be imperfect; even biblical prophecies do not specify exactly how or when they are to be fulfilled. To give a well-known passage a wider meaning than its usual one:

---

[50] D. B. Larsen, *The Neglected Facts of Science* (North Pacific Publishers, 1982). This is the latest of a series of works by this author, giving evidence for a two-part, six-dimensional continuum. My purpose in quoting this source is to resist Laver's suggestion (following Dunne) that one can travel time by moving along a dimension.

For now we see in a bronze mirror — obscurely —
but then face to face;
Now I know partially
but then I shall understand fully.[51]

But although all prophecy is to be regarded as imperfect, providing only a shadowy glimpse of the future, if it is to be regarded as divinely inspired it must at least provide sufficient accurate detail if it is to be of any practical use. We have seen that most of Nostradamus's material falls short of divine inspiration. Most of his predictive material is so obscurely written that it could not, for instance, provide advance warning of a disaster. Where he predicts woe he often, consciously or unconsciously, copies the language of biblical writers. But in saying that Nostradamus was not divinely inspired, and could not travel through time, we are not negating the probability, given the small 'packed' outbursts of relatively accurate prophecies in Centuries II, IX and X, that there were occasions when God 'took over', and provided Nostradamus with sufficient data to 'prove' that the future *can* be foretold, but with insufficient accuracy to place any of his work in the true category of 'divinely-inspired' prophecy. Such knowledge would therefore have resulted from divine concession, rather than from divine inspiration.

But why should this have happened in the case of Nostradamus, if, as we have said, he was guilty of using so many apparently doubtful means to postulate future events? Perhaps it was because of his preoccupation with the future, because it was a lifelong study for him, because he truly desired divine insight, and because his intense desires were occasionally satisfied by his receiving those flashes of insight that approached, but never equalled, perfect prophetic understanding.

Nostradamus is thus a fascinating case study. He is an example of what happens when an aspiring prophet tries to mix occult science with biblical prophecy and its interpretations in his own time. He tried to get the best of both worlds and was partially successful in doing so. But occultism and biblical prophecy are like oil and water: they will not mix naturally. The result of combining the two will be an

---

[51] I Corinthians 13:12 (my translation).

emulsion — man-made, with all the characteristics of human artificiality, including fallibility.

The fallibility of Nostradamus is important, because it shows that 'divine interference' cannot be used to explain the majority of his quatrains, which are confused and arid, whilst most of the remaining stanzas are accounted for by the model with which the previous chapter ended. But why should divine interference be rationed? Perhaps it was because Nostradamus 'dabbled' too much with pre-Christian magic, at the expense of aspiring to a true gift of prophecy — one of the Pentecostal gifts abandoned by the Church. Conversely this may show that the re-development of such gifts would produce much better predictive ability.

A Final Reflection

Nostradamus was no charlatan. His profession as a doctor demanded a high level of altruism, perseverence and ingenuity. He cannot be blamed for using all the sources available to him (including biblical interpretations) as the bases of his prophecies, and he can be excused for playing safe with a confused symbolic style, of the kind that would fire the imagination of future interpreters. Though they warn us of the dangers of 'fake' prophecies (and awaken us to the potential of true prophecy), the Centuries are not patent 'fakes' but, in the main, are likely to have been written with the highest possible motives.

It may be difficult to believe that people such as Napoleon and Hitler would go to such lengths to fulfil Nostradamus's prophecies. Would it not be easier to believe that Nostradamus had genuine prophetic insight? A final illustration may convince readers that what I have been postulating is not so improbable after all.

Nostradamus predicted that within 500 years an interpreter would arise who would provide 'a great revelation' about his works.[52] Many interpreters (Loog, for example) have used this quatrain in reference to themselves, but none of them fit the chronology of the prophecy. Loog, in the 1920s for example, was writing 415 years after Nostradamus's birth and some 350 years after his death. Nostradamus is unlikely

---

[52] Centuries III:94.

to have meant 500 calendar years, for the predicted period would then have terminated in the twenty-first century, which is after his expected date for the end of the world and the Second Advent. Being a Jew, he may have been using lunar years in the prediction (i.e., consisting of 12 months of 29.3 days), or years of 354.3 days: 500 lunar years are roughly equivalent to 484/5 solar (or calendar) years. Calculating from Nostradamus's birth in 1503, this gives a terminating date of about 1987. The most appropriate date for an 'inspired' interpretation of the Centuries is therefore shortly *before* 1987/88, too late for the many claimants of the past, but just before Nostradamus's date for the end of the world (1997). Could it be that the conditions and dating of the quatrain are fulfilled by the present work?

A verdict is therefore required. If Nostradamus genuinely predicted that an interpreter would arise in the 'eighties' of the twentieth century who would provide the real revelation, and the true meaning, of his writings, then it could be claimed that this book demands attention, since it was foreseen by Nostradamus nearly five centuries ago. If, on the other hand, I am simply writing this book to fulfil the conditions of the 'great revelation' quatrain, then I have established that a relatively obscure person, such as myself, can consciously fulfil a Nostradamus prophecy, and if I can do so, then all that I have written about 'participant fulfilment' in connection with powerful leaders like Hitler and Napoleon is substantiated.

It is for you to decide.

Bibliography

Bareste, E. *Nostradamus* (Paris, 1840).

Belland, M. *Napoléon, premier Empereur des Français, prédit par Nostradamus* (Paris, 1806).

Bible (in various translations and versions).

Bouys, T. *Nouvelles Considerations . . . sur Nostradmus* (Paris, 1806).

Centurio, N. *Nostradamus: Der Prophet der Weltgeschichte* (Schikowski, Berlin, 1960).

Cheetham, E. *Nostradamus* (Spearman, 1973 and subsequent reprints by Corgi 1975-1980).

Chytraeus, M. *Explicatio Apocalypsi* (Wittenberg, 1571).

Colligan, D. 'Your Gift of Prophecy' (*Readers Digest*, December 1982, pp. 116-119).

Dupébe, J. *Nostradamus, Lettres Inédites* (Droz, Geneva, 1983).

Elliott, E. *Horae Apocalyptae* (London, 1866).

Encyclopaedia Britannica, Micropaedia (1974 edition, VII:416).

Fontbrune, J. C. de *Nostradamus, Countdown to Apocalypse* (tr. Lykiard) (Hutchinson, 1983).

Fontbrune, M. de *Les Prophéties de Maistre Michel Nostradamus* (Sarlat, 1939).

Foxe *Eicasmi in Apocalypsin* (London, 1586).

Garencieres, T. *A Commentary on the Prophecies of Nostradamus* (London, 1672).

Grattan-Guinness, H. *The Approaching End of the Age* (Hodder and Stoughton, 1878).

Houghton-Brown, G. Several booklets on Nostradamus (Brighton, 1973-80).

Howe, E. *Astrology and Psychological Warfare during World War II* (Rider, 1972).

— *Urania's Children: The Strange World of the Astrologers* (London, 1967). Reprinted as *Astrology and the Third Reich* (Aquarian Press, Wellingborough, 1984).

Jaubert, E. *Eclaircissement des Véritables Quatrains de Maistre Michel Nostradamus* (Amsterdam, 1656).

Jurieu, P. *Accomplishment of the Prophecies* (Rotterdam, 1687).

Krafft, K. E. *Nostradamus Ve o Futuro da Europa* (Alma, Lisbon, 1941).

Larsen, D. B. *The Neglected Facts of Science* (North Pacific Publishers, 1982).

Laver, J. *Nostradamus: The Future Foretold* (Mann, 1940).

Le Pelletier, A. *Les Oracles de Michel de Nostradame* (Paris, 1867).

Le Vert, L. *The Prophecies and Enigmas of Nostradamus* (Firebell, New Jersey, 1979).

Leoni, E. *Nostradamus and His Prophecies* (Bell, New York, 1961, 2nd edition, 1982).

Loog, C. *Die Weissagungen des Nostradamus* (Berlin, 1921).

Lord, G. *Nostradamus' Horoscope* (Hutchinson, 1981).

Luther, M. Preface to the Apocalypse in German translation of the Bible (1517).

Margoliouth, G., and Rodwell, M. (tr.) *The Koran* (Dent, 1909).

Mede, J. *Clavis Apocalyptica* (London, 1627).

Newton, I, *Treatise on the Prophecies of Daniel* (London, 1733).

Nicoullaud, C. *Nostradamus, ses prophéties* (Paris, 1914).

Noorbergen, R. *Nostradamus Forecasts: Invitation to a Holocaust* (New English Library, 1981).

Nostradamus, M. de *Les Propheties de Maistre Michel Nostradamus* (Bonhomme, Lyons 1555). [This is supplemented by two later editions of Pierre Rigaud, published in 1588 and 1566 respectively to Century VII:42, and a later Lyons edition, purporting to be that of Benoist Rigaud, dated 1568.]

Nostradamus, M. *Almanacke for 1559* (London, 1559).

Nostradamus, M. *An Excellent Treatise on Contagious Infirmities* (London, 1559).

O'Brien, E. *The Essential Plotinus* (Mentor, 1964).

Osiander, A. *Conjecturae de Ultimus Temporibus ac de Fine Mundi* (Nurenburg, 1544).

Pitt Francis, D. *Meditations on the Last Message of Jesus* (1973).

—. *The Message of Daniel* (Central London Bible Class Lectures, privately circulated, 1969).

—. *The Most Amazing Message Ever Written* (Castle Books, 1983).

—. 'Predictors of Corporate Failure: Old Models and New Directions', (paper presented at AUTA conference, 1982).

—, and O'Muircheartaigh, C. A. *Statistics* (Arrow, 1981).

Rissault, P. I. *La fine dei tempi. Profezie e predizioni di Nostradamus* (Padua, 1948).

Roberts, H. C. *Complete Prophecies of Nostradamus* (Nostradamus Company, New York, 1947, Granada, 1984).

Rolt, C. E. (ed. and tr.) *Dionysius the Areopagite: The Divine Names and the Mystical Theology* (SPCK, New edition, 1940).

Roux, J. de *La Clef de Nostradamus* (Paris, 1710).

Taffler, R. J., and Tisshaw, H. J., 'Going, going, gone — Four Factors which Predict' (*Accountancy*, March 1977).

Thomas, J. *Eureka: An Exposition of the Apocalypse* (3 vols. Birmingham, 1861-1867).

Torné-Chavigny, H. *Influence de Nostradamus dans le Gouvernement de la France* (Bordeaux, 1878).

Videl, L. *Déclaration des abus, ignorances et séditions de Michel Nostradamus* (Avignon, 1558).

Vignois, E. du *Notre histoire racontée à l'avance par Nostradamus* (Paris, 1910).

Vitringa, A. *Anacrisis Apocalypsis* (Froneker, 1705).

Ward, C. A. *Oracles of Nostradamus* (London, 1891).

Woldben, A. *After Nostradamus* (Spearman, 1973), [translated from an Italian original].

Wolters, C. (ed. and tr.) *The Cloud of Unknowing* (Penguin, 1961).

Woolf, H. I. *Nostradamus* (London, 1944).

Note

The 1555 edition of Nostradamus's Centuries has vanished. I understand that a Soviet Union library contains a second edition, but have not yet checked. The Bibliothéque Nationale contains later editions. Several other early editions and translations are located at a London specialist library.

Statistical Appendices

(1) Bar Charts

There are two main reasons for relegating descriptions of the analytical work on which this book is based to appendices instead of including them in the main body of the text.

In the first place, the text had to be rendered as readable as possible, and, as many readers will not be familiar with methods of statistical testing, it was essential that readability should not be in any way impaired by putting too many statistical terms and diagrams in the text itself. Now that the main message and the 'logical' proofs of the book have been fully explained, some of this back-up proof from statistics can be presented more easily, together with lists of the Centuries and quatrains concerned.

Secondly, since the book was written, calculations could be made much more accurate. When I first became interested in the prophecies of Nostradamus I had little more than an efficient cylindrical slide-rule with which to confirm some of my 'rule of thumb' calculations. While the book was being written I generally used a pocket calculator, but had a small ZX81 home computer available to check calculations if it were needed. Since completing the book, I acquired access to another home computer and have been able quickly and efficiently to double-check some calculations. Further, some of these calculations have been rendered even more accurate, though the benefits of increased accuracy are not as great as may be imagined. This is because some judgements had to be made in categorizing a few of the quatrains, both in respect of alleged fulfilment *and* in terms of the probable reasons for the accuracy of the prediction (e.g., reasonable expectations, use of Bible prophecy, participant fulfilment by a later personality, etc.). The tables earlier in the book place question-marks by some of these and thus all categories could be credited as reasons for the prediction's success.

Because there is greater debate about the fulfilment-dates of some quatrains than about others (e.g., whether the 'Lonole' prediction was fulfilled at the time of Oliver Cromwell or Edward VIII), some quatrains have been listed twice, but most only once. Though there is some subjectiveness in the listing of data, it is small and does not significantly alter either the shapes of the bar charts or the values obtained from the *chi*-squared tests. Lastly, though some *chi*-squared statistics may be regarded as of limited statistical value, for they have expected cell-frequencies of less than 6, they have been included with these limitations for they are useful in determining which relationships are significant and which are not.

For the purpose of these appendices, the data used are confined to the quatrains that were tabulated earlier. Where these occur in two

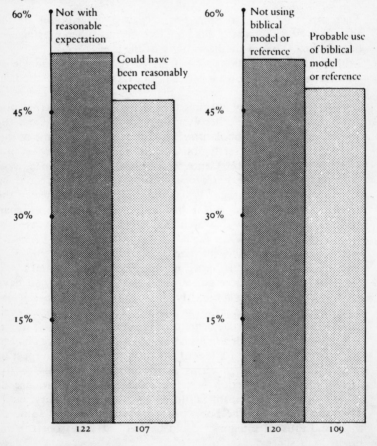

Figure 1: Events that could have been reasonably expected, later 'fudged' by interpreters.

Figure 2: Probable usage of a biblical model or reference.

tables because of double fulfilments, they are sometimes listed twice, and sometimes only once. Thus, the number 229 which is used as a working total in these appendices is not a 'firm' number. It could vary from 227 to over 240 depending on how items could have been included. At all events, just over *a quarter* of the quatrains have been listed as meaningful, given the deficiency of Century VII.

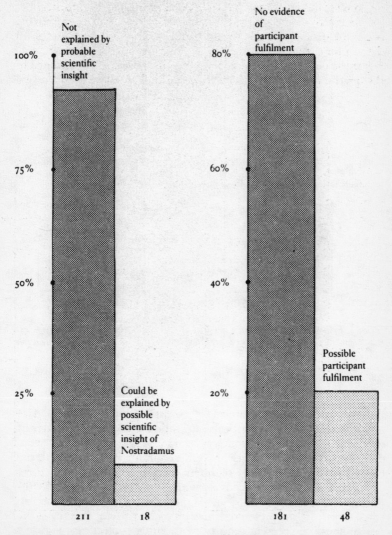

Figure 3: Fulfilments that may have resulted from Nostradamus's scientific insight or superior scientific knowledge.

Figure 4: Fulfilments that may have resulted from deliberate action (participation) by a later historical person (or persons).

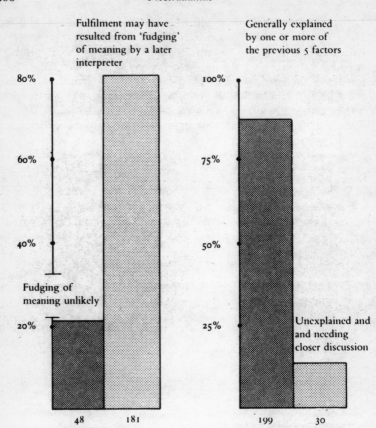

Figure 5: Fulfilments that may have resulted from the 'fudging' or reinterpreting of a prediction intended to mean something else.

Figure 6: Fulfilments explained by the previous five factors compared with those that are largely unexplained.

Before concluding this appendix consisting of bar-charts, it is useful to examine the statistical distribution of the subject matter of the four chapters in which Nostradamus's prophecies were described. There is a danger of double counting but, in general, the bars of the bar chart below represent the subject matter of chapters 2, 3, 4 and 5, dealing respectively with (a) the French Monarchy (b) the period of revolutions in France (and the earlier English revolutions) (c) the present century up to World War II, and (d) the remainder of the present century, with future projections. Figure 7 shows how the 'fulfilled' set of 229 predictions is divided between these four categories.

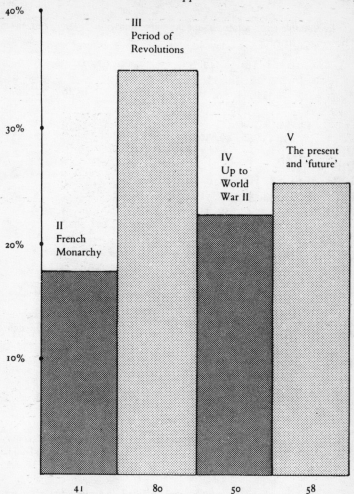

Figure 7: The time-distribution of the main fulfilments (Chapters II-V)

(2) **Ordered Lists of the Main Quatrains**

All the above bar charts were drawn on the assumption that the total number of occurrences of fulfilled predictions in each case was 229 To show how this was achieved, for the first six charts, it will simply be necessary to provide lists of the categories concerned. For Figure 7, however, lists of each of the four categories will be provided. For the first 6 bar charts, the total frequency of items in each list will equal the size of the *right-hand bar* in each of the bar charts, on the assumption that if a quatrain does not occur, it is, in each case, logically a component of the *left-hand bar*.

(a) *Reasonable expectations about the immediate future, later reinterpreted*
These are, in order:

I: 4, 8, 9, 10, 14, 18, 40, 47, 53, 55, 57, 60, 67, 72, 76, 98
II: 7, 12, 16, 24, 29, 38, 53, 55, 68, 75, 94, 97
III: 7, 8, 11, 20, 31, 32, 35, 39, 41, 57, 58, 60, 63, 65, 67, 72, 80, 87,
   99
IV: 21, 47, 54, 61, 96
V: 11, 15, 29, 45, 46, 49, 56, 57, 72, 85, 94
VI: 7, 11, 23, 31, 49, 51, 63, 68, 75, 80
VII: 33, 34
VIII: 15, 19, 28, 31, 38, 40, 52, 64, 71, 76, 77, 80
IX: 7, 18, 22, 34, 36, 45, 51 (twice), 77, 90, 100
X: 22, 39, 40, 44, 45, 59, 86, 100, (twice)
– a total of 107 occurrences, as given in the bar chart.

(b) *Use of biblical prophecy or of a model based on the Bible*
These are, in order:

I: 3, 4, 8, 10, 14 (twice), 15, 16, 28, 29, 30, 34, 40, 48, 50, 51, 53, 55,
   57, 67, 98
II: 6, 7, 12, 16, 28, 29, 38, 39, 40, 46 (twice), 62, 75, 89, 94, 97
III: 7, 20, 32, 35, 39, 41, 57, 58, 59, 60, 63, 64, 65, 67, 72, 75, 94, 97,
   99
IV: 15, 21, 43, 47
V: 11, 15, 29, 45, 46, 49, 67, 72, 90, 92
VI: 5, 6, 7, 11, 23, 26, 33, 49, 51, 63, 75, 80, 84
VII: 33, 34
VIII: 15, 28, 31, 46, 64, 77, 80 (twice)
IX: 7, 20, 22, 36, 38, 51 (twice), 55, 89, 90, 100
X: 44, 72, 86, 100 (twice)
– a total of 109 occurrences, as given in the bar chart.

(c) *Successful quatrains which were fulfilled, because they may simply
    have reflected Nostradamus's scientific knowledge*
These are, in order:

I: 29, 30, 55, 63
II: 6, 16
III: 7, 44, 75
IV: 15, 43, 92
V: 57, 90
VI: 5, 34
IX: 65, 100
– a total of 18 occurrences, as given in the bar chart.

(d) *Quatrains in which there is likely to have been participant fulfilment on the part of the subject of the prediction*
These are, in order:

I: 4, 10, 34, 100
II: 6, 16, 18, 24, 39, 40, 55, 87, 94, 99
III: 37, 39, 57, 58, 63, 94
IV: 2, 15, 54
V: 6, 7, 15, 39, 94
VI: 11, 49, 63, 68, 75, 84
VII: 33, 34
VIII: 38
IX: 7, 18, 64, 89, 93
X: 7, 10, 39, 44, 58, 90
– a total of 48 occurrences, as given in the bar chart

(e) *Cases where obscure predictions and prophecies of contemporary events are likely to have been 'fudged' to suit later events*
These are, in order:

I: 3, 4, 8, 9, 10, 14 (twice), 16, 18, 23, 24, 29, 30, 34, 40, 47, 50, 53, 57, 60, 72, 76, 77, 88, 89, 98, 100 (twice)
II: 1, 6, 12, 16, 18, 24, 28, 29, 38, 39, 40, 44, 51, 53, 55, 57, 67, 68 (twice), 87, 89, 94, 97, 99
III: 7, 8, 11, 20, 31, 32, 35, 37, 39, 44, 45, 57, 58, 59, 60, 63, 64, 67, 68, 80, 81, 83, 87, 94, 99
IV: 2, 15, 21, 32, 54, 41, 82, 89, 92, 96
V: 4, 6, 7, 11, 14, 15, 29, 30, 38, 39, 45, 46, 49, 67, 69, 72, 85, 92, 94
VI: 5, 6, 7, 11, 23, 26, 31, 33, 49, 51, 68, 84, 92
VII: 11, 33, 34
VIII: 15, 19, 31, 33, 37, 38 (twice), 40, 42, 46 (twice), 52, 53, 56, 58, 64, 71, 76, 80 (twice)
IX: 18, 20, 22, 23, 27, 34, 36, 38, 39, 45, 49, 51 (twice), 55, 64, 65, 77, 89, 90, 93, 100
X: 7, 10, 18, 22, 23, 38, 39, 40, 43, 44, 45, 48, 58, 59, 86, 87, 90, 100
– a total of 181 occurrences, as given in the bar chart.

(f) *Fulfilments largely unexplained by the above five factors but with later explanations in Chapter 8.*
There are, in order:

I: 55, 77
II: 51, 53, 55, 68
III: 15, 41, 64, 96
IV: 32, 89
V: 33, 57, 69, 92
VI: 75
VIII: 28, 56, 68, 76

IX: 16, 18, 20, 23, 34, 49, 77
X: 17, 18
– a total of 30 occurrences, as given in the bar chart.

Finally, as a basis of the chi-squared tests which follow, I produce below lists of the contents of my four chapters (which form an approximate chronological sequence), sorted in the order of Nostradamus's Centuries. Thes lists should be read in order of the frequency distribution of Figure 7.

(a) *Nostradamus's Centuries associated with the period of French Monarchy.*
These are, in order:

I: 8, 9, 10
II: 18, 55
III: 11, 15, 20, 31, 39, 41, 87
IV: 2, 47
V: 38, 67, 72
VI: 11, 63, 75
VIII: 38, 52, 68, 71
IX: 7, 18, 27, 36, 38, 39, 45, 64, 93
X: 7, 18, 38, 39, 44, 45, 58, 59
– a total of 41 occurrences, as shown in the bar chart.

(b) *Predictions contained in Chapter 3 and associated with the period of revolutions (including the earlier English revolutions)*
For the purpose of anlysis in the next section, a small change was made. The reference to England's 300-year greatness was removed from this section, and placed in the two remaining sections, as being more appropriate to them. With this improvement, this list reads:

I: 3, 4, 14, 23, 24, 53, 57, 60, 76, 77, 88, 89, 98, 100
II: 12, 29, 44, 51, 53, 67, 68 (twice), 87, 94, 97, 99
III: 35, 37, 45, 57, 59, 80, 81, 83, 96
IV: 54, 82, 89, 96
V: 6, 7, 14, 15, 30, 33, 39, 57, 69, 92
VI: 23, 84, 92
VIII: 19, 37, 38, 40, 42, 46, 53, 56, 58, 76, 80
IX: 20, 22, 23, 34, 49, 51, 77, 89
X: 10, 17, 22, 23, 40, 43, 86, 87, 90
– a total of 80 occurrences, as given in the bar chart (Figure 7).

(c) *Predictions associated with the period leading up to and including World War II, as given in my chapter IV*
With the change mentioned in the above list, these are, in order:

I: 18, 34, 47, 72
II: 1, 6, 16, 24, 38, 39, 40
III: 7, 8, 32, 54, 57, 58, 63, 68, 99
IV: 15, 21, 61
V: 4, 11, 29, 85, 94
VI: 6, 7, 31, 49, 51, 68
VII: 11, 33, 34
VIII: 15, 31, 33, 64, 80
IX: 16, 55, 90, 100
X: 22, 40, 48, 100
– a total of 50 occurrences, as given in the bar chart.

(d) *Predictions in Chapter 5, associated with present-day occurrences, or likely occurrences in the near future*
These are, in order:

I: 14, 15, 16, 29, 30, 40, 48, 50, 51, 55, 63, 67
II: 7, 24, 28 (three times), 46 (twice), 57, 62, 75, 89
III: 44, 60, 64, 65, 67, 72, 75, 94, 96, 97 (twice), 98
IV: 32, 43, 92
V: 45, 46, 49, 56, 90
VI: 5 (twice), 26, 33 (twice), 34, 80
VIII: 28, 46, 77
IX: 51, 65
X: 72 (twice), 100
– a total of 58 occurrences as given in the bar chart.

(3) **The application of Chi-squared Tests**
I have already explained that the use of the chi-squared test is somewhat hazardous. The six categories of explanation are *not* variables (though labelled X_1 to X_6) because, in a work of this kind, it is difficult to 'weight' their importance in each case. There is therefore no question of constructing (and explaining) an appropriate regression model in view of the simplicity of this work. Instead, the chi-squared test is used to measure the frequency of items in each category with the following reservations:

(a) Chi-squared statistics are *not* measures of association and are, at best, indicators of the improbability (at a level of significance) that an association between two category-frequencies has arisen by chance; and

(b) though one set of chi-squared statistics is presented in summary form as a triangular matrix on page 293, there is no suggestion of simultaneous testing or even of rigorous comparison between the chi-squared statistics. At the 5 per cent level of significance, for example, there is a 1 in 20 chance that the statistics result from a 'fluke'.

Each chi-squared statistic should be considered in isolation simply to ascertain whether it is or is not an indicator of (non-random) association at a given level of significance.

The objects of using chi-squared tests in these appendices are fourfold:

(i) to test whether there is significant relationship between any of Nostradamus's Centuries and any one or combination of the six categories studied earlier in this work, and shown in the frequency distributions in the first of these appendices;

(ii) to test whether there is significant relationship between any of the categories themselves; and

(iii) to test whether any one or more of the six categories is/are related significantly to any of the four broad time periods graphically displayed in Figure 7 and discussed respectively in Chapters 2 to 5.

It would be time-consuming and not particularly valuable to tabulate the frequency analysis (cross-category) distributions for all the tests involved.

I shall deal with tests of the relationships between Nostradamus's Centuries and the six categories. The values are:

		Chi-squared statistics
1.	Reasonable expectations (reinterpreted)	4.96
2.	Use of Biblical models or prophecies	21.01
3.	Scientific foresight or knowledge	12.22
4.	Participant fulfilment	14.68
5.	Interpretational 'fudge'	8.21
6.	Unexplained 'hardcore'	10.45

Because there are ten Centuries of Nostradamus and two conditions for each of the factors (i.e., each factor may be either present or absent), there are 9 degrees of freedom $(10 - 1)(2 - 1) = 9 \times 1 = 9$.

The level of significance used for the purpose of testing is the 5 per cent significance level, and for this level of significance to occur (i.e., at or less than 5 per cent probability of the frequencies in categories occurring by chance) the chi-squared statistic at 9 degrees of freedom is about 16.9, and thus the only one of the six categories that seems to be significantly related to Nostradamus's Centuries is his use (or apparent use) of biblical prophecy.

Although the chi-squared statistic is 'significant' in that this distribution does not *appear* to have occurred 'randomly', it does not provide us with a useful pattern of distribution. We are, of course, only dealing with those 229 occurrences that form the main areas of concern about later fulfilments, only a 25 per cent sample of all Nostradamus's quatrains. But if this sample is indicative, Nostradamus appears to have started off using the Bible more often than not, waned in his enthusiasm for biblical references after the Third Century, then revived his interest in Centuries 6 and 7, and waned thereafter – a *double* pattern of 3 Centuries of more than proportionate use of Bible prophecy followed by 2 Centuries of flagging interest in this source of prophetic material. But this is only a theory. At the 5 per cent level of significance it would be most difficult to prove.

Secondly, let me deal with the six major categories which form the subject matter of the book. I shall show the chi-squared statistics in the form of a triangular matrix but as stated earlier this is to provide a summary and not intended to provide comparative measurement.

		X_2	X_3	X_4	X_5	X_6(*)
X_1	Reasonable Expectations (reinterpreted)	19.31	2.05	0.12	3.72	0.62
X_2	Use of Biblical Material		2.07	0.29	0.29	7.06
X_3	Nostradamus's Scientific Insight			0.03	2.71	0.01
X_4	Participative Fulfilment				6.84	1.80
X_5	Interpretational 'Fudge'					4.11
(*) Column value X_6 represents unexplained predictive ability, as in text.						

Note In order to display the descriptions of each category horizontally, this triangular matrix is shown in inverted form.

The chi-squared values in this matrix have to be examined differently from the earlier set. As each of the six factors is either present or absent, there are only two states for each variable, and the number of degrees of freedom is 1 – that is, $(2-1)(2-1)$. Consequently, the test-value for 5 per cent significance is much lower (3.84), and a correction has to be made to the statistics, known as Yates correction. This change (Yates correction) has already been incorporated into the statistics in the above matrix.

We would not expect much significant interplay between the six factors, even though my earlier set of tables showed that often more than one factor could be responsible for the apparent predictive success of a given quatrain. Out of the fifteen possible relationships between thes six factors, only four exceed 3.86 and show that they may not have occurred randomly.

The first of these four is between X_1 and X_2, *Nostradamus's immediate reasoned expectations* and his *use of biblical prophecy*. A significant association is inevitable, because he tended, as we have seen, to use the Bible (or a model based on it) to relate to his expectations about contemporary happenings.

The table relevant to this value is:

	No X_1	X_1	Total
No X_2	81	39	120
X_2	41	68	109
Totals	122	107	229

The uncorrected value is 20.49 and the corrected (Yates) value is 19.31. The table shows association between Nostradamus's use of the Bible and his contemporary expectations, at a *high* level of significance.

The second of the four is negative, and indicates that *participative fulfilment* and *interpretational fudge* are disproportionately associated. The table relevant to this value is:

	No X_4	X_4	Total
No X_5	45	3	48
X_5	136	45	181
Totals	181	48	229

The uncorrected value is 7.93, and the corrected (Yates) value is 6.84. The association is negative in the sense that there is a considerably larger number of cases of interpretational fudge without participant fulfilment than the reverse. If people attempt to fulfil a Nostradamus prophecy and are successful in doing so, there is no need for a later interpreter to 'fudge' the meaning of the original prediction, but the reverse is obviously untrue. The 45 cases where both occur result from an attempt to fulfil an already-'fudged' secondary meaning of the prediction, as in Hitler's invasion of Poland. Clearly, the largest number of cases are those where second meanings have been 'invented' by interpreters, but where there is no apparent participation by subjects of the prediction.

The remaining *two* of these *four* cases concern the relationships between X_2 and X_6, and between X_5 and X_6. Both coefficients *look* significant, but one is dealing with a factor that is not wholly explainable, and has to be understood in that context. Further, I have in Chapter 8 offered reasons why some of the 30 could be removed from the list.

First of all, let us tabulate that between X_2, 'biblical explanation', and X_6 – 'unexplained'.

	No X_2	X_2	*Total*
No X_6	97	102	199
X_6	23	7	30
Totals	120	109	229

The uncorrected value is 8.15 and the corrected (Yates) value is 7.06. This test does little more than prove that, when a biblical model can be used to explain either the structure or apparent fulfilment of one of Nostradamus's quatrains, it ceases to be fully 'unexplained', for the extent to which Nostradamus's use of the Bible can be used to explain his fulfilments considerably outweighs any other form of explanation.

Lastly, let us tabulate that between X_5 'interpretational fudge', and X_6 'unexplained'.

	No X_5	X_5	*Total*
No X_6	37	162	199
X_6	11	19	30
Totals	48	181	229

The uncorrected value is 5.14 and the corrected (Yates) value is 4.11.

This is the one significant *chi*-squared value in the series, about which we may worry least. It simply results from the very large number of cases that have been explained by 'interpretational fudge', and which have therefore been excluded completely from the 'unexplained' category.

We have now carried out two sets of *chi*-squared tests. The first six (between Nostradamus's Centuries and each of the six factors) yielded only one significant statistic, and suggested an interesting pattern of biblical usage in the Centuries. The next fifteen were, in general, insignificant in result, but four were explored, and showed (i) that Nostradamus may have used the Bible alongside his reasonable expectations of the immediate future, and (ii) that interpretational fudge significantly reduces those cases that can be associated with (a) participative fulfilment and (b) the unexplained category; and (iii) that the use of the Bible also significantly reduces the unexplained category.

Our third set of tests relates (or studies the relationship between) the content and time-spans of each of the four chapters 2, 3, 4 and 5 and each of the six factors. Though it does much to confirm the conclusions at which we have already arrived in Chapter 6, it must be borne in mind that the data are slightly different, and that the basic differences result from the following:

(i) in the following tables each factor is counted only once, whereas in the table at the end of Chapter 6, a quatrain is listed separately for each of its factors – hence the total number of occurrences is much greater (493);

(ii) in the following tables, items are listed according to their place in Chapters 2, 3, 4 and 5 – their time-association with the broad themes of Nostradamus's work, whereas in Chapter 6 they were listed according to the actual time of their alleged fulfilment.

There was some overlap between my chapters, and thus their contents cannot be easily classified into fulfilments in the sixteenth, seventeenth, eighteenth, nineteenth and twentieth centuries respectively. For example, most of Chapter 2 relates to sixteenth, seventeenth and eighteenth century fulfilments, while most of Chapter 3 relates to the eighteenth and nineteenth centuries, but does contain some earlier English fulfilments. However, there is some relationship between the order in which I have dealt with items, and the passage of time, so that this next set of six tests will provide useful confirmation of my conclusions at the end of Chapter 6.

First, let me list the six *chi*-squared values that result from tests of significance between the *four* categories of subject-matter based on Chapter 2, 3, 4 and 5, and the six factors. They are:

		Chi-squared statistic
1.	Reasonable expectations (reinterpreted)	16.46
2.	Use of biblical models or prophecies	26.49
3.	Scientific foresight or knowledge	21.82
4.	Participant fulfilment	22.53
5.	Interpretational 'fudge'	57.28
6.	Unexplained 'hardcore'	14.15

There are four chapter divisions, dealing with (a) the French Monarchy, (b) the Revolutions, (c) events leading to World War II and (d) present times. Further, each of the six factors may be present or absent, giving, as earlier, two cross categories in each case. Thus the number of degrees of freedom at which the test may be used is $(4 - 1)(2 - 1) = 3$, and at 3 degrees of freedom the *chi*-squared statistic necessary for testing significance at the 5 per cent level is 7.8, so that *all* the above values are seen to be significant, and the conclusions that one can draw from them confirm all those that were drawn at the end of Chapter 6.

The first significant value (16.46) shows not only the data frequencies but the logic of the approach to Nostradamus, taken in this book.

	No X_1	X_1	Total
Contents of Chapters:			
2	15	26	41
3	48	32	80
4	19	31	50
5	40	18	58
Totals	122	107	229

The probable reason for the high *chi*-squared value is indicated by looking at the second column. Though the fulfilments of reasonably-expected quatrains appear to increase over time and then decrease, it should be appreciated that Chapter 3 contained early fulfilments in English history. The general reason for the significant relationship is as stated in Chapter 6: that fulfilments of Nostradamus's reasonably-expected events *decrease* over time. Where they occur later than Nostradamus imagined, they usually occur because they have been reinterpreted to match later history.

The second significant value is 26.49. It shows that just as Nostradamus's expectations (unaided by the Bible) *decreased* over the time periods which we considered, the relevant use of biblical references, in fact, increased. The table is given below:

	No X_2	X_2	*Total*
Contents of Chapters:			
2	26	15	41
3	56	24	80
4	21	29	50
5	17	41	58
Totals	120	109	229

The significant increase is shown in the X_2 column. Note that, however Nostradamus may originally have used the quatrains that were based on the Bible, interpreters have succeeded in applying most of them to the past two centuries. The lesson of this significant association is, perhaps, that Bible prophecy is always capable of reinterpretation as history unfolds itself, though Nostradamus, of course, 'cashed in' on successful Bible predictions – such as those relating to the return of Jews to Israel in the present century.

The third significant value is 21.82, and relates to distribution of fulfilments of scientific knowledge predictions over time. We would expect the incidence to increase significantly, and this is indeed the case.

	No X_3	X_3	*Total*
Contents of Chapters:			
2	41	0	41
3	79	1	80
4	45	5	50
5	46	12	58
Totals	211	18	229

Again, the reasons for the significant *chi*-squared value may be deduced from the examination of the X_3 column. Note that as time proceeds from the French monarchy to modern times, the number of fulfilments showing Nostradamus's scientific insight increases from 0 to 12, though some of these, as I have shown, betray some imagination on the part of interpreters and Nostradamus may not have intended them to be scientific at all!

The fourth value relates to participant fulfilment. It is 22.53 and occurs mainly because of a 'fluke' in the data. Much of my Chapter 5 relates to future events and for that reason it is quite impossible to identify clear cases of participant fulfilment. In fact, I have only identified one case, which, to some extent, invalidates the *chi*-squared test statistics. When this is taken into consideration there seem to be no significant differences in numbers of participant fulfilments in earlier history. This is shown in the X_4 column below.

	No X_4	X_4	Total
Contents of Chapters:			
2	25	16	41
3	63	17	80
4	36	14	50
5	57	1	58
Totals	181	48	229

Next comes a very high chi-squared statistic, but it arises mainly from the large number of frequencies in Chapter 3, the period of revolutions, and Chapter 4, the Second World War. As I have pointed out earlier, it was at these times that the ingenuity of interpreters was taxed to the utmost. The value is 57.28, and the *chi*-squared contingency table is given below.

	No X_5	X_5	Total
Contents of Chapters:			
2	7	34	41
3	4	76	80
4	5	45	50
5	32	26	58
Totals	48	181	229

The last statistic is 14.15 but still significant at the 5 per cent level of significance.

The relatively high *chi*-squared value simply results from the large number (18) of these occurring in the revolutionary period, i.e., that encompassed by Chapter 3. There is no direct relationship between this factor and the passage of time, and there is no satisfactory explanation of the fact that over 18 of my original 30 unexplained cases occur during and shortly after the French Revolution. It is best to take these cases individually and try to furnish explanations, as I did later in the book.

Index

Aemathein, Aemathion, 68
Air Travel, 166ff
Alais, Peace of, 54
Alexander the Great, 16, 94, 247
Alus, 155
Antibes, 103
Antichrist, 86, 99, 148-158, 213-215, 242, 243
Antoinette, Marie, 86-92, 272
Apollyon (Destroyer), 95, 102
Araxes, 38, 50, 192, 226
Aries (and Bastarniae), 185
Armageddon, 253
Astrology, 15, 17, 128ff, 176-190
Athaliah, 36
Auerbach, Richard, 28
Avignon, 14

Babylon (as Paris), 26, 32-36, 53, 98, 133, 172, 199, 231, 246-8, 249, 253
Bastarnian prediction, 115ff, 185
Belland, M., 221
Bernard of Clairvaux, St, 16
Bible, 16, 24ff, 183, 191-237; *see also* Revelation of John
Blois, 51, 192
Blood, 31, 148-158, 232-233; *see also* Plagues

Bourbons, 23, 26, 59-71
Bouys, Theodore, (Napoleon commentary), 96ff
Bowl (of water), 19
Brezhnev, Leonid, 27
Brissac, 43, 53

Calvin (ism), 54, 117, 192
Cambrai, 61, 62ff, 66, 227
Cancer, 110
Cantril, Hadley, 28
Centuries, 13, 15-20, 31-2
Charles I, 76-9, 196, 265
Charles II, 11, 80, 81
Charles IX (of France), 37, 47-8, 51
Cheetham, Erika, 21n, 29, 32, 41n, 59, 64, 93, 111, 121, 124, 130, 170, 174, 184, 187
Chesterton, G. K., 38
Cinq Mars, 66
Clement VII, 33
Clement, Jacques, 45
Cloud of Unknowing, 20
Coin-tossing, 27
Coligny, Gaspard de, 37, 38, 54, 191
Common Advent (Second Advent), 84, 240, 242
Communism, 153, 164-166
Condé, 54, 260, 267
Copernicus, 14
Creation, Account of, 36

Cromwell, Oliver, 29, 71, 73, 74, 75, 96, 125, 197
Cyrus, 34, 35, 92

Daniel, 10, 31, 101, 150, 153, 179, 232-235, 247, 252
d'Estang, Giscard, 18, 170, 183n
d'Estrees, Gabrielle, 61
da Vinci, Leonardo, 23, 29, 168
de Gaulle, Charles, 133
de Medici, Catherine, 18, 33, 39, 41, 43, 191
de Riviere, 123, 257
de Wohl, Louis, 116, 129
Delphi, 28, 101
Deuteronomy, 5, 100n
Diana, 172
Dionysius (pseudo-), 20
Dixon, Jeanne, 11
D-nebro, 78, 269
Dreyfus, Alfred, 110

Edward VIII, 76-79, 124, 207, 227, 255
Egyptian curse, 40
Elba, 97
Eliott, E., 26
Elizabeth (daughter of Henri II), 37
Elizabeth I, 198, 265
Encyclopaedia Britannica, 12
Ergaste, 92
Evolution, 168
Exegete, 20
Ezekiel (Prophecy against Tyre), 16

Ezra, Apocalypse of (II Esdras), 236

Feetwashing, 20
Ferriere, Dr, 129
Fontbrune, J. C. de, 182n, 240, 243n
Fontbrune, Dr M. de, 124
Fossan, 105, 185, 267
Francis II, 37, 46, 95
Franco, 122-124, 171, 207
French Revolution *see* Revolution
Frondeurs, 31n, 67

Galileo, 14
George VI, 125
Glorious Revolution, 73, 79-83
Goebbels, Joseph, 118, 128
Grattan-Guinness, Dr H., 183
Guise, Duc de, 43

Hadrian, 60, 62ff, 192, 266ff
Hardcore (*see* Unexplained Hardcore)
Helena, St, 97ff
Henri II, 33-37, 41, 252
Henri III, 22, 41-43, 44, 51-53, 191ff, 208-9, 211
Henri IV (Navarre), 42-44, 60, 61, 62ff, 92, 193
Henry VIII (England), 85, 125
Hercules, 69, 70
Hiroshima, 13, 141
Hister, 118-120, 144, 169, 206, 221, 225
Hitler, 13, 28, 93, 112-142, 169, 206, 225, 243, 273, 277
House of Seven, 37ff
Howe, Ellic, 118, 129
Huguenots, 33, 48-49, 53-59, 191-192
Hungary, 133, 136, 173
Hunger, 166ff

Iamblichus, 20
Index Librorum Prohibitorum, 13
Interpretational 'Fudge', 28, 170-175
Inventions, 23-24
Isaiah, 231-237
Israel, 146-150

James II, 80, 82, 197
Jezebel, 33, 36
John XXIII, 164
Joseph, 39, 179

Karnak, 37
Kennedy Brothers, 110
Khomeini, Ayatollah, 94, 173, 216, 265
Krafft, K. E., 116-121, 128ff

Larsen, D. B., 274-5
Laver, J., 20, 29, 31n, 41n, 50, 59, 67, 76, 84, 96, 104, 109, 121, 126, 207
Le Pelletier, Anatole, 104, 114, 115
League of Nations, 238
Leo X & XI, 33
Leo XIII, 109, 270
Lepanto, Battle of, 38, 50, 192, 224, 226
Ligures, Ligurians, 41, 42, 52
London, Fire of, 81
Plague of, 81
Lonole, 29, 75-76, 124, 125, 255
Loog, C., 113-116, 127, 144
Lorraine, Duchess of, 37
Louis XIII, 66, 194
Louis XIV, 31, 66-70, 74, 75, 194
Louix XV, 70, 71
Louis XVI, 71, 86-92, 271
Louis XVIII, 103, 104, 105
Louis-Philippe, 105-7, 202

McGregor, D., 28

Mabus, 155ff
Malachy (of Armagh), 11, 16, 28, 100, 109, 163
Malines, Council of, 64
Marguerite of Navarre, 45
Mark's Gospel, 181
Marie, Sainte, de la Daurade, 228
Mary Stuart, 37, 137
Mede, J., 16, 26, 55, 147, 163
Menorah, *see* Seven-branched Candlestick
Millennium, 146ff, 158, 170
Montargis, 43
Montgolfier brothers, 97, 98, 258
Morocco, 123
Moscow, 244
Moses, 15, 31, 36, 100
Multivariate Discriminant Analysis, 11
Muslim(s), 130, 148-9, 153, 154-6
Mussolini, Benito, 120, 139, 141, 243

Nagasaki, 141
Nantes, Edict of, 54-55
Napoleon I, 73, 86, 92-103, 169, 199-204, 221, 273, 277
Napoleon III, 106
Nazis, 86
Necklace affair, 92
Nelson, Horatio, 265
Newton, Sir Isaac, 16, 26, 55, 147, 163
Nicoullaud, Abbé Charles, 115ff
Nostradamus, life of, 13-15

Ockham's razor, 254
Olivet prophecy, 196

Palma, 60
Papacy, 97ff, 155-166

Paris (as Babylon), 26, 34-35, 53, 60, 86, 98, 133, 172, 199, 231, 246-9, 253
Participative (Participant) Fulfilment, 28, 220ff
Paul (Apostle), 152ff
Paul VI, 164, 169
Pasteur, prophecy of, 23, 234, 258, 262
Pearl Harbour, 136, 258
Peretti, Felice, 17
Perouse, 44
Petain, 86, 133, 134
Phillip II, 60
Phoebe, 146
Phossens, 68
Pi (π), 29
Pius VI, 98
Pius VII, 99
Pius XI, 109
Plagues, Prophecies of, 158-166, 198
Poitiers, 52, 192, 228
Poland, 128ff, 144, 165, 170
Pontefract, 97
Praesepe, 110
Presages, 27, 38
Prescriptive prophecy, 28
Psellus, 19
Pythagoras, 29

Qur'an, 22

Renaissance, 257ff
'Republic', ideas of, 224
Rest Days, 150, 153
Revelation of John (Apocalypse), 10, 15, 25, 34, 36, 55-59, 108, 131, 138, 146, 163, 170, 183, 185, 226, 233-237, 258

Revolution, French (1789), 22, 55, 83-92, 170, 198
(1830), 73, 83, 104-7
(1848), 73, 104-7
Rhone, 97
Richelieu, Cardinal, 66, 194
Rissaut, P. l., 243ff
Russia, 102, 233
Russian Revolution, 111, 205

St Bartholomew's Day massacre, 58
'Salt and Wine', 69, 196
Samarobrin, 167
Saturn, 181, 183
Saulce, 89, 271
Scaliger, J. C., 14, 55
Scientific perceptiveness/ explanations, 23-24, 29, 166-170, 214-5, 222, 254-62
Scythians, 170-1
Second Advent, *see* Common Advent
Seize, 73, 84
Selim II (Selin), 51
Seven-year prophecies, 40, 82
Seven-branched candlestick, 34-46, 191
Sextus V, Pope, 17
Sodom and Gomorrah, 142, 259
Spain, 122-123, 171, 267
Spanish Armada, 225
St Saturnin de Taur, 80
Stalin, Joseph, 127, 131
Statistics, 21
Submarine, 23, 141, 166-170, 260

Suliman the Magnificent, 38, 50, 224-5
Sun City, 67

Toffler, Alvin, 27
Trafalgar, 102
Trinity, 20
Tripod, 19
Tutankahmun, 40
Tyre, Prophecies of, 16, 30, 69

Unexplained 'Hardcore', 32, 262-272
United Nations Organization (UNO), 117

Valois, 53, 94, 223
Varennes stanza, 87, 198, 270-1
Vierge, 261
Venus, 186-7
Verge, 261
Vichy, 132ff

Waterloo, 103
Weighting (coefficients), 11
Wellington, Duke of, 103
William III of Orange, 80-83, 197
Woldben A. (school of interpretation), 243ff
World War I, 111, 205
World War II, 32, 112ff, 205, 259

Xerxes, 101

Z-tests, 10-12

Of further interest:

PROPHECY AND PREDICTION IN THE 20TH CENTURY

CHARLES NEILSON GATTEY

Despite the many theories which attempt to explain it, precognition remains a mystery. The result of many year's study, *Prophecy and Prediction in the 20th Century* will bring you a step closer to understanding the phenomenon.

Lucidly written and meticulously researched, this engrossing case-book is essential reading for the believer, the sceptic and the scholar for, in it, Charles Neilson Gattey—author of the seminal and highly acclaimed *They Saw Tomorrow*—has assembled the best evidence, both anecdotal and experimental, to provide an objective and invaluably comprehensive reference book.

Among the fascinating and bizarre collection of practitioners in precognition from all over the world, examined here are the American prophets Edgar Cayce and Jeane Dixon; Dutch psychic crimebusters Croiset and Hurkos; Elsbeth Ebertin, who cast Hitler's horoscope with uncanny accuracy; France's ace palmist Mme de Thebes; Boriska Silbiger, foreteller of Edward VIII's abdication; Stalin's seer Wolf Messing; Joan Quigley, Nancy Reagan's astrologer, and many more.

The book also reviews the extraordinary experiences of ordinary people who, in dreams or visions—even via radio, TV or films—foresaw murders or danger, travel accidents or wartime deaths, natural disasters or assassinations—some even predicted the winners of races. In addition, it looks at the apparent precognition displayed by writers, such as Jules Verne, as well as such simple divinatory techniques as numerology and the I Ching.

Thoroughly absorbing, *Prophecy and Prediction* will astonish and intrigue, and considers ingenious experiments and theories about time which may explain precognition. It will stand as the definitive overview of the subject in the 20th century to date.